# The White Crane Spirituality Series

White Crane Institute is committed to the certainty that Gay consciousness plays a unique and important role in the evolution of life on Earth. Healthy spirituality entails a healthy sexuality. Our sexuality has led us back to our spiritual selves and history. Same-sex people have, traditionally, been the priests and spiritual leaders of the community. White Crane Books explore aspects of individual sexual life in the service of spiritual growth as well as the positive sexual attitudes and mores of the gay community in the service of humanity.

The White Crane Spirituality Series was established to keep classics of gay spirituality in print employing the most up-to-date publishing technology. Our goal is to provide readers with fine books of insight, discernment and spiritual discovery. White Crane is proud to present these valuable treasures through this Spirituality Series.

# Gay Spirituality

## The Role of Gay Identity in the Transformation of Human Consciousness

## Toby Johnson

This book was first published by Alyson Publications in 2000. This trade paperback edition was published in 2004 by Lethe Press in partnership with White Crane Institute.

White Crane Books is an imprint of Lethe Press. For information write: Lethe Press, 102 Heritage Avenue, Maple Shade, NJ 08052.

lethepress@aol.com        www.lethepressbooks.com

Printed in the United States of America

ISBN 1-59021-022-0

Cover art by Stevee Postman. Photographer & computer artist Stevee Postman is creator of *The Cosmic Tribe Tarot Deck* (with text by Eric Ganther). Prints of his wonderful images are available for purchase at www.stevee.com

**Library of Congress Cataloguing-in-Publication Data**

Johnson, Edwin Clark.
    Gay spirituality: the role of gay identity in the transformation of human consciousness / Toby Johnson.
    — 1st Lethe Press ed.
            p.  cm.
    Includes bibliographical references and index.
    ISBN 1-59021-022-0 (pbk.)
    1. Gays—Religious life. 2. Spiritual life.  I. Title.
BL65.H64J64  2004
204'.4'08664—dc22

                                    2004001408
                                    CIP

**White Crane Institute** is a 501(c)(3) education corporation, committed to the certainty that gay consciousness plays a special and important role in the evolution of life on Earth. White Crane Institute publishes White Crane, the Journal of Gay Wisdom & Culture. Your contributions and support are tax-deductible to the fullest extent of the law.
White Crane Institute, 172 Fifth Avenue, Suite 69, Brooklyn NY 11217.

# CONTENTS

## ACKNOWLEDGMENTS

In the preparation of this manuscript, I have had the assistance of numerous luminaries in the world of gay spirituality. I want to thank Myron McClellan, Philip Kayal, Ralph Walker, and, especially, my Gen-X friend, Eric Ganther, who gave feedback and useful suggestions on the first draft. Daniel Helminiak, Joseph Kramer, Mark Thompson, Arthur Evans, Bert Herrman, Robert Barzan, Gary Hardin, Randy Conner, and Christian de la Huerta commented on later drafts. I want to thank Scott Brassart at Alyson Books, who gave me the idea for this book in the first place, and editor Nancy Lamb, who provided invaluable assistance in trimming excess material and clarifying the meaning of the text.

Still, the ideas are mine. This is my personal vision founded in the experiences and events of my life. These are my insights and understandings. I imagine you'll find some of them wonderful, some incomprehensible, some creative, some brilliant, some ridiculous and outrageous (but, I hope, at least entertaining), and some deeply moving and enlightening.

A lot of the ideas are obvious once you think about them. I hope all this will strike you as what you have always known, though may not have thought about in quite this way—especially as coming directly from the experience of your homosexuality. Nonetheless, I end this preface with a phrase that could save the world were it more frequently uttered:

This is just my opinion. I could be wrong.

—Peregrine's Perspective
Conifer, Colorado, Winter 2000

# INTRODUCTION

There is an enlightenment that goes with being gay, an understanding of the real meaning and message of religion. Not all gay people avail themselves of this enlightenment. Some are blinded to it by momentary attractions of the flesh and the glamour of a liberated gay life. Some are blinded by the guilt and confusion instilled in them by a homophobic society. And some are blinded by the misinformation perpetuated by institutionalized religion. Yet this spiritual enlightenment is there for us, if only we open our eyes.

Gay enlightenment comes, in part, from seeing the world from the perspective of an outsider. It comes also from bringing a different, less polarized, set of assumptions to the process of observing the world. And it comes, for most of us, from not being parents and thus not being caught up in rearing offspring and holding expectations for their lives. The various forms of what is called "gay spirituality" arise from—and facilitate—this enlightened stance. From this position it is possible to understand what religion is really about in the "big picture."

Because gay people are conditioned to step outside the assumptions of society to see sexuality in a more expansive way, we are blessed—and sometimes cursed—with this vanguard vision. If we can deal with this vision successfully, we can assist everybody in understanding the real message of religion.

In fact, it is by our issues that religious people are being tested on the real message of their faith: Do they obey the commandment to love their neighbor or do they give in to prejudice and homophobia? Can religious mentality keep up with cultural change?

It is in regard to our issues that the churches give themselves away. By appealing to homophobia, based in an outmoded view of human nature, instead of helping to cure it for *everybody's* good, they show their failure to abide by the basic teachings they proclaim about love and compassion, they exemplify their inability to cope with the modern world, and they demonstrate (to us, at least) that they are not being led by divine guidance.

## The World Has Changed

Popular religion does not make sense anymore. The traditional myths described the universe as a small disk, not much bigger than the Mediterranean Basin and only about 4,000 years old, floating at the center of a watery firmament, ruled by personal deities with distinctively human traits. Scientific observation shows us a universe that extends billions of light-years into expanding space-time. There is no watery firmament, and the mythical gods couldn't have begun to fathom the modern cosmos. And we've only been looking at it with sophisticated instruments for a few decades. We have barely begun to see what it really is.

The old myths do not address many of the issues that drive modern consciousness: overpopulation, pollution, ecological dynamics, the well-being of the oceans and the rain forests, weapons of mass destruction, exploration of space, cancer, television, automobiles, biotechnology, computers, globalization, evolution, liberty, democracy, psychological sophistication, racial equality, and, of course, sexual orientation.

Religion is supposed to be the conveyor of wisdom. In its myths are supposed to be descriptions—in metaphor and symbol—of how consciousness operates. But the operations of consciousness have become much too complex to be addressed by old myths. Some things that were once important, like human sacrifice and ritual purity, do not even interest us today.

The way to reclaim the positive aspects of religion—sometimes referred to by contemporary religious revolutionaries as "spirituality"— is to rise to a higher perspective from which to understand the wisdom hidden behind the religious myths.

## Gay Consciousness and the Real Meaning of Religion

In the last 100 years a new way of expressing and understanding sexual identity has developed among human beings. We now use words like "homosexual" and "heterosexual." While people obviously had homosexual sex in the past and formed friendship circles and social cliques with other people like themselves, until recently only a rare few identified themselves thereby or experienced that fact as a source of distinctive and positive personality traits. This is something new. This gives us a new perspective on life.

Gay consciousness is trained from an early age to view life from a perspective of critical distance. Gay people are skilled at seeing from over and above and outside. We can model for the rest of humanity how to understand the real wisdom of religion.

Homosexuality and religion are inextricably intertwined. The primary objection to homosexuality in mainstream America remains religious tradition and Scriptural injunction. Yet many homosexuals naturally embody the traits of sensitivity and gentleness that religion is intended to teach. Gay men are often saints and moral exemplars. In spite of the contrary examples that can be offered, there is a goodness and virtue that runs through gay men's lives, and a demonstration of real spirituality in how many of us resolve the problem of making sense of religion in the modern world.

The conflict between church teachings and the reality of gay feelings can create a spiritual crisis that causes homosexuals to reevaluate religion and the meaning of their lives. This spiritual crisis leads some people to reject their religious/spiritual sensitivities, often out of indignation at the blindness and stupidity of conventional religion. While this may be an act of spiritual integrity, it can cost these people an important part of life. After all, spirituality can offer a vision of hope and meaning in a world that sometimes appears to be a hopeless miasma of pain and suffering. At its best, spirituality bestows vision and love of life. It widens our perspective. It sensitizes us to beauty and vitality—the very things at which gay men excel.

Many gay men, however, reject neither their religiousness—their will to be good, kind, and honest and their interest in spiritual matters—nor their homosexuality and their enjoyment of the adventure of being gay.

## The Gay Man as Spiritual Adept

This book is a fleshing out of a particular notion—the gay man as spiritual adept—and an exposition of the insights and speculations of the author, himself a spiritual seeker, a student of comparative religion, and a regular meditator.

The spiritual stereotype of gay men is just that—a stereotype, no more true than any of the others. It applies only to *some* gay men. Other gay men may feel they do not even understand what the stereotype/archetype is about. That's okay. Articulating and promoting the gay spiritual archetype creates the self-fulfilling prophecy that this is how gay men are. In that sense the notion creates what it attempts to describe.

This is not a book about the monumental problems that face the gay community. This is a book about the positive spiritual experience of homosexuality, about an attitude, a way of looking at the world that would resolve many of the problems before they ever got started.

## Everything Possible

This felicitous, problem-solving attitude is based in the model of gay psychotherapy. Central to this gay-oriented, or gay-centered, discipline is the belief that most of the problems homosexuals experience are rooted in "internalized homophobia." Transforming how we think about our homosexuality allows us to discover that the guilt and shame we feel is a shadow that belongs to mainstream society. It allows us to see that homosexuals are the scapegoats for the culture's shame and secret sins. Discovering that we are fundamentally innocent allows us to let go of character deforming, self-afflicting, wrong-making attitudes that generate many of our personal problems. This allows the healthy and adaptive gay personality to shine through.

This is what religion should be doing—both for homosexuals who are discovering their true identity and for heterosexuals who are tormented with anxieties about their own sexual orientation—but is not. Traditional religion, by and large, is not helping people cope with the modern reality. This is partly why psychology is taking over a function religion used to fill.

The song "Everything Possible," composed by Fred Small and popularized by the gay *a cappella* singing group, The Flirtations, beautifully expresses this belief that love and acceptance of homosexuality would positively transform people's lives.

You can be anybody that you want to be,
You can love whomever you will.
You can travel any country where your heart leads
    and know I will love you still.

You can live by yourself,
You can gather friends around,
You can choose one special one.

And the only measure of your words and your deeds
Will be the love you leave behind when you're gone.

Some girls grow up strong and bold,
Some boys are quiet and kind.
Some race on ahead, some follow behind.
Some go in their own way and time.
Some women love women and some men love men.
Some raise children, and some never do.

You can dream all the day,
    never reaching the end
        of everything possible for you.

Don't be rattled by names,
By taunts or games,
      but seek out spirits true.

If you give your friends the best part of yourself,
      they will give the same back to you . . .

And the only measure of your words and your deeds
Will be the love you leave behind when you're gone.[1]

## Homosexual Seers Down Through Time

In the spirit of homosexual seers down through time, we'll look at a series of observations, insights, and speculations on a variety of topics that seem to flow naturally from a modern gay perspective: what religion means in human society, what it should be doing, what has gone wrong with it, where it is going, and what gay men—intentionally or unintentionally—are doing about it. The proposition of this book, then, is that gay spirituality (in contrast to, though not in conflict with, "straight spirituality") is:

1) Experienced from an outside perspective
2) Nondualistic
3) Incarnational (sex-positive and not other-worldly)
4) Evolutionary (and, therefore, challenging to the status quo of traditional religion)
5) Insight-provoking
6) Transformational
7) Adaptively virtuous

As a consequence, we as gay men have a special role to play in the evolution of consciousness. We are playing it through the various incarnations of the "Gay Spirituality Movement" and, whether we mean to or not, by our very existence as self-identified gay people.

The point of all spirituality is to alter our attitude so we live in "heaven" now, that is, in a state of loving acceptance of life and active good will for others. In our homosexuality itself is our experience of "God."

# PART I

## Our Contribution to the Transformation of Human Consciousness

When we talk about gay spirituality, somebody, straight or gay, usually asks, "Why *gay* spirituality? Why not just spirituality or *human* spirituality? What's gay about being spiritual? Or spiritual about being gay?"

Well, here's the answer. And along with it an hypothesis about the true meaning of religion, based in the ideas of comparative religion scholar Joseph Campbell, the Great Teacher and "wise old man" in the life of the author of this book.

Joseph Campbell was an important theoretician and popularizer of a contemporary understanding of religion and myth. He was not gay, though he lived like many gay men. He was a professor at Sarah Lawrence College, and for most of his life he lived with his wife in a modest two-and-a-half room high-rise apartment in New York City's East Village—on Waverly Place overlooking Sheridan Square and Christopher Street. His wife, Jean Erdman, Martha Graham's star pupil, was a successful New York choreographer. They were both acquainted with the sophisticated gay art world. From early on, they decided not to have "earthly children," and to have instead "spirit children": books and plays and creative productions. For the sake of making a larger contribution to society, they chose a lifestyle other than normal heterosexual family life.

Campbell was not a guru. He didn't gather followers. But he understood what myth and religion are really about, and he had an interesting and appealing way of explaining his insights. His books, lectures, and TV programs have transformed the spiritual lives of many people. Campbell's all-inclusive ideas and his lovingly irreverent sarcasm toward religious institutions provide a framework for understanding religion that gay people can readily embrace.

Following Campbell's style of embroidering and weaving together stories from different mythological traditions, we'll take a fresh and sometimes outrageous look at stories of myth, religion, and folklore, using them as guides to a vision for our lives today.

# *Chapter 1*

## PERSPECTIVE: QUEER VICTORY

O n a walking journey, when you come to a rise in the road, the horizon opens up. The world gets bigger and patterns in the lay of the land become apparent. From the summit of even a small hill, you can see more of the world than you could on the plain.

If there happens to be a wall alongside the road, especially if it is high and blocks the view, you might be able to climb to the top of it and then see both sides of the wall. Though you must be careful to keep your balance, if you are daring, you can see what other people cannot see. You can see where you have come from and where you are going. You can see things in relation to one another. From this higher perspective, your journey makes more sense.

### A Higher Perspective

As a consequence of technology and science and the acceleration of the evolution of consciousness on Earth, human beings today are forced to look at the world from a higher perspective than ever before. People are asked to think outside the immediate confines of their own placement in the historical process of the universe, to see "the big picture." Whether they want to or not, they are expected to analyze the forces that construct the popular perception of the world and to understand from over and above the various explanations of reality that have come down to us.

This is especially true and world-shaking in religion. Looking at religions from over and above changes the way their truth is perceived. We see that the wise advice of the ages comes to us through a complex tangle of myths, stories, old wives' tales, legends, and religious doctrines. We recognize the metaphorical nature of religious ideas. We see that out of these metaphors we put together explanations for ourselves of what our lives are about. Such visions are the meat of both religion and spirituality. That is all the mystics and seers who spun the myths were talking about.

All too often, though, driven by practical organizational concerns, the bureaucrats and functionaries of the churches focus on the smaller picture. They inadvertently end up trying to keep people obedient and submissive in order to maintain the status quo.

The human world is full of different myths and explanations for what life is about. Some are contradictory. Most claim to be exclusively true in explicit distinction from all others. How can this be? There is a story that most of us learned in childhood that explains it wisely.

Five blind men are walking down a road in single file. They come upon an obstacle in their path.

"What's this in the way?" the first man asks. The blind men swarm around the obstacle and feel with their hands to determine what it is.

"It is a snake hanging from a tree branch," says the first.

Another calls out, "No, it's just a rope."

Another, alongside, says, "No, no. It's a rock-solid wall."

"I don't understand what you fools are saying," responds the fourth. "It feels just like a thick tree to me."

"Wait a minute, wait a minute," the last man declares, "You don't know what you're talking about. It's waving like the Sultan's fan."

"Get out of the way, get out of the way," shouts a man from atop the obstacle, "Elephant coming through."

Every perception was correct, but not one of the blind men understood what he had encountered. And, notice, the men got angry with one another because they disagreed. Religion and the nature of God are like that. Every myth is true from its own cultural and historical perspective. But no single one actually describes the reality. For that you need to rise to a higher perspective.

While many people today still practice the religions of old, they necessarily adjust the meaning of the doctrines to fit modern reality. That people do this routinely as part of constructing a modern worldview is evidence—and the mechanism—of a transformation of religion. The old myths are passing; a "new myth" is at hand.

## The New Myth

Based in an understanding of human psychology and a view of myth and symbol from over and above any particular tradition, this new and developing myth about ultimate truth is characterized by a self-reflexive awareness of the myth-making process.

Inevitably, the development of this new myth is going to change popular religious consciousness. It is likely to result in a sort of rational, demythologized blend of Christianity, Buddhism, and local nature religion[2]—all embraced with reverence as expressions of wisdom and clues to the nature of consciousness, but none accorded dogmatic dominance. It would be true also to say "remythologized," for, with our new perspective, we can understand and enjoy the mythological presentation of psychological and spiritual wisdom without getting caught up in the strife, confusion, competition, and hostility that come when adherents claim their myth to be right exclusively and demand that others accede to their particular doctrines.

There is a transformation, too, of our planetary ecology. After struggling for millennia just to survive, the human race is now multiplying exponentially and rapidly exceeding the planet's ability to sustain it. The rules of sexual and reproductive behavior, which have been tied to the mystical experience of deeper reality and to the practical concerns of governing society through religious belief, have to change. Part of the "new myth" needs to be a broader understanding of sex and the ecology of reproduction.

Thus the development of gay identification plays an important role in creating the new myth. The very existence of homosexuality in human sexual behavior and the evolution of self-identified gay people in society demand a larger view of things. Any explanation of the nature of sexuality must now include same-sex orientation. A theory of sexuality has to explain all observable phenomena; it cannot dismiss data as irrelevant or distasteful to the majority. So homosexuality expands the view of human nature. From a perspective outside "normal" sexuality, the larger nature of sex becomes more apparent. Likewise, gay experience helps us understand the larger nature of religion and spirituality.

## Earthrise

Human beings today are able to look at history from a broader perspective than ever before. We are able to observe the dynamics of consciousness. This is symbolized by the now familiar image of Earth seen from the surface of the moon—earthrise. For the first time, human beings were able to look at their planet from over and above. Consciousness stepped outside and saw itself.

Such a perspective allows us to see what myth and religion are really about. Gay people are naturals for this perspective. Being homosexual—and specifically identifying as gay—forces us into a higher perspective on life. Because of our homosexual orientation we have available to us insights into the nature of consciousness. We are able to step outside the assumptions and conventions of our culture to see things from a different point of view. In the jargon of management consulting, being gay trains us to think outside the box.

As stated in the introduction, there is a certain kind of enlightenment that goes with being gay, a familiarity with being an outsider and an understanding from over and above of the world in which we live. We naturally see that if the conventions of society are wrong about something as basic as sex, they are probably wrong about a lot of other things as well. With this insight, we can reevaluate what the world says is so. We can see through the metaphors. We can reevaluate what human life is about.

Indeed, many gay men and lesbians have created their own models for the good life and thereby recreated themselves and their world. Every story of "coming out" represents a call to adventure, a profound discovery that many of the important things one was taught are patently wrong. Every story represents a dramatic incident of accepting things as they really are without resistance and disapproval, an heroic effort at transforming negative into positive. Metaphorically, every self-respecting, proud homosexual is an alchemist transforming dross into precious metal, a fairy-tale maiden spinning straw into gold, or an aboriginal medicine man divining the pollen path laid out by the way of nature.

## The Challenge

Unfortunately, the offices of psychotherapists and chemical dependency counselors are packed with homosexually oriented people who have not successfully accomplished this alchemical transformation. Managing to reject social norms and prejudices and then to recreate a whole new interpretation of the world based on personal experience is an enormous task. The function of spiritual wisdom is to assist with such a task.

The deeply personal and idiosyncratic challenge of developing a positive, self-confident, socially contributing homosexuality parallels the struggle of the whole human race to transform the myths and doctrines of the old religions to fit modern, scientifically modulated realities. Philosophically, religiously, all people are being called upon to achieve the perspective on the meaning of life that homosexuals are forced into willy-nilly by not fitting into traditional models. In that sense, modern-day homosexuals are living at the edge of history, and some are helping humanity into the future by setting styles, challenging outmoded cultural assumptions, demonstrating adaptive lifestyles, and participating in a new approach to spirituality—that is to say, by helping devise a new myth.

This new myth is the vision from a higher perspective which modern science and fact-based culture demand. Ideally, achieving perspective does not mean abandoning the past and its models—

some of the metaphors and stories are exquisite—as much as learning to include them with the spiritual equanimity called for by critical distance.

Today, we don't look to the past to discover truth. We no longer find the so-called "argument from authority" very convincing. We wouldn't want to go to a doctor or dentist, or even a building contractor or architect, who looked up what to do for us in a tome from the Middle Ages. We look to the future for truth. We naturally assume modern experimental methods have discovered how things work better than the ancients' guesses, and we expect that what has not been discovered yet will be discovered in time. Why would we look in ancient texts to find out about God? If the ancients were wrong about everything else, why would we think their notions of cosmic reality authoritative?

The rise of gay identity in the last hundred years or so, and particularly in the last 30 years, is an important aspect in the formation of the new myth. Gay people—and our struggle for acceptance and our enterprise of creating gay community—are key players in the transformation. This is so if only because the population imperatives that call for compulsory heterosexuality have been turned upside down and attitudes about sex and reproduction need to change. Having more children, perpetuating one's genes, cannot be the reason for living. There are too many children already. Gay people represent this shift. This transformation in consciousness, this "waking up from history," is what gay spirituality is about.

## An Aristocracy of the Considerate and the Plucky

Homosexuals—either practicing or repressed—have been running the institutions of religion for ages on end. The earliest "religious leaders" were medicine men and shamans, many of whom cross-dressed and behaved homosexually in pursuit of their mystical calling. Homosexual artists, like Leonardo Da Vinci and Michelangelo, helped define religious imagery. Over the centuries, priests, monks, and nuns joined the church to avoid being forced into marriage, family, and the heterosexual lifestyle. This may be why celibate priesthood has been championed by church prelates who, while having no sexual life themselves, could easily dismiss men's need for women because they did not really understand heterosexual drive.

Homosexual orientation and gay identification manifest sensibilities and attitudes that can clearly be thought of as religious: sensitivity to others, desire to be loving, the sense of feeling part of a cause for justice and righteousness, fascination with ritual and history, art and style, and honesty. The point of a gay spirituality is to find and then proclaim the meaning of being homosexual, to answer the question: "What is the message from the Universe, from 'God,' conveyed by my queer nature?"

Some self-identified gay men prefer the term "queer" to "gay." "Queer" was chosen to break with the "gay culture" of the 1980s. Some activists, especially young and academically involved Gen-Xers, understandably felt "gay" had become so mainstreamed and so dominated by consumerism that it had lost its revolutionary edge. More importantly, queer was chosen to be inclusive of all sexual minorities, i.e., gay men, lesbians, bisexuals, transsexuals, and transvestites.

The notion that there is a need for an all-inclusive term has generally come from gay men and has, at various times, been resisted by the other sexual minorities, who recognize they have issues different from those of male homosexuals. It is a gay vision that we are all one and that all sexual minorities should be included in the gay movement's calls for justice, liberation, and respect. And it is a men's blindness that, once included, the other minorities tend to be dismissed.

The message that queer identification contributes to the overall gay movement is that sexuality is much more fluid than previously thought. Queer identification is an embrace of deviance and countercultural values and a rejection of conventional normalcy. Independent of the Foucaultian debate about essence versus construction that founds it philosophically, queer identification is just as much a repudiation of normal heterosexuality as it is of gayness, declaring both as limiting categories.

One of the loveliest uses of the emotionally charged word, queer, with all the spiritual meaning and none of the organizational implications, appears in a quote from early twentieth century novelist E.M. Forster: "An aristocracy of the sensitive, the considerate, and the plucky...are to be found in all nations and classes, and through all the ages. And there is a secret understanding between them when they meet. They represent the true human tradition, the one queer victory of our race over cruelty and chaos."

## Queer Generalizations

Of course, not all of us fit this queer idealization. Terms like "queers" and "gay men" are necessarily generalizations. In a way, anything we say about them can be disproved by a single contrary example. Nonetheless, it makes sense to talk about gay men without having to include each and every gay man and each and every exception to our prototype. The generalizations in this book about the meaning of sexuality or even "human nature" do not apply to everybody. But they do apply to a culturally constructed image of what gay men are like—the myth of the modern gay man.

This myth is a constructed image that helps homosexuals explain their experience to themselves. This image has changed dramatically in the last few decades. The myth of the gay man in the 1940s was of a lonely, tormented, self-hating pervert. The mythical gay man in the mid 1970s was an outlaw and sexual athlete of amazing prowess. In the 1980s, at the height of the AIDS scare, he was a hapless, but self-responsible, victim. By the mid 1990s, he had become a committed spouse clamoring for marriage rights. Overall, in the last half-century, the transformation has been tremendous. We no longer think of ourselves as perverts; we have stopped being victims and become survivors. We have changed our myth.

As soon as we notice these transformations over time, we can see that the generalizations are just images and stereotypes. When we rise to a higher perspective, we are freed from the momentary appearance of things. Within the gay world, of course, we have always known the realities were much more complicated than the stereotypes. But it was precisely by changing these generalizations of what a gay man was that the liberation of modern times was achieved. Gay men changed how they thought about themselves, and the world around them changed, too.

Some of us think of ourselves as spiritual men struggling to create good lives, struggling to "save the world" or, at least, the world of our own experience. As we embrace this new spiritual identity, we transform our interior worlds and the world at large.

# Chapter 2

## PERSPECTIVE: SPIRIT

"Spirituality" is the modern-day term for religiousness apart from the traditional content of religion, i.e., membership in a religious institution and adherence to specific doctrines. Spirituality refers to the meaning behind religion. Not: "What are the true doctrines?" But: "What do the doctrines mean?"

Spirituality is the interface between the doctrines and rituals of traditional religion and the modern effort to expand consciousness and discover the ineffable through the investigation of one's own mind and one's own life story. Spirituality is about the connection between the individual and the transcendent.

"Spiritual," too, is what some people call themselves who are agnostic or unconcerned with religion, but do not consider themselves immoral.

The spiritual life is the interior life: how we think about ourselves and life. It is not about ghosts or angels or powers or miracles. These, after all, are just metaphors for ways to think about and experience life. Technically, spirituality is not about God either. But for many of us "God" is the symbol for the whole experience of being alive and being conscious: How we talk about "God" is how we think about the big picture. God is a thought in our minds. That is why it can be said: God is a spirit.

A spirit is also an attitude. It is the way we feel inside. We speak of a person being mean-spirited or being possessed by a spirit of anger, meaning they are petty or angry all the time. We speak of a school having spirit, meaning there is a general feeling within the student body of camaraderie and good intention (especially for sports victories). We say a person is high-spirited, meaning he or she is generally happy and enthusiastic.

Spirit is the psychological context within which we hold our life. Spirituality is the awareness of that context and the concomitant awareness that we can do things to change it. Indeed, religion is a manifestation of a society's efforts to influence its members' attitudes. Religion and myth explain and dramatize basic attitudes toward life. They help people shape their minds.

The important thing, then, about religious ideas is not whether they are historically true, but how believing in them influences our life. Spirituality refers to the whole complex process by which we are aware of ourselves and devise myths and metaphors to explain ourselves to ourselves. Myths are the clues the universe gives itself to help consciousness realize its own existence.

We might say that the universe is consciousness giving clues to itself about what it is to be conscious. In more mythological-sounding terms, the experience of life is "God" giving clues to "himself" about who "he" really is. But the truth is not in the clues or the metaphors (which are the issues of religion), but in the experience of vitality they facilitate (which is the issue of spirituality).

Spirituality refers to the nature of consciousness and the craving that human beings feel for transcendence. From a perspective of spirituality, we can look for the clues that speak to us. We can search out what makes us feel transcendent.

## Outsider Consciousness

Because so much of religion is appropriately focused on children and teaching them moral values while they are young and impressionable, their lives uncomplicated by adult demands of sex, religion tends to avoid talk of sex. A preacher would have a difficult time explaining a spiritual dimension to coitus to a congregation that includes children who do not understand what "coitus" means—and whose parents probably do not want to have to explain after church.

Mainstream religious imagery—based in the lives of "normal" heterosexuals with families—concerns the issues of family cohesiveness, child-rearing practices, genetic lineage, and preservation of traditions. The popular Christian god is conceived of as a Father who begets a son. His primary command: "Go forth and multiply and subdue the earth." This god is very concerned with primogeniture, apostolic succession, hierarchy, power, etc. The popular images of his religion include the Virgin Mother, the Madonna with Child, the baby Jesus, guardian angels, and the subtle familial relations within the Blessed Trinity.

Gay men's spiritual imagery—based in the lives of outsiders—concerns issues of self-worth, lovableness, finding a soulmate/sex partner, assessing the legitimacy of violating social custom, discovering a relationship with God beyond the rules and traditions, and seeing God differently.

Gay men grow up feeling out of place, not connecting with all the talk of wife and family, not understanding what "normal" people are talking about regarding sex, not getting why jokes about women's breasts, for instance, are funny or provocative. We do not see mommy and daddy, however much we love them, as the models for the life we wish to live.

From our earliest years, we experience being special, often brighter, more obedient—"the best little boy in the world"—or more trouble-making. We learn about secrecy. We learn early to differentiate our ego selves from our parents and siblings. We experience insights other people do not. Many of us compensate for being shunned or made fun of by excelling in school and then career, choosing academic majors and career paths other people would consider peculiar, queer, or eccentric—like the arts or theater or comparative religion—because we are more concerned with "following our bliss" than building a nest in which to raise young.

We may be baffled by other people's obsession with sports and competition. We may prefer womanly interests—the arts, hair, clothes, rearranging the furniture, love, sexual reassurance—to manly interests—athletic prowess, sports scores, hunting, fishing, tools, reassembling an automobile, power, winning. We may be interested in both womanly and manly things, and not understand why other people think them exclusive of one another. We may feel we are the only ones in the world like this.

Gay men's god needs to be concerned about love and friendship and intimacy. He needs to encourage disclosure and relish discovery of other homosexuals. Gay men's god needs to value nonconformity and cherish tradition-breakers.

Of course, because we grow up in mainstream heterosexual culture, we learn its symbols. We, like straights, are concerned about our parents' love for us, and we depend on societal traditions to help us cope with interfamilial relationships. But our deeper issues are concerned with how to succeed without fitting in, how to keep our secrecy, how to find our special friends, how to overcome the taunts and jeers of the other boys on the playground, how to learn what heterosexual humor is about, and how to pretend to be "normal," knowing we are really something else.

Many children today grow up in the world of TV and movies in which homosexuality is relatively accepted. Many may experience few traumas about being gay. Even so, they grow up different from their parents. They have to develop ego-consciousness and a sense of personal identity separate from their parents. For even the most accepting and loving parents cannot model a life other than their own.

## Family Values

People with children have a lifelong concern about their children's welfare, about their roles in the children's lives, the children's behavior, their responsibility for and right to participate in the children's failures and joys. This is what "family values" is about.

The hallmark of good parenting is protecting one's children so they can have as long a childhood as possible. The long childhood of human beings was a major evolutionary development that facilitated our growth of intelligence. The reason families are non-sexual and why sexuality "threatens families" is that a child's becoming sexually active signals the end of the innocence and simplicity of childhood.

Parents try to deny children the knowledge of sex in order to allow their complex psychological personalities to form before being further complicated by sex. This is why sexual molestation of children is so vilified. This deliberate denial causes straight people with children to repress sexuality and to project their fears of erotic power onto sexually "deviant" people—i.e., us.

Homosexuals have different material in our minds. We are concerned about different things. We have no reason to reenter a sexual latency period for the sake of our children's maturation. We find ourselves facing spiritual questions about our sexuality and our embodiment, not about the family power structure.

Instead of behaving toward God as a pre-pubescent boy to his big, strong, protective but demanding father, gay men seek a god who is a loving and forgiving playmate. We look for a friend who will understand what it is like to have been called names by the other boys, to have been embarrassed among peers because we accidentally made a gender inappropriate remark and everybody laughed, a friend who will say it is okay to have feelings of admiration and desire to gaze upon—and even to touch—other boys' bare chests, a friend who will say: "I'll do it with you to prove it's okay."

For gay boys growing up, it is not necessary to change their fascination with their own bodies and other boys' bodies with the onset of sexual desire. Fascination with male bodies simply becomes erotic desire. Straight boys, on the other hand, must shift their fascination from their own developing maleness and their ability to pleasure themselves to the desire for a female body and the acquisition of performance skills to seduce and give pleasure to a woman.

In a way, gay sex is simply an extension of learning how to enjoy pleasure and to share it with others. It is always boyish play. It never has to take on the meaning of heterosexual bonding and procreation or the heavy responsibility of creating a family.

There are, of course, gay people with families. For them, perhaps, these dynamics are even more complicated, because both interests are intermingled, though the parental responsibilities necessarily overshadow the sexual. Gay people who do have children, as gay people, probably make better parents, because to become parents they must make an active decision to go through with what it takes to give birth or adopt. Gay men do not become parents by accident or whim. Some gay people probably choose parenting so they can do it right, not because they have a right to do it.

There is a more complicated development of sexuality in straight people. Straight men, for instance, often have to prove to themselves and their peers they are not gay. A whole strain of homophobia is internal to heterosexuals' self-image. While gay people suffer the external brunt of homophobia, the greatest damage is probably done to straight men who cannot allow themselves to relax and be themselves out of fear of how others will judge their masculinity.

The god gay men love and obey and seek mystical union with is concerned about issues different from the god of straight people with families. One of the blind men who approached the elephant at the genitals would have had a very different experience from the others.

With the perspective of "spirituality" rather than religion, gay men can see how to transform their religious attitudes and select the mythic explanations that address their lives. Our sexual orientation makes our lives different. We can expect it to make our souls different too.

# Chapter 3

## NON-DUALISM: SEXUAL ORIENTATION

Attraction—sexual and nonsexual—between a woman and a man witnesses to the interplay of opposites. The polarities are the primal forces called yin and yang, dark and light, receptive and creative, passive and active, feminine and masculine, which generate the world. Female and male are special cases of these polarities. The attraction between male and female manifests the duality that stirs creation.

In the same way, attraction—nonsexual and sexual—between two men or two women witnesses to the ultimate unity of the world beyond duality. Beneath the apparent swirl of polarities, ever growing, ever changing, clashing in conflict and cooperating in love, lies a deeper stratum in which all is at rest and the opposites are illusory. The attraction between same-sex individuals manifests the unity that precedes and transcends the duality.

When the polarities are thought of as male and female, they seem exclusive of one another. That is the dualistic way to see them. Another way to think about the polarities is as left and right. Then they are just opposite sides of each other, necessary to each other's existence. They are no longer mutually exclusive; instead, they are mutually inclusive.

Shifting the model from mutually exclusive qualities to mutually inclusive qualities helps explain the nature of homosexuality.

## *The Causes of Homosexuality*

There is much discussion about the cause(s) of homosexuality. Part of this is a debate about the legitimacy of paralleling sexual orientation with race in determining "minority status." Some people argue that if sexual orientation is genetically or congenitally determined, then homosexuality is just like being black (or brown, yellow or red)—something people cannot do anything about. Others argue that because some homosexually oriented people succeed at suppressing their sexual behavior and learn to function heterosexually, then this is something people can do something about and therefore should.

Handedness—that most people are right-handed and a small minority are left-handed—provides a better model for the apparent polarization of homosexuality and heterosexuality. Most people are right-handed; most of the things in the world are designed for right-handed people. But there is a significant portion of people who are naturally left-handed. This is not a choice. It is determined by brain structure, and is relatively unchangeable, though a few people do succeed at suppressing left-handedness and developing right-handed skills, while some people are naturally ambidextrous.

In the past, left-handedness was sometimes considered a sign of demonic possession. People have been burned at the stake as witches because they were left-handed. The Bible uses left as a metaphor for damnation. The word "sinister," meaning evil and suspicious, comes from the Latin for left-hand. Until quite recently, left-handers were punished in grade school for writing with their dominant hand. Teachers sometimes tied the child's left hand behind his or her back to force right-handedness. These efforts were seldom successful, and sometimes resulted in neurological disabilities like stuttering.

Today, with psychological and physiological sophistication, nobody even thinks of condemning left-handedness or trying to force people to change their natural tendency. Indeed, modern brain study has shown that left-handers have a more developed connection between their right and left hemispheres that may result in "better" brain function. Nonetheless, the left-handers will have problems throughout their lives that righties do not; they will scrape their knuckles more often because of right-handed door knobs; they will smear their penmanship because writing goes from left to right. But left-handedness is no longer a moral issue. This is the proper parallel to homosexuality.

## A Different Understanding of the Polarities

Gay people experience the world differently, just as men experience the world differently from women. We have a different understanding of the polarities. Many straight people cannot understand homosexuality and think it is a choice. The fact that we feel no choice in our orientation is evidence that we have a different way of experiencing these matters.

Heterosexuals feel a compulsive drive to link up with someone opposite them, a person as different as day from night who, at least during the time of sexual arousal and romance, seems their "other half." What a joy!

But they necessarily cannot understand the motivations or the personality patterns of the person they are drawn to. For the very thing they are drawn to is the differentness. "Men are from Mars; women from Venus" goes the chestnut. Men do not understand "what women want." Women continually ask: "What is it with men?" They say of one another, "You can't live with 'em and you can't live without 'em."

Males have a natural drive to seek variety in sex and hence to have sex with more and different partners. Men experience sex in the eyes, in the pang of desire. Females have a drive to have more and deeper emotional sex with a stable partner. Women experience sex in the heart, with the throb of feeling.

Men have different desires from women; they see the world differently. Importantly, men and women view the feelings and motivations and goals of sex differently. They therefore experience turmoil, confusion, and anger, because the very thing they most desire is so elusive. They see the world as separate and different from them; they experience the world as characterized by duality.

Husbands and wives have a hard time talking to one another, especially about matters of sex and love. They find it difficult to discuss feelings. Archetypally, men cannot manage the words "I love you," and women cannot describe the kind of sexual stimulation they crave. This difficulty with open communication reverberates through people's lives so that all sorts of simple problems become intractable.

These issues form the basis of a lot of comedy, but they are not always funny. They are sometimes a source of violence. A shockingly high percentage of women have been sexually assaulted in their lives. Men get angry. Testosterone drives them to fight for what eludes them. They compete with one another over the right to impress and possess women. They assault women out of anger that they cannot truly possess them.

Homosexuals, on the other hand, experience the compulsive drive to find someone basically like themselves. At the level of worldview and, especially, motivation for and attitudes about sex, gay people choose a world of agreement and harmony. When we are infatuated and in love, we may see our beloved as a manifestation of who we want to be. Our beloved is less our "other half" than an image of our idealized self.

We know what our lover's body feels like inside because it is how our own body feels. We know how to give and to receive pleasure with such a body. It is possible for us to perfectly mirror our partner's sexual stimulation of us. It is possible for us to alternate active and passive roles.

Of course, we live in a world pervaded by the notion that opposites attract, and so we often interpret our attraction to another person of the same sex according to this cliché. And there is some truth to this. Any two people are almost always going to have differences and those differences are going to seem like opposite, complementary traits. In fact, since in all relationships—straight, gay, sexual, and non-sexual—human beings are looking to expand their experience, we are going to be connecting with people different from us.

Of course, any two people are not always on the same wavelength, and so gay relationships also experience turmoil, confusion, and anger. But the essence of our vision is not dual but unitary. We see the world not as an elusive opposite ever evading our grasp, but as a reflection of our own being, manifesting in three dimensional space as an other who triggers deep psychological mechanisms and therefore appears to us sexually attractive.

Straight men certainly feel wonder and joy in seeing and loving an attractive woman, especially a "soul mate" who seems their perfect complement. Heterosexuals also enjoy the glories of sex, and for them sex is participation in God's process of creating the world—in their case, through the intersection of opposites.

Their experience, however, is different from ours. It does not contain the sense of being part of the other's beauty. A straight man does not look at a woman and wonder if he could look like her or if the qualities of attractiveness that he sees in her might be in him also. A gay man does. Our self-image is formed by our attraction to other men. We learn to value ourselves by the people to whom we are attracted and who are attracted to us.

A straight man is proud to have a beautiful woman on his arm. Other men will envy and honor him for his prowess. A gay man sees that he becomes more attractive in his own eyes and in the eyes of other men when he is with an attractive man. It is, perhaps, less prowess and more the beauty itself that the gay man displays and longs for.

A layer of gay sexual attraction is the fantasy that we could be the person we are attracted to. Indeed, in sexual arousal sometimes we do want to be him, to have his body, to be what it is we love about him, to feel what he is like inside, and to be attractive and loved as we perceive him to be because we are in love with him. We long to see through his eyes so that we can see ourselves as he sees us—as he loves us and perceives us as attractive and desirable. For such vision both allays our own fears and self-consciousness and helps us transcend ego by showing us the world from another person's perspective.

There is no real correlate in heterosexual experience. Straight men do not long to be women and to experience what it is like to be in a female body no matter how attracted they are to that woman's body.

The experience of the polarities—especially as they are inculcated by religious beliefs—influences how we see the whole world.

## Black and White Thinking

A manifestation of such polarization, for instance, is what is called "black and white thinking." This means not recognizing the shades of gray that make up the real world of human interaction. It is also called the fallacy of the excluded middle, an obsession with extremes: virgin/whore, saint/sinner, American/Communist, conservative/liberal, straight/gay. The answer, politically and morally, always lies between the two extremes. That is why the adversarial system we live under prizes compromise, even as both sides hurl epithets at the compromisers. It is a hopeless political strategy and a personal neurosis to see the issues only in black and white terms.

In politics, one side of the polarity is usually concerned with figuring out who was wrong and who is to blame for bad behavior (forcing the other side to exonerate that behavior because of poverty, poor education, and racial prejudice, which really are the issues). These people, all too often embraced by religion, actually seem more concerned with finding somebody to blame than in solving problems, as though figuring out who is wrong or who has been morally weak somehow addresses social issues. This is how even religious people with loving motivation can end up on the side of hatred and vengeance all in the name of "being right."

Many world problems are based in racial hatred and genetic competition. One group of people—primarily identifiable as racial and/or religious—want to dominate another group of people. The issue is genetic dominance. It is based in that very rudimentary (heterosexual) notion of sexuality: Go forth and multiply and subdue the earth. The polarization built into the heterosexual worldview is obvious.

Somebody has to show that this adversarial stance toward other people and toward life itself is not helping. By holding a nondualistic vision, we can help overcome the polarities. To be able to rise above polarity and contradiction is a great ability. It is the only way to achieve peace.

Most people live in an intensely dualistic world, gay and straight alike. We are always confronted with things we like and things we don't like. We are always experiencing opposition. The world is always at odds with itself. We overcome this not by denying the polarities but by transcending them, incorporating both sides. The gay personality is not neuter, it is inclusive.

## The American Melting Pot

America stands for just this kind of overview in which racial, religious, and ethnic differences are supposed to be transcended. It is not surprising, therefore, that gay consciousness should have developed primarily in the United States. The evidence that gay consciousness is more advanced is the bafflement gay people experience when we see how "normal" people behave. That the world is in the mess it is in is proof that being "normal" is not always the best way to approach the world.

Nondualistic, spiritual insight is needed to solve the mess and transform the world.

# *Chapter 4*

## INCARNATION: SEX

A gay spirituality is necessarily concerned about sex—and is necessarily sex-positive. People who choose to identify themselves openly as gay are more sexually motivated and more sexually aware than others. If their sexual and affectional urges were insignificant to them, they would never have come out in the first place. Because gay people have experienced their sexual drive as so intense and consuming that it sets them on a different course from their peers, they are more motivated to find deeper levels of meaning for sex and to discover more variety in ways of experiencing it.

Of course, there are highly sexualized straight people. But they do not have a great need to tease out new meaning for sexuality. It comes to them. This is not to deny that for everybody, straight and gay, discovering sex can be difficult or that straight people cannot find new meanings for their sexuality on their own. But the culture supports heterosexuals with a ready explanation of what sex is for, though usually relegating it to a simply biological, reproductive role. As gay people we have to create our own explanations, our own myths, our own visions of why "God" created us this way and of what it means to be homosexual. We often have to do this on a person-by-person basis with little help from either mainstream or gay culture.

When we seek spiritual answers as gay people, we are necessarily looking for sex-positive and gay-positive answers. This puts us in a special place in the evolution of religion.

Gay consciousness gives insights into sex by demanding that it be viewed from the perspective of the exceptions, not the norm. What forces a theory—or a theology—to expand and rise to a higher perspective are not the findings that fit the theory, but those that do not. The accumulation of knowledge is founded on seeking explanations for what does not meet expectations and assumptions.

## The Function of Sex

Sex is a state of heightened awareness of consciousness incarnated in flesh, an altered state of consciousness in which individuality is momentarily transcended and consciousness merges with the collective. It is consciousness delighting in its own evolution into human bodies that can feel pleasure and joy.

The most important function of sex in human evolution has been reproduction. You could even say the purpose of sex is to produce babies. A lot of people do say that. Unfortunately, they often go on to say, looking from their own limited perspective, that reproduction is the *only* purpose of sex, and if sex cannot lead to reproduction then it should not be allowed. They do not see things from a high enough perspective. That there are self-aware and self-identifying gay people tells us that there is more to sex than reproduction. The issue is not what some sort of creator/biodesigner had in mind. The issue is what is real. Homosexuality is real. Therefore, it is part of the design.

It is homosexuals' responsibility to create an understanding of functions for ourselves. And we have. This is a major part of our contribution to evolution. As consciousness has evolved, new layers of reality of sex have developed. Certainly, human beings have sex in a much more complex way, more rich, more prolonged than other animals. In addition to a biological process, in human beings sex has evolved into a psychological process.

Modern gay-sensitive research demonstrates broader functions of sex in refuting the notion that homosexuality does not exist among animals. Giving evidence of homosexual activity in more than 450 species, for example, biologist Bruce Bagemihl offers a new paradigm of "biological exuberance." Nature is driven as much by abundance and excess as it is by limitation and practicality. The conventional model of evolution based in Darwin's experience of nineteenth century British capitalism presumed scarcity and competition with a winner-take-all mentality called "survival of the fittest." In fact, perhaps, nature simply delights in variety. Efficiency and cost effectiveness are modern economic ideas. Biological exuberance may be "God's" idea. And gay people represent the exuberance for fun and pleasure.

## Psychological Aspects

Sex has psychological aspects. Entering the altered state of consciousness with another person opens us to him and him to us. Sharing orgasms with another person stirs feelings of connection and intimacy. It opens us to his "karmic patterns" (which is why we should exercise caution about whom we get involved with). It deepens true love when that is present. It boosts our self-image and raises our energy level. Being in love and full of sexual vibrancy makes us feel good. Even without the emotions of "true love," having a satisfying sexual connection with another man makes us feel alive.

Having sex that feels good and makes us self-assured and confident in our worth as a person and as an attractive human body changes our behavior. We can be kind and loving, happy and generous, sharing our joy with other people. "Everybody loves a lover" says the old song lyric.

The experience of attraction to another man (or, for a lesbian, to another woman) is a source of joy for the beauty of life itself.

Much of gay life has always seemed to be about getting sex. That is what all the advertising promises. But the truth is that for most of us, most of the time, the experience of our homosexuality is the pang of joy and poignancy we feel when we see the amazing beauty of other men's bodies. This is so whether we get to have them or not. There is a joy and fascination in seeing a man bare-chested, an experience of wonder, an evocation of desire and longing, a thrill and an affirmation that life is grand and that the world is infinitely lovable. That such male beauty exists is reason for living. That is why we can enjoy photographs and movies, why we can enjoy even without possessing. It is not about possessing as much as appreciating. It is not about our own ego as much as life itself.

Not only do we experience sexual attraction to other men and a desire to touch them, to become sexually aroused with them, and to come to orgasm through mutual stimulation, we also experience a simple delight in being homosexual. Independent of actually having homosexual sex, there is an excitement and a sense of being special in the realization "I am gay." Scary at first, this insight into the nature of our own consciousness becomes an invitation to a fuller life. Once we have come out to ourselves, we have the opportunity to seek greater meaning for sex.

## In the Flesh

Bioenergetics and other body-oriented forms of psychotherapy theorize that orgasm has a healing function in the psyche quite independent of biological reproduction. They suggest that traumas, fears, negative conditioning and the like result in tightness and restriction in the body that distort both psychological and purely physiological processes. These can result not only in neurosis and mental illness, but also in psychosomatic disorders, cardiovascular disease, perhaps even cancer. The surge of energy during orgasm can break the blocks and keep the system clear of restrictions to the vital flow. The role of orgasm then is more than just ejaculation or reception of genetic material. It is activation of important self-regulating mechanisms in the mind-body system.

Perhaps the function of sex and orgasm in human beings has been not only to clear the individual's nervous system but also—and consequently—to affect the way the nervous system has evolved. The sexuality of human beings is different from almost all other species on the planet. Partly because women's sexual interest is not restricted by an estrus cycle, human beings are sexually and psychologically available and motivated all the time. We engage in sexual foreplay beyond instinctual seduction ritual. We experience orgasm more completely, it appears, than most other animals. And, at least among land animals, we alone have developed sophisticated language and complex brain functions. It seems that our sexuality may have been in some ways responsible for, or at least intrinsic to, our evolution of intelligence and conscious thought. Perhaps it was human beings' evolution of orgasm and complex sexual emotions separate from pure reproductive imperatives that caused us to develop intelligence.

## In the Soul

Sexual attraction can be understood as the experience in the flesh of what in the mind is wonder and curiosity. Sexual attraction is the desire to know another's body, to feel the flesh, to experience the rhythms of the other's movement. It is the drive to enter into relationship with the other, to try to see from the other's perspective, and so to add complexity to one's own experience of life. What directed the path of survival up toward consciousness and humanity may have been our ability to experience wonder, to feel curiosity, to develop myth, to desire connection, and to ask questions which force open neural pathways.

Within the act of lovemaking itself, sex is the experience of being caught up by a deeply primal, transpersonal force. It is not surprising that one consequence of such an experience should be genetic transfer and reproduction of life through time and through evolutionary advance. Our sexuality, far from being a distraction from "God," can be understood as the instrument by which God created us and continues to manifest himself to us.

People are blinded to the holiness of the flesh by fear and desire. They are blinded by the tendency of the senses to get stuck in what is familiar and expected, by our human failure to see the whole and to see life in context, by our failure to see the forest for the trees. But we will never develop vision by fleeing the flesh, by condemning our sexuality, by refusing to love God's manifestations in the flesh.

## *Mystical Aspects*

Sex also has mystical aspects. The experience of sexual arousal feels like moving beyond yourself. It is as though something primal and pre-rational is taking you over. You feel as though your unconscious is taking control. Sex in some way feels instinctual: We do not have to be taught to know how to do it (though we can certainly be taught how to do it better—and that is one of the reasons for experiencing sex with a variety of partners).

Becoming sexually aroused feels like being possessed by a god, what the Greeks called a *daimon*. And the pleasure of sex is called ecstasy, for in that surge of pleasure one feels outside oneself.

Our experience of loving another person is our participation in the divine love for creation. And our experience of being loved is our perception of God's love for us. Indeed, God has no way to demonstrate love for creatures except through the creatures' love for one another. This love for creation is not some curious will that creatures overcome their corporeality. The flesh is the mode of creation. God's love for us and our love for God is experienced in our flesh.

In the Gnostic Gospel of Thomas, the disciples asked Jesus, "When will you appear to us, and when will we see you?" Jesus answered, "When you strip without being ashamed, and you take your clothes and . . . trample them, then [you] will see the son of the living one and you will not be afraid." (Logion 34) In our nakedness to one another, we see Jesus/God in the flesh.

We might say that God created human beings because he loves to have sex. The way he experiences the pang of beauty and poignancy we experience when we gaze on a lovely young man in the height of his sexual maturity and erotic arousal is through *our* experience. The way he touches and caresses strong manly flesh and pleasures a man as a man would pleasure another man is through our doing it.

The mystical aspects were commonly known among primitive peoples for whom sexual activity and religious rituals were intertwined. The gods were metaphors for sex, and they were worshipped by having sex. The men masturbated into the earth to fructify the fields; the women offered themselves to the moon or the sun, opening their legs to allow the light from the heavenly bodies to enter their wombs; then, when the men returned from the fields, the women were waiting with holy organs for the men to fructify again with their bodily pleasure. And, in all likelihood, we know now, the men's ritual was led by a homosexual shaman and the women's by a lesbian witch/wisewoman.

Western Christian civilization "matured" beyond the sexual taboos and the public sexual acting out of these "primitive" peoples, but, in so doing, lost the connection between sex and spirit. Indeed, sex became the major sin. Like the latency period in childhood when the sex play of infancy goes into the unconscious to allow the personality (and self-awareness) to grow before the onset of full-blown sexuality in adolescence, this repression served humankind through centuries of psychological evolution.

But now, as the imperative to reproduce changes, it is time for further maturation of the interplay between sexuality and spirituality, between rejoicing in the flesh and deepening consciousness. Achieving a perspective on sex and on religiousness—exemplified by the gay experience of critical distance—allows us to see they should not be at odds. Indeed, the consequences of their having been divided for two millennia have been severe.

Somebody has to say, "Hey, this is not working." That is one of the roles of gay identity in the development of religion. We have to remind them that religion should not be anti-sexual, and the evidence of that is what the anti-sex bias in religion has done to us.

## What Is Wrong With the World

Saint Paul said the relationship between husband and wife parallels the relationship between God and his church. This Scriptural text is read at weddings, and it is taken to be Christianity's affirmation of sexuality. The image, unfortunately, is not very sex-positive. It does not seem to say anything about the joys of the flesh or to even hint at the intense sensations and feelings that flood the body and sweep the soul when people make love.

Saint Paul's image tends to be about power and authority in heterosexual relationships, not about the divinity of the sexual experience. Indeed, Christians ended up with a model of sexual relationship founded primarily in male dominance for the sake of controlling the genetic makeup of offspring. It did not have anything to do with pleasure. The early Christians—and all their followers thereafter—were intensely negative about incarnation in the flesh. Life was hard. People were cruel. Nature was harsh. Death was everywhere. Life in the flesh looked like a poor alternative to life in the mind. And for much of human evolution the function of religion was to offer an escape from the hardships of the world. How much better to end up in a dream in the mind, free of the sufferings of the body!

Life is still hard, harder than it needs to be. But we have learned to prevent many of the sufferings of the flesh. In today's technologically advanced world, there does not have to be inequality or cruelty, privation or disease, hunger or war. We could have "heaven on earth" if we just decided to. That we do not indicates that our model of the world and of life is not good enough: too much duality; too much domination by one person, one group, one set of beliefs and ideas over others; too much resentment and disapproval about other people's pleasure; and not enough well-wishing and collective joy for the good feelings everybody could be sharing.

What is wrong with the world has a lot to do with the collective model of what sex is—and it flows out of the male dominant heterosexual pattern. Males are driven to propagate their genes by subduing females, by preventing the females from having sex with other males, and by trying to stop other males from having sex with anybody. This is the alpha male dynamic.

It shows up in relation to power and money exactly the same way. The alpha male is driven to exercise power by controlling his associates and followers, and denying power to his competitors.

What are called "normal people" sometimes behave abominably about sex. Some of them seem more concerned with competition and imposition of power than with love and affection. They harass one another. They use one another. They commit rape. They murder their partners. The crimes of heterosexuality are accepted as an inevitable part of human nature. That this does not make sense to most gay men (and most women) is further evidence there is a superiority to not being "normal."

Of course, there are homosexual criminals and even liberated gay men (and women) who sometimes harass, batter, or use other people. But, with a few sensationalized exceptions, we do not commit rape and we are not killers (and those who are prove themselves terribly conflicted about their sexual orientation and are not liberated gay people).

## As Equals, In Unity

Gay relationships, at least in the abstract, offer a model of a different way of relating—as equals, in unity not duality.

It is wonderful that we can give one another sexual consciousness; beautiful that through an induction of touch, feeling, sensation, and wonderment we can stir up in one another the sense of well-being, of vitality, of feeling loved and shown affection. Sexual consciousness is being one with the *elan vital* that rises up through the universe. In the metaphorical language of religious mysticism, sex is the direct experience of God's love that sweeps through us, affirming and glorying in incarnation. Isn't it what God was feeling when he looked on all that he had made and said, "It is good"?

What a generous thing to be able to give to another what you want so much for yourself! And do we not truly want sex—not just as a frivolous whim or a vanity—but as a metaphysical reality of our consciousness as human beings? We need to feel loved. We need to be touched in order to grow and to stay healthy and vibrant.

## Spiritual Paths That Are Not Sexual

Perhaps we need to acknowledge that there are spiritual paths that are not sexual and that do not have anything to do with celebrating incarnation. These may involve a transcending of the world of the senses, an escape from incarnation for a radically different merging of consciousness with Spirit.

There are those, gay and straight, who realize oneness with

God—or feel a sense of moral obligation independent of the image of God—and lose, thereby, all interest in personal pleasure and satisfaction. For some of them this is an admirable state beyond self and selfishness. There are those who for biological or karmic reasons have just never had a lot of interest in sex in the first place. For them, perhaps, the gnawing distraction of sex is best discarded.

Of course, sexual need can be transcended and, with Freudian determination, sublimated. There are rewards for redirecting sexual energy—rewards in intensity of experience, maybe especially in prayer and religious enthusiasm.

## Sex With God

In its own wonderful—and wonderfully human—way, however, sex bestows similar intensities. For those who have opened their eyes to it and thus made it so for themselves, sex is God's bestowal of grace and love.

Our having sex is God's way of experiencing joy in creation. And our being loved by another is our way of experiencing God's love for us. God's love manifests as our beloved. In a way, all sex is sex with God.

# Chapter 5

## EVOLUTION: TEST FOR RELIGION

The mainstream, popular religions of the West, Christianity and Judaism, are being challenged by the way they deal with sex and homosexuality. The mystical core teachings of the religions urge unconditional love and acceptance of all people. But the popular manifestations of the religions encourage xenophobia, prejudice, pettiness, and narrow-mindedness. Religious leaders cite made-up statistics and literally lie about the behavior of gay people.

Because the religious nature of human beings deserves to be saved from the ephemeral institutions that represent it, we can hope that, in its own way, the gay issue will be the straw that breaks the camel's back, precipitating a modern reformation in religious thinking.

### The Ability to Keep Up With Social Change

The religious impulse in humankind has resulted in some of the greatest works of art and highest cultural achievements. Religion has bestowed upon us both a mystical sensitivity and a moral sensibility. The Ten Commandments and the teachings of Jesus Christ helped tame primitive human instincts and instill sentiments of compassion and mercy in warlike and barbaric people. Islam drew together the disparate and quarrelsome nomadic tribes of the Middle East and northern Africa. Hindu, Buddhist, and Taoist attitudes shaped the great civilizations of Asia.

Religion civilized Western culture and, in turn, the gradual maturation of civilization tamed religion. Notions of personal freedom and human rights supplanted theocracy. The First Amendment to the U.S. Constitution beat back the forces of religious oppression. By taking religion out of government, the liberal humanism of the American Founding Fathers freed religion from politics and allowed it to focus on what it was supposed to be about: love and compassion, not authority and power.

To those of us who have experienced moving liturgies and inspiring rituals, it is obvious that there is something beautiful about our love of God and our fellowship with other human beings. We have joined in a twilight procession through autumn fields singing Gregorian chant. Or we have sung rousing hymns on a Sunday morning and felt exultation and joy. Or we have sat in disciplined meditation and seen through the illusion of the world. These have all been good for us. They would be good experiences for everybody.

Our religious impulse makes us want to live good lives, to be in harmony with life, to make our lives worthwhile. It impels us not to hurt others—certainly never to kill or steal or behave in ways that would cause pain and suffering to others. Our religiousness has taught us to feel others' pain as our own, to recoil from the thought of causing pain just as we recoil from the thought of suffering pain.

Unfortunately, these same religious impulses inspired the Crusades, stoked the pyres of the Inquisition, sent Muslim armies marauding through India, rallied the Conquistadors against the Meso-American Indians and the Union cavalry against the Plains Indians, and drove people all through history to turn against their neighbors in righteousness, missionary zeal, and fear of taboo violation. The same exalted emotions that gave us high art and culture also have given us hypocrisy, cruelty, racism and anti-Semitism, and, of course, homophobia. Religion has kept the poor enslaved and justified oppression and social hierarchy. Religion teaches bigotry and judgmentalism even as it preaches love and gentleness.

There are many issues involved here; deep layers of the individual and the public psyche are being affected. What gets acted out is not always pretty. Certainly, one of the complex issues here is the ability of religious ideas to keep up with social change. The traditional myths that make up the world's great religions developed over long periods of time. Religion has always tried to respond to the issues of the present by seeking wisdom from the past. Perhaps most of its failures have happened because events occurred too suddenly for the deep and unconscious processes of religious impulse and mythmaking to cope. That is certainly what is happening now.

You hear statistics like: 70 percent of the accumulated knowledge of the human race has been acquired in the last 50 years and an eighth grader has been exposed to more information in his or her life than all the philosophers of Greece put together. It's mind-boggling. How are the processes of the collective psyche going to keep up?

## Trapped in the Myth of Religious Authority

The defenders of religion explain that it is supposed to be a conservative, stabilizing force. And that is why it does not always have answers for modern problems. But it is precisely religion that is supposed to provide those answers. Religious leaders decry the collapse of morality and decency in modern society. They are right: Terrible things are happening. But if there is a breakdown in the public's observance of religious propriety, the place to look for the cause has to be in religion. It is too late to blame modernization and call for a return to past ignorance. If religious symbols do not move people to behave harmoniously, isn't it because there is something wrong with religion? The symbols have lost their power.

Most religious, church-going people really mean to be good and loving. And most of them are. They often demonstrate remarkable generosity, conscientiousness, and self-sacrifice. The problem is that traditional popular religion operates out of an inadequate notion of right and wrong. Religious people are told to think they are right and others are wrong. Fundamentalists complain that liberal attitudes in society toward abortion and homosexuality deny their basic American rights to stop sin and determine how the people who live around them behave.

Religious people think they are doing good by stirring up negative judgments of sexuality in general and of homosexuality in particular. They think they are preventing pain and suffering, preserving propriety, championing tried and true solutions to the problems of the human condition. But many of them do not see the big picture. They do not see that other people have differing and valid perceptions. They are trapped in the myth of religious authority which insists that if they are right, others must be wrong. They are trapped in dualistic thinking. That this is so indicates a failure of their mythological system to force open their eyes to current reality. Instead of expanding consciousness and encouraging growth, most popular religions champion the status quo and shrink awareness with simplistic answers to complex problems. Curiously, the main answer the churches offer to complex social problems is: Join the church.

## Saving Religion

If we are going to "save" religion, we must do it by developing religious sensibilities and myths that make sense in today's cosmology and respond to today's problems. And, since religion is one of the biggest problems the gay community faces, we would do well to encourage and support its transformation.

It is nice that the Catholic Church has finally exonerated Galileo for introducing the world to scientific observation and experimental method as tools for exploring reality. But it is not enough to admit change happens by rectifying a wrong of the seventeenth century. Religion has to admit it is wrong about current matters. The nature of homosexuality and sexual variance is an essential one for them to confront because it affects real people's lives now. If religion fails to adapt, it invalidates its role as spiritual teacher and guide.

The evolution of self-aware, intentional gay identification presents a test for traditional religion. The teachings of almost all the Masters around the world call for loving kindness and good intentions for other people. That religious people are so virulently anti-gay and feel justified in hating homosexuality (if not homosexuals) is an indication of the failure of their mythological system to convey the teachings it proclaims.

For instance, Jesus said to love your enemies and do good to those that hate you. Most gay people, of course, do not hate Fundamentalist Christians, but political realities have made us enemies of theirs. Should the Christians not, therefore, do good to us by giving us the marriage rights we ask for and the legal protections we say we need? "If a man asks for your shirt, give him your coat also." (Matthew 5:40) How can the followers of Jesus refuse our pleading?

Fundamentalists say they do not hate homosexuals. They claim they love us. Is that why they say such false and horrible things about us? Their speech belies their claims. Hate, after all, is in the eye of the victim. That we experience their attitudes toward us as hateful is the proof that that is what it is.

The New Testament gives advice about how the gay rights movement should be treated. Soon after the death of Jesus, the Temple elders were discussing what to do about the Christian heresy that was growing in Jerusalem. Some wanted to slay all the disciples of Jesus and end Christianity before it caused any more trouble. A wise Elder named Gamaliel, the teacher of St. Paul, proposed leaving it up to God. "Let these men alone," he said, "if their work is of man, it will be overthrown. But if it is of God, you will not be able to overthrow it, and you will find yourselves fighting against God" (Acts 5:38-39).

## *Woe Unto You Scribes and Pharisees*

The only people Jesus specifically condemned in any way were "the Scribes and the Pharisees." And it is telling that Bible translations generally keep these words as antiquated terms instead of translating them into modern idiom. For "Scribes and Pharisees" translates directly to "Church officials and conservative religious leaders."

As the word suggests, the Scribes were the temple bureaucrats and the lawyers who could read and write and who, therefore, kept the records and managed the business of the Temple. The Pharisees were members of a lay reform movement in Judaism that called for a return to the old ways—to the "fundamentals"—insisting on literal interpretation of the Torah. They believed in angels and supernatural interventions and were always preaching that the end of the world was imminent.

All Jewish men dressed for prayer by strapping phylacteries (little wooden boxes containing the written text of the prayer *Shema Israel*) to their forehead and left arm in literal obedience to the text which said to keep these words as a sign for the hand and a pendant on the forehead, and by covering their heads with a prayer shawl with fringes, knotted to signify the 613 rules of the Mishnah (the oral tradition extrapolated from the Ten Commandments to cover every aspect of Jewish life).

The Pharisees were ostentatiously religious: They wore elaborate phylacteries with broad straps and oversized shawls with extra long fringe to demonstrate how obedient they were to the letter of the law. The Pharisees were clearly the predecessors of our modern day conservative evangelists and TV preachers who bemoan the present state of the world, predict that according to Bible prophecies the end of the world is nigh, and proclaim how saved they are.

To paraphrase Matthew 23:13: "Woe unto you," Jesus said, "Church officials and conservative religious leaders, hypocrites. Because you close the gates of heaven to those who are going in, you won't go in yourselves."

## The Way to Get to Heaven

A published analysis of the work of French existentialist playwright Jean Anouilh describes the Last Judgment as he sees it.

> The good are densely clustered at the gate of heaven, eager to march in, sure of their reserved seats, keyed up and bursting with impatience.
>
> All at once, a rumor starts spreading: "It seems He's going to forgive those others, too!"
>
> For a minute, everybody's dumbfounded. They look at one another in disbelief, gasping and sputtering, "After all the trouble I went through!" "If only I'd known this..." "I just cannot get over it!"
>
> Exasperated, they work themselves into a fury and start cursing God; and at that very instant they're damned. That was the final judgment. (Louis Evely, *That Man is You*).

The way to get into heaven is to want other people to get in, too. The tragedy of the anti-homosexual stance of most religions is not so much what it does to the gay people. (We can wake up and leave, after all!) It is what it does to the faithful.

If you take Jesus's prediction in Matthew 25:45 seriously, at the Last Judgment, the Judge is going to have to say to the Fundamentalists: "Behold, when I was thrown out of the military or was fired from my job or evicted from my apartment, you didn't care. When I was sick, you didn't visit me or lobby Congress for research funds. When I wanted to sacramentalize my relationship, you passed laws to prevent me. When I needed civil rights, you vilified me and misrepresented my claims. When I complained about injustice and demonstrated politically, you sensationalized my cause as a fundraising tactic to gather more wealth into your coffers. When I died, you picketed my funeral. Behold, what you didn't do for the least of these, my lesbian and gay sisters and brothers, you didn't do for me. Because you were not hospitable to these strangers in your midst, heaven holds no hospitality for you. Get thee into everlasting damnation."

Perhaps the reason spiritually oriented gay people have to work for the transformation of religion is to save the Christians from their own hell-fire!

## Transformation of the Ideas of Morality

The reality that population imperatives have changed demands an evolution in religious notions. The recognition of psychological dynamics demands change in how we understand human nature. The willingness of religions to entertain the idea that they are wrong about homosexuality is an indication of how willing they are to cope with all the tremendous changes that are occurring in the world today.

Because gay people have loudly proclaimed our existence, the religions must eventually develop a theology of sex that includes homosexuality. The behavior of ten percent of the population cannot be dismissed or vilified just because the ancients were not psychologically sophisticated enough to understand it. The churches and religious traditions that fail to keep up with change show themselves deficient by their attitudes toward gay identity.

The issue of homosexuality demands a transformation of the old ideas of morality. This issue reveals that a workable morality must come from reason, good sense, and compassion, not from rules handed down from ancient authority.

## Traditional Family Values

There is an element of blindness and hypocrisy in what is called "family values." In order to be in favor of families, you are supposed to ignore the reality of sexual activity in society and pretend it does not exist—like parents hiding sex from their children. Yet the ability to do even this is an artifact of modern architecture. When people lived in tents or one room huts, sex was not private and they could not hide it from the kids by locking the bedroom door and keeping the noise down.

Part of what is offensive to "family values" about gay identity is that, for better or worse, it undermines that hypocrisy. Advocates of family values are appalled that gay people have marches to demand justice and celebrate past victories, because the whole idea of the marches is to proclaim sexuality. Open gay identity rejects such denial and hypocrisy. Indeed, part of the positive popular gay stereo-type is that we "tell it like it is."

The other face of family values is xenophobia and concern for preservation of gene lines. Central is the notion that nobody outside blood family can really be trusted: Blood is thicker than water. Family values make wrong anything that is different. Hence, for some, racial animosity can be justified as a family value. In the dual-istic world, it is us against them. And "them" is anybody we cannot understand or who does not agree with "us" or participate in our cultural styles.

Many non-gay people simply cannot understand homosexuality. That is the problem with being in the majority: Your way seems like the only way. Homosexuals are more capable of understanding heterosexuality. We see it all around us. We can understand that our sexual drive could have been like theirs, but isn't. We can see the diversity because we are part of it. If nothing else, conscious homosexuality necessarily encourages open-mindedness.

The push for gay marriage, for instance, is about demanding that society pay attention to actual situations—telling it like it is. For better or worse, gay couples exist. They have legal and financial involvements that need to be recognized in law. Owning property together creates legal entanglements. In the case of a breakup or death, legal mechanisms are needed to untangle these matters.

Gay marriage is not about undermining the sacrament of matrimony. It is about dealing with reality. Society does not decline to make laws about banking just because the Bible did not mention banks. Thousands of years ago we may not have needed legal acknowledgment of same-sex relationships. But in today's complex and legalized world, we do.

## The Highest Form of Love

There is an irony of history in the fact that the Catholic Church's position on sex—at times seeming to condemn everything sexual that is not loving married heterosexual coitus for the purpose of reproduction in positions that minimize pleasure and maximize possibilities for fertilization—originated in a doctrinal effort to affirm the goodness of the flesh and the legitimacy of sex.

Early in its life, Christianity competed with Manicheism, a religion that merged Christian myth with Greek Gnosticism and Persian Zoroastrianism into an exaggeratedly dualistic mystical theology that taught that incarnation in flesh was evil. Sparks of spiritual substance were said to be snatched away from the realm of light and spirit, and trapped in base material reality by acts of sex that led to conception.

For some Manicheans this meant sex was wrong. They vowed abstinence and practiced celibacy and asceticism to escape the bonds of flesh. But others, recognizing that sexual consciousness is a kind of mystical state, believed that it was not sex that should be avoided but reproduction. Sexual ecstasy, in fact, helped them escape the base material existence. Indeed, some believed the "ritual eating of semen" freed spirit from its entrapment in matter, and this became a sort of sacrament. Manicheans developed methods of contraception to allow sexual activity but prevent the unwanted assault on the spirit realm. There is a recognizably homosexual spin in this. What else is "ritual eating of semen" but fellating the priest—or vice versa? Paradoxically, at the same time the Gnostic notions were anti-sexual, they were liberated and pro-homosexual.

These same ideas reappeared in the Middle Ages as Catharism (also called Albigensianism) in Provence and Languedoc in the south of France. Catharism had the odd side effect of creating for a while a liberated counterculture and a flourishing of the arts. Indirectly, this society created the idea of Romantic Love—that one should be sexually attracted to a person one mates with—an idea we today understand to be basic to love and affection.

In explaining how courtly love developed into modern romance, Joseph Campbell delighted in proclaiming that in the Middle Ages the highest form of love was adultery. Marital love was participation in societal, familial concerns. But forbidden love was participation in a mystery of the soul. This was passion that risked burning at the stake and eternal damnation for the sake of the beloved.

Even to the present day, homosexuals have been faced with this same dilemma. To be true to themselves and their deepest personal needs and feelings, they have had to accept the risk of eternal damnation as proof of their love and integrity.

Gay classics scholar John Boswell argued that homosexual unions were different from heterosexual marriages precisely because they were chosen out of love and emotional connection. Though his research has been questioned even by pro-gay scholars, Boswell contended in *Same-Sex Unions in Premodern Europe* that faith communities used liturgies, like the Office for Same-Sex Unions under the patronage of the holy martyrs (and lovers) Saints Serge and Bacchus, to recognize gay unions, even before the Church began to perform straight marriages. Because heterosexual unions were usually arranged, they were obvious to family and society. But because homosexual unions were chosen intimately and invisibly, they needed to be proclaimed since, as the liturgies said, the lovers were "united not in the bond of birth but in spiritual faith and love."

The Catholic Church fought against both Manicheism and Catharism by condemning them as heresies and persecuting the believers. In order to affirm fleshly, material existence and proclaim the goodness of sex and procreation, church officials specifically condemned the heretics' practice of contraception and championed the notion that the proper purpose of sex was reproduction.

A thousand years later, when Pope Pius XII was trying to deal with the discoveries of modern medicine, he was constrained by an official condemnation of birth control. And so, in 1958, in a speech to a group of Italian midwives, Pius XII forbid Catholic parents from using "artificial means" to regulate family size, supposedly bound by the official declaration of *magisterium* (the Church's teaching authority) condemning Manichean contraception. Because of the papal need not only to be right, but also to have always been right, the Church's pro-sex stand in the third century ended up casting a sex-negative and anti-female pall over all religion in the twentieth century.

## The Goal of Spiritual Growth

The goal of spiritual growth is to transcend religion and see through the metaphors of religious beliefs. Thus, institutional religion presents a puzzle: In order to attain spiritual maturity, we need religion to show us the way. But that means we need religion in order to learn to leave it behind or, at least, to develop a more profound understanding of it than most popular religions allow.

Perhaps gay people are lucky in having been thrown out of their churches. This gives them the opportunity to see beyond religion. Somebody—let it be us gay people!—has to say to the religious masses of the world: "Do not take all this so seriously. It's just a metaphor."

The point of religion is to stir up in people positive, loving attitudes toward life. Religion often fails in this regard. The modern mind sees that the Fundamentalist churches that rail against homosexuals are only a few generations distant from the Inquisitors who burned homosexuals at the stake. That the Inquisitors behaved as they did in the name of God is evidence that God is not guiding and controlling the church.

It is the life-enhancing, mystical-consciousness-inspiring, all-loving spiritual core of the religious instinct that must be saved from religion.

Gay people are, in a way, at an advantage from the start. We feel the loving, religious sentiments deeply, yet we do not fit into the church. Our exclusion demonstrates to us that these deep-felt sentiments transcend religion and religious beliefs.

As the general public becomes gradually more inured to homosexuality and the presence of a vocal gay minority as part of modern life, the anti-gay behavior of Fundamentalist religions (Christian, Jewish, and Islamic) will tend to look more and more bigoted and out-of-touch. In the long run, the know-nothing stance of the Fundamentalists regarding homosexuality will further isolate the churches and temples from mainstream reality. This will hopefully help foment the necessary reformation in religion.

# Chapter 6

## EVOLUTION: THE BIBLE

Gay perspective helps us understand how to think about the Bible. We can see how dated the Bible's religious notions are by examining how they fail to recognize the psychological reality that we are living. Indeed, the interpretation of the Bible by mainstream Christians is seriously challenged by the way they deal with the texts that are supposedly about homosexuality. These verses are routinely taken out of context and presented as though the ancient writers knew what homosexuality was as a modern psychological/behavioral category.

Modern Biblical exegesis, the science of understanding what the texts meant to the people who composed them, shows that the anti-gay texts are generally misinterpreted. The story of Sodom and Gomorrah, for example, does not really have anything to do with homosexuality. And the condemnation in Leviticus of sex between men as an abomination is not about homosexual love, but about preventing religious assimilation.

### Sodom and Gomorrah

The real sin of Sodom and Gomorrah was inhospitality to strangers, a notion that sounds pretty wishy-washy in modern culture. But in an ancient desert culture, inhospitality to strangers who came to an oasis for water and protection from the elements was deadly serious, tantamount to murder. That is how Jesus understood the story. Not recognizing any sort of anti-homosexual content, he used Sodom and Gomorrah as an example of simple inhospitality and, by extension, refusal to welcome the Christian gospel (Luke 10:12).

The story goes as follows: God was talking with Abraham the Patriarch about how mean and selfish the people were in Sodom and Gomorrah. He said he was going to come down and smite them. Abraham objected, perhaps because Lot, his relative, old friend, and competitor in the sheepherding business (they had split the territory up between them) was living in Sodom. Abraham begged God not to destroy the inhabitants of the city if there were as many as 50 righteous men among them. God agreed. Abraham then pressed for 45. When God agreed again, Abraham talked him down to 40, then 30, 20, and finally ten.

So God arrives, in the form of two angels, to check out Sodom and to see if there are even ten righteous men there. The angels go straight to the house of Lot, who hospitably invites them to stay at his place. But they decline, saying they want to spend the night in the town square.

Lot warns the angels that that would be dangerous, and gets them to come in for dinner. About that time, townsfolk show up at the door wanting Lot to bring the visitors out so they can "know" them. Lot was a foreigner himself and a newcomer; the Sodomites might have been suspicious of just who he was entertaining.

Lot declines. When the townsfolk try to force their way in the door, the angels strike them blind, then warn Lot to take his family and get out of town. "Leave and don't look back," they say. The next morning fire falls out of the sky and burns up the cities, a column of smoke rising to the heavens.

There is no specific mention of sex in the story. The townsfolk want to "know" the strangers. It is true that the Hebrew verb "to know" was sometimes used as a euphemism for "to have sex," but out of its 943 occurrences in the Old Testament it is clearly used to mean sex only ten times. The argument for a sexual meaning in the story of Sodom is that Lot offers his daughters to the unruly townsfolk as distractions. But this really speaks more about how little women were regarded than what the townsfolk wanted to "know."

If anything, this story is an example of a familiar theme in myth that wicked people are not able to recognize divine or angelic visitors even when they are right in front of them. The Greek myth of Baucis and Philemon tells practically the same story. In this tale Zeus and Hermes are wandering the countryside. As it approaches time for dinner, they knock at several doors but nobody will invite them in. Finally they come to the humble home of an aged couple, Baucis and Philemon. In spite of being impoverished, the old couple invites the strangers in and serves them a meal. The gods reward them by changing their little hut into a golden temple (and also by flooding the homes of all the people who hadn't shown such hospitality).

The townsfolk of Sodom were annihilated for not recognizing who was in their midst because they were too suspicious, selfish, petty, and mean-spirited, not because they were homosexual.

Though the story dates back to ancient times, the anti-homosexual twist that the townsfolk wanted to gang rape the angels became popular in Christian thinking in the fourteenth century. This interpretation helped explain the dual catastrophes of the Hundred Years War and the Black Death, and served the dual purpose of providing a cause/scapegoat and motivating repopulation. Blaming non-reproductive sex, including sodomy, for God's wrath encouraged reproduction and helped to get the agrarian economy going again after the decimation of the work force.

It is ironic that the Christian activists of the present day, behaving inhospitably to gay people, are looking like the Sodomites—unable to see the angelic presences in their midst, or at least the innocence and good will of most gay people. And gay people are looking like the angels—fighting for health funding, volunteering as AIDS caregivers, reaching out to their suffering brethren in a true act of compassion, creating community in spite of adversity. To use another Biblical image, gay people are the Samaritans, hated and despised because of religious animosity, who nevertheless demonstrate love of neighbor. These are the "least of my brethren."

## *Onan Spills His Seed*

A similar misreading of Scripture is the basis of the Christian condemnation of masturbation and objection to ejaculation outside a vagina. In the Book of Genesis is the tale of Onan, who was killed by God because he spilled his seed (Genesis 38:10). In popular legend, Onan was swallowed up when a crack in the earth opened—ostensibly because his semen touched the ground.

But, in fact, that is not what the story is about at all. The punishment of Onan is about the ancient Hebrew laws of inheritance. "The law of levirate marriage" required that if a man died without a proper heir, his brother, the person closest to him by blood, should father a child by his widow in order to give him an heir. If the brother did not succeed in fathering an heir, then the deceased's possessions reverted back to the paternal line of succession. Onan practiced *coitus interruptus*, withdrawing just before ejaculation, a form of contraception, in order to contravene the law of levirate marriage so that he could get his brother's fortune. It had nothing whatsoever to do with masturbation, semen or even contraception. Onan was punished for being disobedient, selfish, and greedy.

## *Abominations*

It is hard to know what the ancient Hebrews actually thought about homosexual sex. The verse quoted so regularly condemning sex with a man as with a woman may well have been a rule against anally raping vanquished soldiers in battle as a proclamation of masculinity. That should have been prohibited and it is not mentioned anywhere else. Besides, the supposed objection to homosexuality in Leviticus 18 is not to homosexual sex or anal intercourse per se, but to a man being treated like a woman. This is more about what ancient Hebrew men thought of women than same-sex sexual relationships.

Literally, in Hebrew, Leviticus 18:22 says: "With a male you shall not lie the lyings of a woman." The verse appears in a chapter concerned with describing things the Hebrews were not supposed to do because the Canaanites did them. The chapter begins and ends with the command: "You shall not do what is done in the land where you live; you shall not walk in the way of their laws and customs." That was the real issue: keeping Hebrew culture from picking up Canaanite influences. Most of the verses concern the blood relationships that constitute incest. Appended to the end of this discussion is the prohibition of intercourse with a woman during her menstruation, of sex with animals, of child sacrifice to the god Molech, and the aforementioned odd line about not lying the lyings of a woman—nothing about the proper function of the anus or incompatibility of same sex organs.

The simple fact is, the commandment not to have sex with a man as with a woman is satisfied by having sex with a man as with a man, that is, as equals, honoring one another, giving each other pleasure out of respect and affection, with no expectation of reproducing, just out of joy in each other's physicality.

Furthermore, the condemnation of homosexual intercourse is as an "abomination." While that word sounds particularly egregious, in fact, it is used in the Bible specifically to distinguish an act as taboo from one that is ethically wrong. Murder or theft or lying are wrong and sinful. They violate another person. An abomination is a violation of ritual or social propriety.

Picking your nose in public is an abomination. In modern parlance, it's "gross." That is not the same thing as sin, even though, being a primitive tribe, the Hebrews stoned people for bad manners and taboo violations. Abominations were violations of ritual purity, things that prevented a person from participating in tribal religious life. Doing anything the Canaanites did in their worship was an abomination, like sacred male "prostitution." A more modern example would be a Jew making the sign of the cross as he comes up to bat in a game of baseball: That is something Catholics do. It is a violation of Jewish identity. But certainly not a sin or crime.

This is not to suggest that the Hebrews were not homophobic. They did stone homosexuals. But so what? The taboos of ancient Hebrew culture have nothing to do with homosexual identity in modern, psychologically aware society.

Most of the outdated commandments from Scripture are ignored anyway: The rule against blending fibers in fabric; the rule against shaving or cutting one's hair; the rule against allowing menstruating women to be in the presence of men; the elaborate rules of food preparation; the rules about land reform and reallocation of wealth to the poor every 50 years; the laws against gleaning of grain fields and hybridizing of animals; the rules forbidding loaning money at interest; the laws requiring prayer and the ritual garbing with phylacteries and shawls; the rule requiring men to keep their heads covered; the commandments about offering tithes of spices and herbs; the commandments about animal sacrifice—all are dismissed because everybody can see they belong to a distant, primitive time and have no application to modern pluralistic society.

So how come the disputed texts about homosexuality are taken to be God's unchangeable revelation? This kind of selective reading of Scripture is itself a disproof of the Evangelical declarations of Biblical inerrancy.

## The Bible Is Not About Modern Life

We don't know what homosexuality was in a desert nomadic society 3,000 years ago. But it certainly was not what it is now in the twenty-first century. The Bible is not about modern life. Its model of the solar system is inaccurate. Its understanding of disease is inconsistent with scientific germ theory. The Biblical authors did not know about genetics and heredity. It is not that the Bible is "wrong," but parts of it are just "not applicable." The Bible's sexual rules and cleanliness taboos do not make sense in a world of daily bathing, antiseptic soaps, deodorants, condoms, and tampons.

The Hebrews had no notion of romantic love. Sex was for reproduction, for dominance, and for satisfaction of lust, not expression of affection and interpersonal romance, though certainly interpersonal bonds developed. Ironically, one of the few stories in the Bible about such an interpersonal bond is that of David and Jonathan who "loved one another with a love surpassing the love of women." (2 Samuel 1:26) There are no loving heterosexual couples in the Bible, no nuclear families. The Bible never says Adam and Eve loved each other or lived in a three-bedroom tent with little Cain and Abel.

We do wrong to project our notions of romance and interpersonal bonding into Old Testament times. This was more than 1,000 years before medieval Provence, courtly love, and the valorization of sexual attraction as a basis for forming marriages that color our modern ideas. The ancient Hebrews would have been thoroughly befuddled by our ideas of love at first sight or falling in love or finding a soulmate by sexual attraction. For them sexual attraction was lust, not an invitation to personal intimacy. It was the urge to dominate and use another person's body for one's own purposes. Much of the time for a man—and that is who mattered, since women were chattel—sexual attraction was more like pride in possessions or desire to acquire property. That is why there is more mention in the Ten Commandments of sins of covetousness than sins of eroticism.

There is eroticism in the Bible. The book called The Song of Solomon or Canticle of Canticles is an example of Hebrew erotic poetry. It demonstrates sexual desire, but not interpersonal intimacy. King Solomon, to whom authorship is attributed, had 700 wives and 300 concubines. He would have been singing his erotic canticles to a different woman every night. (Medieval scholars had a difficult time explaining what this book was doing in the Bible. They explained the sexual imagery as a metaphor for the soul's desire for God.)

And, curiously, what is also in the Bible is concern about penis size. Biblical characters occasionally rhapsodizes with highfalutin Biblical eloquence: "The Lord exalteth my horn" (1 Sam 2:1,10; Psalms 18:2; Luke 1:69). What else does that mean but "God gives me a large, lasting erection"?

## Not an Instruction Book of Modern Family Values

The Bible does not lay out the design for family values. It does forbid adultery, but not because it jeopardizes the affection of husband and wife, but because adultery was a violation of a man's property rights and a threat to the integrity of his line of inheritance. The

Bible does not forbid masturbation. It does not distinguish between the urethral drip of gonorrhea and emission of seminal fluid. It does not mention pedophilia. It does not define monogamy. There is no commandment against abortion, no Biblical definition of when life begins. There is no commandment against pornography. Though it does warn against overindulgence in alcohol, the Bible does not mention drugs. Or cigarettes.

The Bible is not an "instruction book for life." It is an anthology of Hebrew literature: The Psalms are a book of poetry, the Canticle of Canticles a collection of popular songs, the Book of Job a play written in the style of a Greek tragedy. The Book of Numbers contains a census report; the Prophecy of Ezechial might be an account of a UFO sighting. Some of the stories, like Adam and Eve and Jonah and the whale, are pure fable or *midrash*.[3] Some are faithful recordings of history, while others are merely folk legends devised to explain natural phenomena.

The fateful story of Sodom and Gomorrah seems to be of this last kind. In all likelihood, there really were two little towns in the desert called Sodom and Gomorrah. They may even have had a reputation for being mean-spirited and unwelcoming. Some sort of disaster probably befell these cities on the plain, and religious imagination and pedagogical opportunity figured out a lesson to draw from the catastrophic event.

Most likely the towns were destroyed by an earthquake, volcanic eruption, or even a meteor. Some modern astronomers now think the Great Chicago Fire was caused by a rain of space debris. (There were sudden, unexplained fires all across the upper Midwest that night.) The story about Mrs. O'Leary's cow was a fanciful explanation for that disaster, not a great deal different from the story of Lot and the angels.

Perhaps the best evidence for this interpretation is the inclusion in the story of Lot's wife being turned into a pillar of salt for looking back to see what was happening. (Why would that little, so human, foible incur God's furious wrath against deviant sexuality?) The area around the Dead Sea, where Sodom and Gomorrah were located, because it is below sea-level, is full of unusual geological formations—some of them rock columns, like aboveground stalagmites or, specifically, like the calcium carbonate deposits called *tufa* that ring Mono Lake in northern California. These could easily look to the imaginative mind like running people turned to mineral. Bad science, but appealing folk-legend.

To finish the story: After Lot's poor wife was petrified for looking over her shoulder, his daughters took him into the mountains to a cave. There they got him drunk and seduced him so they could get pregnant. The daughters' offspring went on to father the Moabites and the Ammonites, tribes the Hebrews later had to deal with politically. This story is far more about racial power dynamics in Canaan than God's plan for nuclear families.

A similar story appears in the Book of Judges (Chapters 20 and 21). A Levite and his concubine are traveling from Bethlehem to Ephrain. They stop overnight in the town of Gibeah of the Benjamites. At first no one will invite them in, and they prepare to sleep in the town square. Then an old man, a fellow countryman of the Levite now living in Gibeah, invites them in for dinner. While they are eating, a couple of men identified as worshippers of Belial (a Canaanite deity) come to the door demanding to "know" the Levite. When they won't go away, even when the host offers his virgin daughter, the Levite seizes his concubine and gives her to them. The men rape her repeatedly and leave her to die on the old man's doorstep. The Levite carries her body back to his home in Ephraim, then cuts the body into twelve pieces and in outrage sends the pieces to the twelve tribes of Israel. When the leaders of the tribe of Benjamin decline to extradite the guilty parties, a war starts against them. An army comprised of representatives from all the other tribes attack Gibeah. They set the town afire so that a column of smoke rises to heaven.

This story sounds just like the destruction of Sodom and Gomorrah without the divine intervention. It is a story about flagrant lawlessness. It is included in the Book of Judges as evidence for why a king over all of Israel was needed.

## *Not Derived But Projected*

Trying to figure out the morals of the Old Testament stories is hopeless. The specifics of the morality that Christianity preaches may be founded in Biblical passages, but they are not derived from the text as much as they are projected back into it.

Pro-gay Scripture scholars, for instance, show how the possible references to homosexuality in the Epistles of Saint Paul are based on interpretation choices made for uncertain Greek expressions. Saint Paul condemned "soft" men and "male-fuckers." Bible translators centuries later decided he must have meant homosexuals. But is a soft man effeminate or weak-willed? Is a male-fucker a person who fucks males or a male who fucks? John Boswell offered the example of "lady killer." Is a lady killer a person who kills ladies or a lady who kills? In fact, it is neither. It is a dashing, sexually attractive man. How could you tell that except from context and usage? The words assumed to mean homosexuals do not appear elsewhere in Paul's writing. Who could know what he meant when there's no context except the translator's prejudices?

Even if St. Paul did mean sissies and queers, so what? He was an uptight preacher from a Middle Eastern country where everybody was uptight about their bodies and kept themselves covered from head to foot. When he came to Greece to proclaim Jesus's gospel of universal love, he discovered a country where, just the opposite, men and, to a lesser degree, women were proud of their bodies and showed themselves freely. St. Paul was demonstrating culture shock, not divine revelation.

St. Paul turned Jesus's commandment of love upside down. Quoting the Book of Proverbs, he says: "If your enemy is hungry, feed him, and if he is thirsty, give him a drink; for in so doing you will heap burning coals upon his head" (Romans 12:20). Heaping burning coals on somebody's head is not what Jesus meant by "Love your neighbor as yourself."

This is not to deny Scripture, but to recognize it for what it is, a literary anthology of an ancient foreign culture, and to recognize that things change. The world of today is radically different from that of two or three thousand years ago.

Why did the omniscient God think it was so important to specify minute details about such insignificant things as what the Hebrews ate or who they undressed in front of, but neglected in his book of rules for all future generations such issues as nuclear and biological warfare or destruction of the rain forests? With all the prophecies in the Bible that TV evangelists say predict various political maneuvers in the Middle East today, how come the landing on the moon was not predicted? How come sexual morality is so important to Christianity when Jesus gave no rules about sex at all except to forbid divorce, which is now widely accepted among Protestants? If homosexuality was such an important issue in Christian morals, how come Jesus forgot to mention it?

How come the accumulation of Christian Scriptures ended with the Council of Nicea in 325 A.D.? How come God stopped revealing things once the institution of the church got established? Does this not seem like an organizational imperative of the institution to prevent "new revelations" from creating competitors, rather than the wise guidance of a loving God?

For a prehistoric, generally illiterate people, written Scripture was special: proof of something magical and powerful. Today the Bible is just another book in a world overflowing with written texts. There is nothing mystical anymore about something being written down. As far as written things go, the Declaration of Independence and the U.S. Bill of Rights are far more influential and relevant in our lives than the purity codes in the books of Leviticus and Deuteronomy.

The Bible certainly contains spiritually inspiring words. The Psalms contain insightful verses that address basic human questions about existence. The New Testament teachings of Jesus are profound and important. Like the Sermons of the Buddha, the poetry of the Sufis, the Dialogues of Plato, and the *Tao Te Ching*, there is wisdom contained in Holy Scriptures. The Bible is qualitatively different from all the others because of its status in Christianity as "revealed," but there is a lot of the Bible that is meaningless to us today. Old

Testament strictures are ignored even by the preachers who claim every word was dictated directly by the Almighty.

## The Gay Perspective

Certainly the Bible is not affirmative of homosexual love. Christianity has a long history of condemning homosexuality. But the pro-gay findings of modern Biblical analysis give the churches an easy way out. They could claim these discoveries. They could even claim them as their own. All they would have to do is call for consistency with the Christian commandment to love your neighbor. They could embrace the discoveries of gay Scripture scholars as evidence that God is still working in the world and helping people to understand his Word.

Whatever happens, the churches must start to reform and restructure religion. They must proclaim a new understanding of the meaning of religion. They must make sense of the multiplicity of religions on Earth. And probably they must return to the teachings of Jesus. Changing the way they treat homosexuals is a good place to start. This one act would allow Christians to be modern and Christlike at the same time.

The gay perspective dramatizes the inconsistency with which Biblical texts are treated. Our struggle is to let loving kindness, goodness, and compassion determine morality, not ancient texts read out of context. Curiously (or not so curiously), this moral paradigm shift was the "good news" proclaimed by Jesus 2000 years ago. Whatever happened to it? Our struggle helps to push religion into the future, transforming it from superstition that limits people's lives to a force that opens up symbolic vistas with which people can enhance their lives.

As we will see, traditional Christian religion will inevitably fade away, and a scientifically sound and psychologically sophisticated worldview—based in Buddhistic moral and mystical notions, stripped of Orientalisms, liberated from traditional anti-sex bias, and enriched with the social teachings of Jesus, stripped of their supernaturalisms—will replace it. Helping dramatize and accelerate this transformation is a major contribution gay people make.

# Chapter 7

## EVOLUTION: TRANSFER OF THE FOCAL
## POINT OF WONDER

Religion is undergoing a transformation today because of the recognition of the metaphorical nature of myth and doctrine. The rise of gay identity is an important part of this evolutionary development, both demonstrating it and helping to bring it about.

This transformation is happening, in great part, because 1) science has replaced the old mythological worldviews with a new empirically based cosmology, 2) the development of a global society has forced a kind of cultural pluralism in which the various religions are exposed as symbolical culture forms, not special revelations of Absolute Truth, and 3) the human population has grown to the point that it threatens to exhaust the resources of the planet and overwhelm the environment.

### The Post-Modern Worldview

What has come to characterize our "post-modern" worldview is the stance of observing from over and above, from an Archimedian perspective. We are aware of process. Modern technology, global communication, easy travel, and historical and cultural awareness have forced human beings into a higher perspective on what it means to be human. We live in a world so different from the ancients, they could not even have begun to imagine our lives. It would all look like magic.

We—modern, educated, sophisticated global citizens—for better or worse, are unlike any human beings who have ever lived. We know about the possibility of global events. This changes our way of understanding the explanations of life that have come down to us, especially religion.

## All Myths Are False and All Are True

The only attitude toward myth and religion that makes any sense today is that all are equally false as literal accounts of real-time events or as factual descriptions of metaphysical realities. At the same time, all are true as clues to that mysterious reality that sometimes breaks through into everyday life as miracles, powers, and inexplicable occurrences. Whether religious myths are factually true or not, they are pointers to the nature of consciousness. They are metaphors for how to live rich and full lives. They are interesting, important, and sometimes inspiring. But they are not factual statements of Absolute Truth.

All myths are equally false and equally true. But not all myths are equal. Some are more effective than others in conveying life-affirming wisdom. The way to judge a myth or a religious tradition is to look at how its believers behave.

## The Development of Religion and Myth

Historical perspective and the modern attitude of scientific objectivity allow us to observe the development of religion and myth as anthropological phenomena. We can see that the primary figures of myth arose from the earliest human experience of wonder, mystery, and danger.

For the hunting peoples of prehistory, the sabertooth tiger, the woolly mammoth, and the other animals upon which they depended for food—and for tutorship—were the source of both danger and sustenance. Humans had to learn how to share the wilderness with the animals. For the animals, through long-evolved instinct, knew how to find food. They seemed to know the weather, to be able to anticipate the changes of the season, and to live in accord with nature—things primitive humans had to learn and incorporate into the collective instincts of the tribe passed down through its religion and lore. Thus, the earliest surviving religious images and prehistoric cave paintings show half-human, half-animal figures that were the mythological totem-ancestors, anthropomorphizations of the powers of nature. Through meditating on them, ritually honoring them, and repeating stories about them, hunters believed they appeased the animal spirits and were granted their wisdom—and their flesh for food.

Primitive tribes dependent on plants for food developed agriculture, and in so doing shifted the imagery of their religion from the animal spirits to the patterns of plant growth and cyclic time. The rituals of planting and harvesting were identified with the patterns of human procreation, birth, and growth.

With further cultural evolution, humankind brought both the animal world and the plant world under control. They were no longer the source of mystery and danger. From the primitive fascination with—and dependence upon—the cycles of nature, the early humans developed knowledge of the stars and celestial bodies that moved across the heavens in their orderly pattern. They observed that these seemed to correlate with human life cycles. Thus the great field of instructive wonder shifted to the skies. People worshipped sun gods and moon goddesses and told stories about them to explain human experience.

Further evolution in consciousness and culture shifted these myths into higher and more abstract realms. The gods became invisible philosophical forces that dominated the realm of conscience, volition, and behavior. God was not a beast to appease so humans could righteously take its body for food or a field of grain to coax to fruition, but an overseeing judge to please by one's cooperation in the social order. Still, that God looked down from a heaven situated just above the sky, and his realm of power and punishment was situated somewhere underground.

Today these mysteries of the heavens no longer move the soul. We no longer believe God is watching from heaven overhead, for that heaven has proved to be only sky. We know, from observation, that the sky extends light-years beyond imagination into an infinity that none of the gods of human mythology could have even begun to imagine. Beneath us is planetary rock. God has moved out of the sky and into the realm of consciousness and mind.

## A Prodigious Transfer

According to Joseph Campbell in *The Hero With A Thousand Faces*, the development of science from seventeenth century astronomy to nineteenth century biology to twentieth century anthropology and psychology marks "the path of a prodigious transfer of the focal point of human wonder." Not the animals or the plants, not the march of the spheres, not the notion of cosmic law, but now humankind's own consciousness is the crucial mystery.

The "fringe phenomena," like UFOs, angelic apparitions, psychic powers, miracles, weeping icons, stigmatas, etc., that once justified religion are understood to be at least partly psychological. Nonetheless, they manifest mysterious aspects of human consciousness. They point to powers we do not understand, powers that belong to the human mind, but not to beings from the sky.

The religious impulse—what we call spirituality—is no longer about the gods, but about humankind itself. Our consciousness is the mysterious alien presence we both fear and look to for sustenance—now not of the flesh, but of the soul. Psychology has taken the place that religion once held as arbiter of what is right and natural. No longer in an underground hell, the force of the devil is now identified as the "id." No longer above the sky, heaven is now identified as the higher consciousness. It is understanding what and who we are that fascinates and motivates us.

In the last half of the twentieth century, in part because of pollution and technological damage to the planet, a new paradigm has appeared, a new way of thinking about what human beings are. This is ecology, the understanding of the biological systems of the earth and our place in those larger systems.

Yet to interpret ourselves to ourselves we still have only metaphors and myths. It is our own consciousness—our psychological health and well-being—to which we look to discover how to transform our experience.

The lessons of the ages turn out to be about how to take responsibility for our own growth and evolution. We can learn from the past, we can look to the metaphors of old and model our lives on them, we can investigate the wisdom written in sacred texts. But the gods we imagine live more in our hearts and minds than in outside space. Outside space has been taken over by science and discovered to be empty.

Of course, space is not empty at all. Modern physics tells us that the universe expands by continually creating new space and new particles that flicker in and out of existence. Three-dimensional space is bubbling up everywhere, like suds pouring out of an over-soaped washing machine, out of what the cosmologists call with mystical vagueness the "quantum foam." Space is alive with energy patterns and streams of electromagnetic waves. But no gods, no heavenly throne rooms. They are in a different kind of "space" entirely.

## The Place of Mystery

We may be moved and spiritually changed by the mythological traditions of the past, but what they reveal to us is not the gods in the sky, but the patterns of our own evolution from plant to animal to primate to human being and beyond. The place of mystery is in the working of the human mind.

This is, in fact, the high teaching of the great mystical traditions worldwide, despite the retrograde superstition of most popular religions. From Jesus to Buddha to the Hindu Upanishads, from Hermes Trismegistus through medieval alchemy, the message is basically the same: "The Kingdom of God is spread upon the face of the earth, and men do not see it." "Behold, the gods are within you." "As above, so below. As within, so without." "Brahman is Atman." "Thou art That."

There will never be a new myth like the myths of old. No world savior can arise and declare that he or she is the incarnation of God on earth. No one would believe him or her. Actually, it happens all the time and nobody cares except the cult-watchers and maybe the police and psychiatrists. The memory of the myths of the past will serve as the source of metaphors about how to live and how to transform consciousness. But the epistemological foundations will have shifted. No longer is the truth in the myth. Now we understand that the truth is the psychological awareness of what the myth means.

Interest in spirituality is based on an intuition that there is more to life than meets the eye, that greater forces influence the outcome of human events than human beings are used to seeing.

Science, the modern worldview, provides models for thinking about these forces. We can call them wave patterns or field phenomena. To the modern mind, it makes more sense to talk about scientific laws than personalities embedded in natural phenomena. The latter is obviously projection and anthropomorphism. But the divergent descriptions are just two ways of saying the same thing. It is how people put it all together inside their heads, how they interpret the world and themselves to themselves, how they understand it "in human terms" that is myth.

Curiously, in modern America, the efforts to influence and control people's inner consciousness have shifted away from religion into mass media and, in particular, advertising. Special effects wizardry now allows a purveyor of consumer goods to transmit a wonderful, funny, educational, life-positive message to the world, giving people, perhaps, a moment of near mystical rapture—and all tagged with a product name.

## Not an Extremist Faction of the Sexual Revolution

The rise of gay awareness and the development of a gay cultural movement are part of the general transformation of human consciousness. Rather than as an extremist faction of the Sexual Revolution, the gay movement is better understood as a manifestation of new ways of understanding human life.

In explaining the role that gay consciousness plays in the evolution—and transformation—of human consciousness and, especially, religious sensibility, we are, in fact, creating a myth, constructing a meaning for what homosexuality is. Let us be clear not to claim to be right in opposition to other ways of thinking. Let us not be out to "make other people wrong," so we can be "right." Let us not commit the same error of which we accuse the Fundamentalists. Our quest is not about who is right and who is wrong.

All the myths are right, and all are likewise wrong, in the sense that all are metaphors. And the truth of the myths is not in the content of the metaphors but in the response they elicit. The demonstration of the validity of a myth is how it improves the lives of those who hold it in mind. If they become loving, generous, honest, compassionate people, then the myth is working. If they become belligerent, mean, greedy, and self-righteous, then something has gone wrong.

The issue is not what is true or false. Of course, there are some things that are true and some that are false in the sense of being correct or not: Napoleon died on St. Helena, not Elba; one plus one is two, not three; heavy objects fall at the same speed as light objects, not faster. Fact-finding and science tell us how the physical world behaves. But religious truths, like the Resurrection of Jesus or the Ascension of Mohammed or whether it is better to be loving than hateful, are not based on experimental facts. They defy classification into true or false.

The issue in religion should be how choosing certain metaphors will affect our consciousness in such a way that we behave well toward others and cooperate with them in the creation of a good and harmonious world. The metaphor that moves and awakens the mind, that communicates wonder and describes our place in the cosmos today is that we are all parts of greater planetary ecology.

# Chapter 8

## EVOLUTION: THE NEW PARADIGM

Throughout history, people we would now identify as "gay" have been in the vanguard of social change. They have been the artists, painters, poets, philosophers, and saints. Gay people naturally belong in the vanguard of today's prodigious paradigm shifts.[4]

We are living at a time of tremendous change. The old imperatives of reproducing offspring to keep alive certain races or cultures are outdated. Overpopulation is now the problem.

Introductory psychology texts usually report on studies of rat behavior. Among the things that have been discovered is that rats in overcrowded conditions begin to kill their offspring and behave homosexually. This discovery provides an experimental demonstration of a cause for sexual deviance, though such a model seems a little insulting. In all likelihood, homosexuality among human beings is far more complicated than the instinctive behavior of rats in captivity. Nonetheless, there is a message here. Built into nature are self-adjusting mechanisms. Nature changes in response to planetary conditions. Through sexuality, nature communicates its imperatives for the future.

The new paradigm, the new myth, developing as part of the continuing evolution of humankind at the level of consciousness, is evolutionary and ecological. It is expressed in terms that sound simultaneously scientific and mystical. Four illustrative models are: the Gaia

Hypothesis, the Holographic Universe, the theory of Morphogenetic Fields, and the Jungian notion of the Collective Unconscious.

## The Gaia Hypothesis

According to this new paradigm, we are all part of the complex life of planet Earth. The name given to the organism of the planet is that of the Greek Earth Goddess Gaia.

This notion was first suggested by evolutionary biologists James Lovelock and Lynn Margulis as a code name for the observation that the earth demonstrates homeostatic mechanisms. The planet has changed and adjusted its atmosphere to accommodate life. It has produced living organisms that could adapt themselves to the atmosphere and then change the atmosphere to suit them. The simplest example is that when plant life, which inhales carbon dioxide and exhales oxygen, flourished and took over the planet, animal life appeared that inhales oxygen and exhales carbon dioxide. A necessary balance was achieved.

The Gaia Hypothesis says the earth can be understood as functioning like a single organism. Extrapolated and mythologized, this has become the notion that the earth is a living organism. And that we are parts of it.

Ecology and environmentalism, both as the modern scientific discovery of the interplay of species and as a political cause against pollution and destruction of nature, give additional flesh to the hypothesis. The web of life is like the vast and intricate interplay of cells in our own bodies, a process going on automatically without conscious control, always working smoothly for the continuation of life and the growth of intelligence and consciousness.

Perhaps the development of life and intelligence is built into the structure of the universe. Life happens in just the same way beautiful crystals grow in rocks and order forms out of disorder. It takes no special intervention or miracle to make life. The universe itself is alive.

Saying the universe is alive is a little different from saying it is full of living things. But electron microscopy has shown that the world around us swarms with infinitesimal life: Everywhere are nematodes, mites, amoebas and paramecia, bacteria, molds, and viruses. In a single ounce of fertile soil, there has been found to be well over a mile of fungus mycelium, comparable lengths of other roots, and more than 20 times as many bacteria as the total number of men, women, and children on Earth. Even our own bodies are colonized by microbes, molds, and tiny insects that look more ferocious than dinosaurs. How can we distinguish what is alive and what is not?

## The Holographic Universe

There is a parallel notion that says the universe can be thought of as a great hologram. This recent invention of laser technology provides a model for understanding how everything is interconnected. A hologram is like a photograph, but the gimmick of holography is that instead of storing an image that maps point-to-point (as with a snapshot), a hologram stores a pattern of wave interference that holds more information than a photograph and holds it in a different way. Every point maps with every other point. The entire image is stored everywhere on the surface.

The holographic model for the universe says that what we are experiencing in our mind's eye that looks like a movie of a three-dimensional world of separate objects is really a vast pattern of interference waves of energy. Everything is part of everything else.

The holographic model is another way of expressing in modern terms the notion that we are all part of something bigger than ourselves. What we are only just now coming to see is that we are not really isolated egos, fighting with one another and fearing God's retribution, but cells of a larger planetary being. We all have a place in the ecology of Earth.

## Gaia Is Growing

Individual human beings are organs of Gaia, patterns in the great hologram of planet Earth. At least in metaphor, individual people are to Gaia as the individual neurons in our brains are to us. Furthermore, the life of Gaia parallels the life of an individual human being, growing from infancy through childhood, adolescence, and young adulthood, to maturity, dealing with the predictable stages of growth and tasks of psychological development.

Gaia is growing, just like a human being. We cannot tell where we are in the life cycle of the planet because we have nothing to compare it to. But we can hypothesize that the planet is near the end of childhood. The body has reached its mature proportions by evolving intelligence and filling the globe. If this is so, it is time for the adult personality to form by becoming self-aware, eschewing superstition, and taking responsibility for the direction of evolution and the outcome of life on Earth.

The consciousness that sees from a higher perspective is the way we experience being part of the evolving planetary consciousness. We are evolution become conscious.

Perhaps this will result in a profound awakening of the planetary mind into a collective consciousness. In such a collective consciousness, human individuality will not be lost. Instead, the isolation of individuals will be overcome in a general awareness of everybody being part of everybody else.

This connectedness could be a mystical phenomenon, perhaps a sort of telepathy. You might imagine this awareness as a vivid experience of compassion for other people and for the world itself. You might imagine it as a direct perception of how other people see things, the feeling of "walking in their shoes," perhaps even the intuition of what it is like to see through their eyes. You might imagine it as the immediate sense of the Golden Rule so you feel consciously, like a sixth sense, that what you do to others is really being done to you.

Perhaps this evolution will happen less mystically and more technologically. The Internet and instantaneous worldwide communications are constructing fiber optic networks that will serve as neural pathways for a collective brain for planet Earth. We are now exposed to the lives of people around the globe. We see their pain when disaster strikes. We cannot avoid knowing what is happening. The whole world now responds to the plight of refugees or victims of disasters. A hundred years ago no one would have bothered because no one would have known about them.

The danger is that violence and greed will dominate the further evolution of humankind. That is why a genuine transformation is needed. We cannot go on as we have. The world cannot keep getting more and more crowded. We have to change. To do this the human race must recognize and value the place of non-reproducing people.

## Outside and Inside

Perhaps the next step in evolution will happen both outside and inside human beings as consciousness evolves beyond us. Outside, electronic neural pathways will connect us to one another and to a group consciousness. Inside, we shall develop telepathic and empathetic abilities that will help us understand and care for one another. That would be a real change in human nature, but one consistent with the direction evolution has taken so far.

Inevitably, computers will become more and more directly interfaced with human consciousness, "wet-wired" into the cerebrum. Then all human beings will be interconnected like neurons of a global brain.

This will certainly change how human beings experience sex. Already the Internet has created new ways of meeting and new flirtation rituals. It permits long distance mutual masturbation. There is no possibility of genetic or biological transfer over the Web: no pregnancy, no disease. What will sex be like when people can connect brain to brain, pleasure-center to pleasure-center, through the phone lines? Will we be able to masturbate somebody else from inside his or her brain? What will happen to heterosexuality and homosexuality if we can get inside both men's and women's bodies? What will it be like to have actual physical sex with another person while being electronically linked to him?

This is the stuff of science fiction. Yet it is the logical—and probably desirable—extension of computer interfaces: a modem that connects us to a central, common memory bank, that feels like a sixth sense, and that gives us access to the wisdom and accumulated information from all the lives that are and have ever been connected to the network.

Maybe, just maybe, if this assembled network turns out to be sensitive to "karmic resonances" in the planetary spirit field, like a radio receiver picking up signals from the ether, *all* human lives will be accessible, *all* previous incarnations of the human race "remembered" by the Super-Internet of the future.

## Gaydar

It is possible what is called "gaydar," by which we recognize something about one another at the level of soul, might be a hint at a kind of telepathy or psychic connection, a forerunner of the birth of collective planetary consciousness.

A certain amount of gaydar, of course, is return of mutual interest and flirtation, holding a gaze just a little too long, for instance. A certain amount is recognition of traits most people do not know enough about to be sensitive to: slender wrists or a particular cant of the hips. A certain amount is wishful thinking. And a certain amount of gaydar seems to be almost psychic. There is a parallel phenomenon in New Age mysticism and spiritualism in the ability to "see auras."

## Morphogenetic Fields

The notion of morphogenetic fields says evolution goes on, not at the level of individual organisms, but at the level of collective "fields." These fields influence the structure of organisms' DNA the way magnetic fields influence the arrangement of iron filings around a magnet. Repetition of certain behaviors alters the fields through "morphic resonance" so that all organisms partaking in that field are affected.

The notion of resonance addresses the problem in Darwinian evolution that acquired traits cannot be passed on. Conventional theory holds that evolution occurs by natural selection of *randomly occurring* mutations. What is passed on can only contain what an organism inherited from its parents. None of its experience matters (except whether it lives long enough to reproduce). The theory of morphogenetic fields explains how acquired traits, the results of the forces of natural selection and cooperative adaptation, can influence how mutation proceeds. This makes the whole process more efficient and less dependent on serendipity and coincidence.

The idea of morphogenetic fields, proposed by biologist Rupert Sheldrake and officially called "the theory of formative causation," has entered pop-consciousness in the notion of the so-called "hundredth-monkey effect." The partly apocryphal story about how a tribe of monkeys living on a chain of islands off the coast of Japan learned to wash sweet potatoes researchers put out for them goes as follows: At first the monkeys scraped sand from the potatoes to make them more palatable. Then one day one of them carried a potato to the seashore and washed it in the surf. Noticing, a few others followed suit. Suddenly, to the surprise of the researchers, *all* the monkeys were washing their sweet potatoes. And this was so not only on the island where the practice started, but on all the islands where this species of monkey lived. When "critical mass" was achieved, all the monkeys, even those outside the possibility of direct communication, knew to carry the potatoes to the water. The discovery had affected the morphogenetic field of the monkeys, creating a sudden jump in their development.

Proponents say a demonstration of morphogenetic fields can be found in the high-tech chemical industry. Science is constantly working to form new chemical compounds. But it is often difficult to get a new compound to form. Yet it has been observed that once a compound crystallizes in the desired way, it becomes increasingly easier to get it to do so again. Soon this elusive compound can be mass produced. And this is so around the world. The mechanical explanation for this phenomenon is that seed crystals from the original successful batch get into the environment, carried in the hair and beards of scientists. A more elegant explanation is that the crystallization of the compound establishes a "field" with which the other crystals resonate and fall into place. This same phenomenon might have happened with the formation of the organic compounds that gave rise to life on Earth.

Applied to human culture, morphogenetic fields may affect all sorts of functions in human physical development and consciousness. The continual breaking of athletic records is a simple example. Before Roger Bannister's accomplishment, running the four-minute mile was thought impossible. Now it is routine. The apparent ease with which each new generation copes with technology may be a similar example. Children understand computers while their parents still struggle with VCRs. The activity and achievements of some people affect other people.

Perhaps, for instance, when I fasten my seat belt every time I get in the car, I influence the human complex of morphogenetic fields so that using the seat belt becomes more natural for everybody. My personal behavior then affects the whole world. My commitment to using a condom for penetrative sex may make it easier for somebody else to think to do so. My virtue can change the world. My beliefs put out morphic resonances that change other people's beliefs. It matters what I think.

If the planet has self-adjusting mechanisms, then the appearance of gay people could be a direct response to the crisis of overpopulation. And if we are indeed special productions of Gaia, might not we have a natural vocation to be concerned with ecological issues? Environmentalism and concern for the planet's well-being, recycling, eating good food, not polluting or wasting energy should come to us naturally as we play out our role in the evolutionary life of Gaia.

## The Collective Unconscious

"Every man is more than just himself; he also represents the unique, the very special and always significant and remarkable point at which the world's phenomena intersect, only once in this way and never again.... Each represents a gamble on the part of nature in creation of the human." (Herman Hesse, *Demian*)

Patterns in human culture, especially in myth and religion, represent what might be called the "great thoughts" of Gaia. The planetary mind might be thought of as an immense hologram—of which all of us are particular "interference patterns," remarkable points at which the world's phenomena intersect to form self-aware beings. Similarly, the planetary mind might be thought of as the interplay of morphogenetic fields—itself a super "field" of conscious awareness through which flow the patterns that comprise individual lives.

In mythological terms, these great thoughts of Gaia might be considered "karmic patterns," the resonances from all the lives of all the sentient beings who've lived before us. It is against the cacophony of these resonances that we must each orchestrate our own lives. Indeed, each of us might be thought of as an instrument in a common band. The orchestra of Earth is performing a grand improvisational jam session in which each player responds to the melodies he or she hears. Each of us adds new nuances and creative variations to the vast interplay of lives.

This interplay is what Jungian psychology, a major branch of psychological theory that values the nature of religion and symbology, calls the Collective Unconscious. The personal unconscious is the part of our mind created by the events and accidents that have made us who we are as individuals. But our individual minds are part of the interplay of larger patterns, all of which is the material of the collective unconscious.

How all these patterns and phenomena intersect is like a game of drawing straws. We do not know whether we are going to get a short straw or a long straw. At every moment, we wait to see how the world will unfold.

## Part of Something Bigger

The immediate cause of our experiences, good or bad, is what is happening in our life: what the problems are, the accomplishments, the joys, the sorrows. But we are also picking up the great flow of human consciousness of which we are a part, the mind of the planet that resonates with all the experience of life. C. G. Jung hypothesized this collective mind as a kind of planetary memory to explain the similarity of myths, legends, and symbols around the world.

Quantum physics and new paradigm science is showing that consciousness is one of the factors of space-time reality just like extension, breadth, volume, duration, and gravitation. Consciousness grows with the increase of complexity of the activity propagating across the surface of space-time. Our consciousness is composed of the opening and closing of the DNA molecules that generate our "life field" and the secretion and reabsorption of neurotransmitters across the synapses of our complex network of nerve cells that generate our "mind and spirit field."

Our bodies are our minds' conception of itself. What "we" are is a learned set of patterns for ordering, interpreting, and making sense of the barrage of data our senses are continuously sending us. There is a lot more going on around us than ever gets through our filters or incorporated into our patterns. Our bodies are our minds' sensory organ. The sensations that produce the consciousness that is "us" come from our interaction with other sentient beings. Indeed, everything around us is something somebody else did, their time and attention and consciousness patterns solidified into the world. Our bodies are the perspective we are taking on that world. Our perspective is how we relate to the collective, cosmic mind.

Our perspective is also called our "ego." Ego is how we think of ourselves, our placement in the barrage. Ego is based on what we think other people think about us. This idealized image of ourselves which we try to project to other people the Jungians call persona or mask.

Our egos are the lens through which we view the universe. Because we each see only from the limited perspective of our own egos and our own place in space and time, we tend to think of ourselves as isolated individuals. Perhaps the single most important discovery we make from the history of religion and mysticism is that there is more to human beings than individual consciousness recognizes. We are all part of something bigger—and subtler—than ourselves.

It is the modern perspective, facilitated by technology, communications, and high-speed travel, that allows us to observe the functioning of the planetary mind. It is the world-shaking ideas of people like Freud, Jung, Darwin, Marx, and Einstein that allow us to understand paradigm shifts. And it is the chaos of the modern day, especially in religion, that allows us to discover who we really are in the great thoughts of Gaia.

Gay consciousness, with its outsider perspective and dissatisfaction with the status quo and conventional social values, gives us insight into the nature of religion and myth. We have special reason to want a new paradigm for what it means to be human.

# Chapter 9

## INSIGHT: RELIGION AND MYTH

Just as psychological sophistication allows us to name and understand homosexuality, so "spiritual sophistication" allows us to understand religion. Science and technology is about how the world works; religion and myth is about how the mind works. Off and on throughout history, science and religion have been considered contradictory.

Most of us learned that "myths" were *other people's* religions: falsities. Our myths and our religion were true. But, in its technical meaning, a myth is not a falsehood, though many myths would be judged false by scientific standards. Myths are poetic, symbolic, metaphorical ways of talking about the mysterious and meaningful aspects of human experience. Love, for instance, is hard to quantify or describe scientifically, but it is real. And it is often best talked about by telling stories of people who have demonstrated love.

Myths are ways of talking about what cannot be talked about. Myths provide context for interpreting experience. Myths are the way people explain patterns in life, the way they explain the relations of things to one another and the purpose of things existing at all. Myths describe the big picture. They represent the great thoughts of the planet.

### Myths Are Not Hard to Believe
Myths are not mysteries that are hard to believe. They are obvi-

ous. The current myths are what everybody thinks are the explanations for things. When you hear a myth, if it works for you, you agree because it is consistent with everything else you think.

When the ancients looked up at the night sky, they saw it circling around them. The stories of the gods—and of God—were based in the observable world and practical political and social realities. The notion that the gods demanded sacrifice to assure fertility and prosperity was obvious. The king expected taxes to be paid; God would, too. That God would issue commandments was no surprise; tribal leaders issued commands all the time.

When we moderns look out into the night sky, we see how the spheres move around the sun, and how we are situated on one of them. The explanations of reality have to make sense to us in terms of our observation of things. We no longer have kings. The modern Western worldview strives toward democracy and egalitarianism. We expect to participate in the world process, not be dominated by it.

This experience seems contrary to what preachers have to say about "faith." They say that the truths of religion must be acceded to, sometimes against good sense. They say it takes courage and commitment to believe. That they have to preach this way is indicative of their problem: Their myth does not fit experience. So believers have to be browbeaten into agreement, and enemies identified and vilified to show what happens to people who do not accede to the preachers' doctrines.

The preachers are right when they complain that modern society is run amok, that people do not hold proper values, and that everything is falling apart. What they don't understand is that a major reason for this is that religion has failed to keep up with cultural change. If the myths don't speak to people, it isn't the people's fault. It is the failure of the myths.

The point of believing in certain dogmas or celebrating certain rituals or commemorating certain events is not that the dogmas or rituals or commemorations are true. The point is that believing and participating in the rituals affects our consciousness and transforms how we perceive our world. Science tells us facts. Religion and myth explain what the facts mean by telling stories. If the stories are inconsistent with the facts, they do not convey meaning.

To believe in a religion does not mean agreeing with it as fact. Rather, to believe means to allow the imagery to work on us, letting these mythically rich thoughts be the things we think about. It is wonderful, for instance, to associate events in our life—especially the painful ones—with the gentle touch of a benevolent, loving Father. That does not mean there has to actually exist a personal god who has feelings like a human father. The benevolence is a metaphor about the proper attitude to hold toward all of life.

Life is not an exam. There are no right and wrong answers. After death, we are not going to be given a pop quiz in Catechism. If it even makes sense to talk of such a thing, the fact is, "Absolute Truth" is so beyond human understanding that we can never be right about it. How could an ant, for instance, comprehend the great geo-political conflicts that beset human beings and, indirectly, threaten the anthill's very existence?

## The Real Big Bang

Partly tongue-in-cheek, let us consider that our whole universe is, in fact, a subatomic particle in a universe at the next level up; what we see as the cosmos, they call an electron or a meson cloud or an atomic nucleus. And consider that this subatomic particle is in a tungsten atom in the filament of a light bulb in a refrigerator that belongs to a being so huge we cannot even imagine it, but from whose own perspective is just the right size to live in his or her universe.

And perhaps this fellow has come down to the kitchen to have a midnight snack. When he opens the door, the light bulb that contains our universe comes on. Power pours through the filament, exciting the atoms so they emit light and heat. From the point of view of that huge being, the light came on so he could hunt for something to eat in his fridge. But from our point of view the light coming on was what we call the Big Bang—the creation of our universe.

It is impossible for us to detect that universe above us, impossible for us to know anything about the fellow that opened the door and started the whole process, absolutely impossible for us to figure out or comprehend what woke him from sleep or what he chose for his midnight snack.

And that is only imagining that the next level up would be by order of size. What if it is by some other order of difference?

Modern science has shown us a universe that—just at our own level—is beyond comprehension. How we explain things to ourselves is how we cope with the immensity of the universe. From the point of view of the midnight snacker, virtually everything we think about the nature of the universe is wrong, a sheer supposition based on inadequate information.

That should not surprise us. Everything our predecessors thought has turned out to be wrong, too. Plato and Aristotle did not have the faintest idea of what we now know the world to be. Certainly scientific method has uncovered some basic facts that we can be sure of, we can also be sure that in a thousand years, or even a hundred years, what we now think is true will be understood to have been just a rough approximation. At every stage of cultural evolution, people have thought they knew what was really going on, and were wrong: the sun was not circling the earth; the world was not flat; babies were not planted by men in the wombs of women like seeds planted in a field. Why should we think we are any different? There will be new paradigms in the future that explain phenomena much more elegantly than current paradigms and that will give us new powers and new responsibilities.

A major lesson from the history of science is that it is hubris to think you have all the answers. And we can be sure that anybody who claims they do is wrong. That is a strong indictment of religious leaders who declare the Bible as truth and claim to know the mind of God, of gurus who tell us how we should live, and of religious traditions that hand down "revealed truths" from the distant past.

Indeed, what the history of religion provides us with is not a collection of facts, but the indication that human consciousness is bigger than we imagine; that there are more layers to reality that we can see; that our world is just the surface of a cosmic wonder. What religion, with its fascination with signs, miracles, supernatural happenings, and mystical experience, actually tells us about is consciousness itself.

## All We Have Are Metaphors And Symbols

Perhaps there is some great cosmic process going on that is the universe becoming conscious of itself. Perhaps we are a part of the process, but we can never achieve a high enough perspective to comprehend it. How would we understand our place in the universe's evolution of consciousness? How would a Jurassic-era fish comprehend its contribution to the evolution of the microchip?

All we really have are metaphors and symbols. And they are not about Absolute Truth as much as how we should think about our lives for the sake of our emotional and psychological well-being. What we believe is about how we want our world to be. Isn't it better to believe in a loving universe than a hostile one? We will be different people if we believe everything is motivated by love rather than if we believe everything is motivated by greed or hatred.

Beliefs are less statements about reality than meditative practices to change the believer's attitudes. God is an idea that forces open the boundaries of consciousness. To try to think about God is to hold in mind something that by definition cannot be contained. Thus, holding God in mind stretches imagination, calls us to see beyond ourselves, to rise to a higher perspective.

## Consciousness Itself

The primary focus of religion is the experience of consciousness. God is the image consciousness offers itself for itself. With this insight, we can understand what the myths are actually about. We can see patterns from different mythological systems and understand how each tradition emphasizes certain notions for historical, political, and cultural reasons. We can see how beliefs shape culture and how culture shapes beliefs.

Understanding mythic patterns does not necessarily deny the content of a specific myth, nor does it invalidate the positive benefits of believing a certain myth or myth tradition. Interpreting the myths is not explaining them away, though it does change our stance toward them. That the story of the Resurrection of Jesus is a manifestation in Hellenized Jewish culture of the myth-motif of the sacrificed king fructifying the soil at the start of spring does not mean Jesus did not rise from the dead. It shifts the discussion into a whole different realm about the "great thoughts" that appear throughout human history, rather than about a specific moment in history. The myth of Resurrection is about the cycle of Eternal Return, about the observation that while everything living seems to die, life goes on and on. It is the promise that death is just a part of greater life.

At the same time, once we discover that resurrection from the dead was not uncommon among heroes of legend, Jesus's resurrection necessarily seems less amazing. Learning that Tibetan masters, for instance, have seemed to die and then return in miraculous ways helps us understand that Jesus's reanimation was possible.

Ironically, if we are open to it, shifting the discussion to a higher perspective strengthens the significance of the myth. The discovery of the body of Jesus in an anthropological dig—unlikely though that is—would disprove the literal historicity of the myth, but it would not in any way invalidate the belief in the symbol of Resurrection from the Dead.

Holding in mind the wonder and marvel evoked by the story of the resurrection of Jesus can bestow a sense of how we participate in the round of seasons, how the body can be transfigured, how the focus can shift from the physical body to the ethereal body, how we can see beyond ourselves to discover we are part of something bigger. That something bigger is itself enfolded into the myth of the Resurrection of Jesus as the image of the Mystical Body of Christ made up of the spiritual substance of all believers. All sentient beings are likewise said to constitute the *Dharmakaya*, the "wisdom body," of the Buddha. Perhaps these mythological notions were efforts to describe the Gaia Hypothesis discussed in the preceding chapter.

## The Arbitrariness of Truth

At any rate, changing one's religion—especially by rejecting the general cultural myth, like Christianity in America, and embracing, say, a New Age revival of pagan Goddess worship—bestows a certain sense of distance from the myth and a sense of the arbitrariness of its truth.

The gay Radical Faeries, for instance, who perform a ritual under the full moon to the Goddess, in all likelihood, do not attach the kind of dogmatic realism to their notion of divinity as do Christians who perform a ritual on Sunday morning and who have never changed religions or questioned the truth of their tradition.

And the Faeries do not worship the moon goddess as did the pagans of old they imitate. They know better than to believe the moon is the face of a personal female. There is a subtlety of meaning here. The modern revival of ancient traditions presupposes an arbitrariness of truth and presumes that worship is about metaphor and that metaphors can change.

# Chapter 10

## TRANSFORMATION: THE NATURE OF EVIL

The world is what you make it. In the New Age paradigm, each of us "creates" the universe of our own experience. How we think about life, how we make decisions, what we feel about other people and intend or wish to happen to them—these, and a multitude of other factors, determine what our own experienced world is like and how we participate in the construction of the experienced world of all the other people with whom we interact. This phenomenon is what, in hippie jargon, was called "giving off vibes." The vibes we give off affect everything and everyone around us, especially ourselves.

"Evil" is the result of the confused and conflicting intentions of all the people in the world, unaware of their power to "put out vibes," using the power willy-nilly and for all the wrong reasons.

The intention that "good things happen to me" unwittingly contains the intention that good things do not happen to other people. If good things happened to everybody I would not be any different from everybody else; I want *especially* good things to happen to me. The intention that I be rich entails the intention that other people be poor. The intention that I be right entails the intention that others be wrong. Intentions are slippery; they have more than one way of becoming true: The intention that there be no death on earth by hunger, for instance, would clearly be satisfied by the appearance of a plague that kills off 60 percent of the population and thereby increases the availability of food.

Everything's bad for somebody. Good and bad look different from different perspectives. A building boom and needed job opportunities in an economically disadvantaged town in east Texas was once a tornado that destroyed people's homes and devastated their lives. A bonus for investors in consolidating industries is a job loss and family destitution to employees of the companies that merged and downsized.

Bad things happen because conflicting intentions for other people create "karmic resonances" and practical, self-fulfilling prophecies that bad things will happen to people.

When you see somebody driving recklessly, perhaps speeding up behind you in the outside lane and abruptly cutting in front of you, you are likely to think: "Damn him, I hope he has an accident," or, "I hope he gets a ticket." The latter is certainly more benign than the former, but isn't the better attitude: "Oh, I hope he'll be safe and get to his destination on time"? This compassionate response puts out good vibes and reduces the possibility of your becoming enraged and causing an accident.

## The Creation of Evil

The definition of homosexuality as a sin, disease, or crime is a demonstration of this mechanism of the creation of evil. Our oppressors did not have to use force; they created a definition and their victims punished themselves by believing it. In the old days, homosexuals became "perverts" because that is what they were told they were. They felt worthless and guilt-ridden as a consequence. Some could not maintain relationships. Some became sex-obsessed. Some killed themselves. Some spent their lives unhappy and dissatisfied.

Taking a walk down Castro Street or Christopher Street provides a dramatic experience of this dynamic. Depending on our mood and attitudes, we can see different things. If we are feeling unloved or jaded or just scared of the unfamiliar, these gay ghetto streets can look terribly depressing. We can see unhappy, dissipated men hungrily hunting for sex and connection while avoiding eye contact with anybody for fear they will connect with the wrong person. We can see men with seriously damaged self-images trying desperately to make themselves look sexy in ways that instead look pathetic. We can see mortally ill men trudging dispiritedly—and invisibly and perhaps resentfully—among the men cruising for sex. We can see the tawdry lights of gay capitalism calling all these men inside to soothe the pain with alcoholic stupor.

Or, if we are in a good mood, feeling loved and loving, we might see an entirely different scene. We might see friendly neighbors bantering jovially with one another in the golden sunlight. We might see kind, gentle men celebrating their liberation, feeling free to show one another affection and sexual attention. We might see sexy, appealing men smiling at one another—and at us. We might see heroic men bearing the ordeals of sickness and mortality with admirable strength and perseverance, brimming with life in spite of their infirmity. We might see the infrastructure of a supportive gay community.

What we see and how we value or judge it is more determined by the complex array of experiences that have colored our vision than by what is "really" out there. And how we—and all the other people—see things determines what is going to be "out there."

AIDS itself is a demonstration of this mechanism. Out of rather understandable, if misguided, motives, "good people" intended that "bad people" be punished. They created a consensual universe in which bad things happened to people whose sexual behavior they disapproved of, considering that to be a major part of why they could think of themselves as "good."

This is not new. There were debates in medical ethics in the not-so-distant past about whether it was morally acceptable to research treatments for venereal diseases. Since these diseases were God's punishment of sin, opponents said, it would be interfering in divine retribution to develop a cure for syphilis. Ironically, scholars now believe the disease called leprosy in Biblical times and that Jesus became famous for curing included various manifestations of syphilis.

When AIDS appeared among homosexuals, the self-fulfilling prophecies were triggered. The ill-will did not exactly cause the virus, but it dramatically altered the response to the virus. In the early days, most doctors and researchers avoided dealing with AIDS because it might suggest they were homosexual (i.e., one of the "bad people"). The president could not use the words involved in talking about it. Organized gay people, unable to trust the medical profession or the government, ignored warnings about possible transmission and boycotted screening efforts. So the virus was inadvertently allowed to spread widely before any response was made.

The treatment of gay teenagers is another example. The cultural notion that gay youth are "sick" results in suicidal teenagers. The self-fulfilling prophecy that gay teenage runaways are wanton and incorrigible results in incorrigible, wanton teenagers surviving through prostitution. The "good people" cannot see that rules and biases against homosexuality are what cause the youths' problems and prevent their solution—through being rescued by gay adults, for example. Because gay adults are afraid to get involved with needy teenagers because of the presumption (and maybe the reality) that they would be having illegal sex with them, the logical refuge for youth seeking entry to gay life is excluded. So back to the streets they go to hustle some more.

The most obvious and pervasive example of the cultural manufacture of a problem is the "war against drugs." As everyone in America knows, like whiskey during the 1920s, prohibition of certain drugs drives an underworld economy that generates crime. The police involvement to suppress the drugs "for people's own good" ruins more lives than it helps. Perhaps the worst aspect of this problem is that the wide range of drugs, from botanicals to pharmaceuticals to homemade concoctions of who-knows-what are all lumped together as illegal so that people do not appreciate the significant differences between them. And, all the while, alcohol, perhaps the most seriously destructive drug of all, is embraced at the highest levels of society and government.

## *Making Other People Wrong*

What causes "evil" is "making other people wrong." The very act of judging another's behavior and then entertaining feelings of disapproval, resentment, and revulsion puts out vibes and generates self-fulfilling prophecies that the others will suffer misfortune. The fact that this mechanism works is taken for proof that the judged behavior was indeed wrong and deserved punishment. By projecting this whole process of ill-wishing onto an externally existing Devil, the people who put out the bad vibes are blinded to what they are doing.

Just as patterns of good vibes come together to produce loving, effective people who make the world better around them, patterns of bad vibes can come together to produce serial killers, urban cannibals, and seriously disturbed individuals who commit horrendous crimes. Their existence notwithstanding, the answer is to reduce the general level of bad vibes, not stir up more in the name of righteously opposing evil. "Resist not evil," Jesus said. (Matthew 5:39) Let it go. Forgive. Respond to everything with love and compassion.

The fact is, all of us make people wrong all the time. It is a natural consequence of seeing the world as dual and of seeing only from our own limited perspective. We project our negative feelings about ourselves onto others, getting compulsively annoyed by behavior in others we try to suppress in ourselves. What we internalize as bad about ourselves, we tend to see exaggeratedly in others, and we judge them to protect ourselves from our own self-judgment. This is what in Jungian psychology is called "the Shadow."

## *The Shadow*

Here is one of the places where gay people succumb to the negative consequences of the dualistic worldview of heterosexuals. Straight men, not wanting to seem to themselves like women whom they cannot understand, project negative attitudes toward nonpolarized men, i.e., homosexuals. This is homophobia. Homosexuals, especially during early adolescence, take on these negative judgments and feel bad about themselves. This is called internalized homophobia. We then project our bad feelings about ourselves onto other homosexuals. We see our own suppressed traits acted out in them: selfishness, bitchiness, fickleness. We get caught in the negative dynamics of the straight world's dualistic thinking. It is this that causes most of our difficulties. The major work of gay psychotherapy and gay spirituality is to recognize and stop this self-defeating process.

Ironically, most of the time our experience of being victims of straight people's homophobia is probably projection. It is what psychiatry calls "delusions of reference": If you are feeling vulnerable, for instance, when you hear somebody laughing, you are likely to think they are laughing at you, even when they are not. Because we have seen such horrendous examples of victimization of homosexuals, we imagine straight people are more disapproving than they probably really are. Straight people often do have real reactions to seeing gay people, but it is probably less often disgust they feel than curiosity or simple anxiety over sex-role violations. Straight people are easily sent into a tizzy by anything that crosses the gulf between male and female: a man wearing high heels, a woman using the men's bathroom. These are familiar humorous situations on "Candid Camera." It is less disapproval and disgust they feel than confusion, because this area of their experience is so tightly regimented.

Perhaps the reason drag and cross-dressing are such familiar elements of comedy is that in a controlled situation, an accomplished comedian can easily transmute the anxiety into laughter.

In like manner, the expressed homophobia and anti-gay sentiment in society is an example of straight people's projection. Non-gay people project onto gay people (the polar opposite of straight) many of the sexual traits they necessarily—and perhaps even appropriately—suppress in themselves. We are their Shadow. We get blamed for their fears and their sexual feelings toward people of their same sex.

Because straight men—compelled by church and myth, indoctrination and population imperatives—have learned to suppress homosexual desire and accelerate heterosexual desire, they are necessarily disturbed by homosexuality. People are always annoyed by their own

Shadow. This is less a justification of behavior than a call for increased consciousness and acknowledgment of Shadow dynamics.

## The Golden Rule

Clearly there are behaviors that are bad. They hurt other people. They result in strife and disharmony in society. Few of us have any problem recognizing that we should not murder, we should not steal, and we should not cause other people pain and suffering. These are all obvious when you apply the Golden Rule. And we can apply the Golden Rule without ever "making anybody else wrong." The Golden Rule does not call for judgment, though it might call you to admonish someone for their error—but out of love and support, not judgment. The Golden Rule is not about right and wrong, but it does give us a mechanism for determining our behavior without projecting anything onto other people.

Indeed, the Golden Rule is about *introjecting* other's experience, feeling their feelings, realizing our oneness with them. On the other hand, obedience to rules of propriety and cleanliness, for example, stirs up feelings of wrong-making, causes internalization of negative judgment, and consequently encourages projection of ill-will toward others. Such rules of propriety and cleanliness are what in Biblical language is called The Law.

What got Jesus in trouble with the Temple officials and the political authorities was his teaching that the Golden Rule should preempt The Law, that love was the one commandment that prevailed over the multitude of rules that religion promulgates. This same teaching is what is at the heart of the countercultural values from which gay liberation rose. And it is this teaching that keeps gay culture at odds with the religious establishment. We look to our present experience and our sensibilities to tell us what is right and wrong. They look to rules written down 3,000 years ago.

Jesus said something about the nature of evil that suggests this collective view. Referring to a local disaster in which a tower fell and killed 18 people, he asked rhetorically if this was because the victims were particularly guilty of sin. He answered himself, saying, no, that is not why disasters happen. Those people were no more sinful than everybody else. Then he added, "But if you do not stop your sinning, you will all likewise perish." (Luke 13: 1-5)

That is, individual people are not punished for sins by accidents and bad fortune. But the sin and thoughtlessness in the world generate a reality in which bad things happen. That is not necessarily so mystical: In a world in which everybody is "sinning," where, for instance, contractors skimp on materials and the towers they build fall down, it is collective "sin" that results in misfortune because it allows people not to care. "What goes around comes around," says the cliché about karma.

## Prayer as Weapon

Perhaps there is a mystical side to this as well. The image of the Creator God is a metaphor for the power of intention human beings possess, usually unconsciously. Prayer is one of the ways to focus that intention. The metaphor is that a personal God answers prayers, but if intentions have power in themselves, you do not need a God to have prayers answered.

In the tragic battle that has developed between gay people and the Religious Right, for instance, Christians have gained power by their collective prayers. They have a mythology that explains how they can join their intentions together. The gay side of the battle does not possess such a "weapon." Here, prayer has become a weapon.

In a way, the greatest tragedy is not so much the suffering that is caused by religious righteousness, but the deforming of what started out as good intentions. The Religious Right, after all, does not really mean to hate homosexuals. They think they are being loving, trying to save us. But because they are blinded to our difference (perhaps by the deliberate misinformation they are given by money-crazed leaders), their focused intentions end up creating hateful consequences—like AIDS.

We cannot exactly blame the appearance of AIDS on the Christian churches. There is surely a way in which we "brought it upon ourselves" by creating a "sexual ecology"—or better, an inadvertent sexual ecological imbalance—that a virus could take advantage of. But, still, we have to ask why the good, loving Christians, trying to imitate the example of Jesus, were more interested in blaming the victims than praying and working for the eradication of the virus. We have to wonder how the Roman Catholic Church, for instance, could be more interested in furthering its campaign against condoms than in stopping the spread of a deadly disease.

Poor Jesus! One time he managed to stop people from stoning a hapless woman caught in adultery by reminding them of their own sinfulness. But ever since, believing that his death on the cross has taken away their sins, his followers have brandished their stones proudly. Turning Jesus's admonition upside down, every born-again Christian now seems to believe he has authorization to cast his stone first. And so, out of love of Jesus and the admirable desire to be sinless, born-again Christians throw their stones at their own shadows. Unfortunately, the rocks hit us, the homosexuals hidden in those shadows.

# *Chapter 11*

## TRANSFORMATION: CONSCIOUSNESS CHANGE

All mythologies are about transformation: turning straw into gold, frogs into princes, bread into the body of Jesus, evil into good. Transformation through consciousness change is at the heart of gay spirituality. It is the cure for internalized homophobia and conflicting projections.

Transformation is different from change. If you paint a black car red, you have changed its color. But if you paint it with yellow checkers, you have transformed it—into a taxicab. You have altered its relation to the larger context. Transformation is about altering context—either by creating a new context or by expanding an existing one.

The rise of gay identity—and the experience of each individual in coming out—demonstrates a dramatic transformation. Before, homosexuality looked like the worst thing in the world. After, it looks like a gift from God, a blessing from the Great Mother, a boon from nature, a long straw picked from the draw.

Our ability to transform the world by the way we look at it shows us the secret for breaking the cycle of the creation of evil.

Such transformation has been a perennial theme in modern American thinking. It appeared especially dramatically in the 1960s with the "Age of Aquarius." That thrust for social transformation flowed out of the fact that a numerically powerful generation was

going through its idealistic, naïve young adulthood just when unprece-
dented world-changing events and technological advances were happening. This movement to transform the world came to be called the
counterculture, and gay people responded to it enthusiastically.

## Counterculture

There have always been "countercultures," small enclaves of people who thought themselves above the conventions of society. These
groups have almost always, out of necessity, originated among the
upper classes. People with excess money and leisure time are able to
say life ought to be about the development of one's talents. They can
devote themselves to art and poetry and high culture, including, of
course, mystical religion. They can see that life ought to be about the
enhancement of experience, about generating good feelings with
other people, about seeking truth over social convention, about transcending the law and liberating themselves sexually. They can see
that sex could and should be about more than reproduction.

The counterculture of the 1960s proclaimed that liberated, self-
actualizing, psychologically sophisticated values of the upper class
ought to be accorded to everybody. Indeed, in a burst of enthusiasm
for the common man and an idealistic revulsion at the excesses of the
wealthy class, they championed mingling lower class simplicity,
earthiness, and lack of "phoniness" with upper class freedom and liberation from convention.

The counterculture, thus, called for abolition of class differences,
freedom from the work ethic, self-actualization, and enhancement of
the joys of consciousness through new religions and sex, drugs, and
rock 'n roll. Of course, they were also rebelling against authority and
the military-industrial complex involved in the inscrutable war in
Southeast Asia that represented a real threat to the young.

In an odd mix of Marxist historical analysis and astrology, the
counterculture proclaimed that transformation—"The Revolution"—
was just around the corner. The world was going to be saved by a
rediscovery of the teachings of Jesus (reiterated by John Lennon):
All you need is love.

## *The Flower of the Counterculture*

Gay people were naturally drawn to the counterculture. This was partly geographical. The hippies congregated in New York and San Francisco, cities with large homosexual populations. The anti-establishment countercultural values—calling for psychological introspection and truthtelling, eschewing phoniness, affirming the wisdom of the body and the goodness of pleasure—promised young homosexuals a supportive environment in which to come out and discover themselves.

In many ways, gay liberation was "the flower of the counterculture," demonstrating the success of revolution through consciousness change. This was the revolutionary method: We would change how we thought about ourselves and the world and, consequently, the world (and our experience) would change. And it did.

Nevertheless, the problems of internalizing homophobia and projecting shadow traits onto other people still beset liberated homosexuals. The political and cultural events that set the revolution in motion did not necessarily liberate people internally.

In some ways, however, the counterculture succeeded. The revolution did happen. Sometime in the late 1960s, following the assassination of President Kennedy and the U.S. involvement in Vietnam—symbolized by the Summer of Love and the walk on the moon—everything changed.

Now in truth what changed were mostly styles: carrot cake became a staple of the American diet; tofu appeared at the local grocery store. But some of these style changes were permanent and deep: the informalization of society, frankness about sex, the incorporation into everyday speech of taboo words, the disappearance of dress codes, the shattering of familiar family structure, and, of course, the visibility of gay men and lesbians.

## *A New Sexual Paradigm*

Courtesy of the 1960s counterculture, sexual mores today are different from those in the 1940s. Of course, many elements of sexual behavior are determined by people's relationship status.

And, as the counterculture's youth grew older and developed relationships, their need to be unconventional diminished. The people who championed promiscuity in the 1960s called for marriage rights in the 1990s.

On a more personal level, the frank acknowledgment of masturbation and its acceptance as normal is a change that has endured. In the not-so-distant past, people thought masturbation sinful or at best an inadequate alternative to procreative intercourse. Masturbation was fraught with guilt and shame because it did not lead to reproduction. People were thus expected to live with sexual tension if they were not ready to become parents. Today that tension is easily and guiltlessly released. The enjoyment of bodily pleasure is accepted as natural and perfectly human, indeed, psychologically beneficial.

This was a watershed event, and it demonstrates a paradigm shift in people's understanding of what sex is. Sex used to be acceptable only for reproduction. The pleasure of sex was a trick played on us by nature to get us to breed. But we weren't supposed to have sex in ways that precluded the possibility of conception.

Today, we understand that the sexual pleasure is a worthwhile goal in itself. The pleasure of sex with another person can enhance an intimate relationship with them. Sex with oneself stimulates needed physical processes. Relishing bodily experience and coming to orgasm releases neurotransmitters that benefit bodily and psychological functioning. The pleasure-bestowing aspects of sex can be separated from the reproductive. Because we are conscious, self-directing moral agents, we can trick nature. Human beings are not bound by instinctive drives. We determine what our sexuality means to us. This shift in thought has made gay consciousness possible.

## What Happened to the Counterculture?

The counterculture was as much a symptom of change in society as it was a cause. The hippies and fellow travelers did not cause the revolution as much as personify it. And then it all got "co-opted"—to use the jargon of that day—by being absorbed into mainstream society.

In some ways, the counterculture just faded away. The kids who championed these values grew up, got married, and had children. And children have a dampening effect on an individual's freedom and capacity to nonconform.

In gay culture much of the early idealism of the movement was lost. This was, paradoxically, in great part because of its success. The general co-opting of the counterculture into mainstream society appeared in gay society as the rise of "gay capitalism," glamour, and sexual excess that were the natural consequences of liberation. There was a youthful, lustful enthusiasm for freedom that exploded in the creation of gay cultures, gay communities, and gay ghettos—and a sexual ecology ripe for infection.

Actually, much of the glamour and so-called excess of the 1970s, though it did bring the very real tragedy of AIDS into people's lives, was illusory. The men you saw on Castro Street or Christopher Street looking like hungry, lustful, manly debauchees went home from the bars or the baths or sex clubs, changed clothes, and turned into friendly next door neighbors and bankers and nurses—regular people. Of course, there were some, especially the young and sexy professionals of the gay subculture, like bartenders, porn stars, and hustlers, who lived the illusion 24 hours a day. But most gay men were never really the fantasies they acted out in the wake of their liberation.

## Technologies of Transformation

Liberation, transformation, and revolution were in the air. New religions appeared. Gurus arrived from India. Psychologists announced techniques that could ease lifelong neuroses: encounter groups, primal screaming, nude therapy. Everybody wanted to improve themselves.

A spate of seminars and workshops about transformation sprung up around the United States. Part relationship therapy and part motivational seminar, these programs called themselves "technologies of transformation." (The most famous—and notorious—is *est*). These seminars taught a version of the "Perennial Philosophy" blended with modern-day marketing techniques.

The Perennial Philosophy is the basis of most Western esotericism and occultism, including freemasonry. Coming out of Gnosticism and Platonism, it teaches, loosely, that everything is a transient manifestation or emanation of the Absolute. These emanations include human souls that reincarnate through lifetime after lifetime. Human beings potentially have creative powers and can perform miracles, especially if they've been initiated into esoteric wisdom and understand the power of words to create what they say. (The Perennial Philosophy is remarkably Buddhistic.)

The cultural and countercultural fascination with transformation introduced modern Americans to spiritual principles gleaned from Buddhism, Vedanta, and mystical Christianity that were modernized through Scientology, Dale Carnegie, and high-powered salesmanship training. The technologies of transformation had—and continue to have—influence in modern consciousness. And, because the publisher of the *Advocate* magazine developed a specifically gay version called The Advocate Experience, this influence extended to gay consciousness, especially on the West Coast.

The use of aphorisms and jargon was a major technique. While these clichés became the butt of TV jokes, they really did express important spiritual wisdom and provide techniques for enhancing interpersonal relationships and bringing about life transformation. The fundamental transformation, of course, that we are all always engaged in is coping with the barrage of problems of everyday life.

## Coping With Problems

The simple practice of transformation is exemplified in the *est*-ian parable of "changing the tire." When you have a flat tire, you can react in two different ways. You can get angry and annoyed that this has happened to you. You can fuss at the universe and curse your fate. You can throw open the trunk with a bang and crash about getting the jack untangled, probably hitting your head on the trunk lid at least once. And every time something goes wrong you can get more upset and bungle the job even more.

Or you can just change the tire.

If you cope with problems one by one as they come up, not

resisting and not taking them personally, then you can solve them one by one. The way you transform things in the outside world is by changing the way you hold them in your mind.

A demonstration of this effect has appeared through medical technology in the creation of mood and self-concept altering drugs called Serotonin Specific Re-uptake Inhibitors (SSRIs). Prozac is the brand name of the most familiar SSRI. By slowing the speed with which the neurotransmitter serotonin is broken down and reabsorbed by receptor sites at the synapses of nerve cells, these drugs change the ratio of the various chemicals in the brain. It is the ratios of these neurotransmitters to one another that create the interplay of patterns of activity in our brains that we experience as consciousness. These are the patterns that intersect in us to make us and to make up our world.

When you take Prozac, you discover you feel a little better. Things that had been needling you disappear. And, curiously, the people around you change, too. They stop doing the things that were bothering you. In part, this is a result of selective perception and self-fulfilling prophecy. And, in part, it is a result of your changing how you interact with the others in your world. The obvious fact is that when you take a drug to change your brain chemistry, *other people's* behavior changes. You transform your experience, not by dealing with the content, but by going to the root of the experience.

## *A Kind of Magic*

Transformation is a kind of magic or, better said, magic is a symbolic practice of transformation. The real magic in life is not levitating or becoming invisible or twitching your nose to get chores to happen by themselves. The real magic is experiencing that life moves smoothly and that we can cope with everything that comes along. With that outlook, life is interesting and wonderful and feels like it is helping us to grow and mature and to find and fulfill patterns of meaning and beauty.

There is a Talmudic saying that the reward for doing a good deed is the inclination to do another good deed. Similarly, the consequence of performing an act of transformation is the opportunity to perform another act of transformation, i.e., as we get more done, there is more to do. The problems keep on coming. But our attitude changes.

We might say the whole function of the universe is to evolve consciousness through an unimaginably long and complex series of solving problems and thereby expanding awareness. As we work our way through life, solving problems, transforming difficulties, we are in harmony with the great growth of everything. We transform things by loving them. We transform the world by loving the world, holding unconditional good intentions for everybody and not making others wrong.

The thing that most needs transformation, of course, is the evil that comes from the clashing of intentions about how to solve problems. When we see the effects of that evil—violence, intolerance, bigotry, injustice—we have to remind ourselves that this is exactly what needs transforming, and that transformation will occur, not by resisting evil, but by loving it the way it is.

This does not mean we do not try to change things. In fact, one of the things to love is our inclination to change injustice, stupidity, and bigotry through political and cultural activism.

Looking at the world and seeing the suffering and violence and learning to say, "It is great just the way it is," does not mean giving in. It means holding it all in a larger context. For, from the larger context, it is easier to cope with and easier to change.

## I Have a Right to Be Here

The great magnanimous gesture is to look on all the suffering in our lives that other people have caused, all the sadness and tragedy we have experienced because of the way things are, all the injustice and inequity and selfishness, and—like Jesus on the cross—to forgive them all. That raises us above the suffering, and it releases the resistance we feel.

During his final meditation the Buddha was assaulted by Kama-Mara, the god of love and death, and by his daughters, Desire,

Pining, and Lust. In a classic gesture, Buddha ended the assault to his meditation by touching the earth to proclaim: "I have a right to be here." That is always the way to transform experience.

This is the essential declaration of gay liberation. We are here. And we have a right to be here. We are generating consciousness-change.

## Chapter 12

### *Transformation: Flesh*

AIDS created an unexpected transformation in the burgeoning gay culture that formed after liberation. The epidemic took the movement in a new direction, one that demonstrated and solidified gay men's caring and sense of loyalty to one another. It called us to bear witness to suffering and mortality, to experience a certain kinship with Third World and downtrodden peoples we might not have otherwise discovered. But it also further stigmatized our sexuality and allowed anti-gay activists to blame us for a world-threatening plague. In fact, gay sex was not the cause of the disease. If anything, AIDS among gay men was the symptom that caused the industrialized world to wake up to a worldwide ecological catastrophe. In America, the AIDS crisis was a call for compassion and a reminder that American society is not insulated from the world.

AIDS revealed the fragility of the flesh. As Buddha discovered, being incarnate means getting sick, suffering privation, growing old, and dying. These are the conditions of flesh. We therefore struggle to make peace with the flesh, finding in it the source of our joy and pleasure, as well as the cause of our decrepitude and death.

### *Physical Hygiene*

Occasionally in some very superstitious and medically inaccurate ways and occasionally in appropriate and sensible ways, hygiene has long been a concern of religion. Washing of hands, feet, and head before entering a mosque or temple ritualized cleanliness and gave desert people an opportunity to bathe. Not eating pork or oysters, as mandated by the dietary rules of the Torah, protected people from trichinosis and spoiled shellfish. However, the basis of those laws was more superstitious and symbolic than medical. Perhaps Hebrews saw people die after eating pork, but they were much more apt to understand that as punishment for eating a meat sacred to Canaanite gods than as contamination of the meat or the result of unsanitary food-preparation. The Hebrews did not know why they did not eat pork any more than Americans know why we don't eat horse, dog, guinea pig, or fried grasshoppers.

The ancients were unaware of modern germ theory, and most of their cleanliness taboos, while part of the religion, were not really "spiritual." But there is still a way in which hygiene and good health practices in general are spiritual: They protect life.

## Failure to Observe Biological Hygiene

It is interesting that the countercultural commitment to egalitarianism, in part, motivated the failure to observe biological hygiene among hippies and gay men that resulted in such horrendous health problems. It was a matter of political and social conviction—as well as ritual—for counterculturalists to drink from a common glass. Based on the idealistic sci-fi novel *Stranger in a Strange Land*, "sharing water" became a communal practice. So did drinking wine from a common jug and drawing on a joint passed around the circle.

One of the reasons AIDS moved through the gay community with such alacrity is that countercultural political awareness called for rejection of old-fashioned roles and oppressive sexual identities. It was a matter of principle widely accepted throughout the community that gay men should not divide themselves into "butch" and "femme" or follow rigid sex roles in lovemaking. Egalitarianism required that if you wanted to be a "top" you also had to be a "bottom" and vice versa. "Versatility" was championed.

Pairings which did not fit the butch-femme model and in which the roles of top and bottom were interchanged or switched during sex were a manifestation of seeing in one's sexual partner a reflection of oneself. But since, because of simple fluid mechanics, HIV is more readily passed from top to bottom, it was just this alternation of positions that helped propel the spread of infection.

## Transformation in Attitudes About the Body

Identifying as homosexual or, at least, engaging in anal sex demands a transformation in attitudes about the body and cleanliness. We are taught in our culture that the anus is intrinsically dirty because fecal matter passes through the orifice. Reorienting our ideas about the body "down there" is necessary for us to discover the erotic potential. When properly washed on the outside and evacuated on the inside, the anus is no more dirty than other parts of the body.

The notion that the anus is always dirty actually works against basic sexual hygiene. At least before AIDS forced us to pay attention to such matters, people were less apt to be concerned with protecting their anuses from infection, because it seemed as if they were already contaminated anyway. It didn't matter what you introduced into them. That, of course, is terribly wrong.

Just as vaginal intercourse permits exposure to blood and blood-borne pathogens, anal intercourse permits exposure to feces and fecal-borne pathogens. The fecal-oral route can spread hepatitis, dysentery, and the amoebic diseases that had created serious health problems for gay men before AIDS overshadowed other STDs. Yet these diseases can result in chronic debilitating conditions as serious as HIV infection. Transmission of these fecal-borne diseases is not particularly affected by condom use.

Foreplay for anal intercourse, however, often includes "rimming." Such oral-anal stimulation is one of the highest sexual pleasures, often exceeding that of penetration. In the Christian hysteria over witchcraft and Satanism, and out of Christianity's fear and condemnation of sexual positions not specifically open to procreation, this staple of gay men's pleasuring was mythologized as the "Devil's

Kiss." The level of denunciation was, perhaps, an indication of how good it feels.

Passionately kissing another's anus is a sign of ultimate submission, a breakdown of boundaries. Though the symbolism has been diluted in our modern everything-goes, no-holds-barred, drug-enhanced sex culture, mutual rimming signifies intense intimacy and adoration of each other's body. Perhaps the Christians condemned it because, metaphorically speaking, it was such a powerful affirmation of incarnation in pleasure-relishing flesh.

## More Important as a Nerve Center Than an Orifice

The colon and rectum are part of the body's fluid transport system, actively involved with reclaiming water used in digestion and metabolism. The anus is entry to the delicate, sensitive membranes of the body, rich in blood vessels and nerve-endings. Freud taught that the anus is more important as a nerve center than as an orifice for excretion. Symbolically, subconsciously, the growth of personality and consciousness goes through a so-called anal stage. A whole range of attitudes about life are involved with learning control of the anal sphincter.

On the other hand, anality itself is not of the essence of homosexuality. There is a popular confusion of homoeroticism and expression of male affection with sodomy, as though the essence of homosexual desire is to be receptive in anal sex. Anal intercourse is a heterosexual as well as homosexual practice, an easy and natural means of avoiding conception.

Some gay men like being tops. Many prefer being bottoms. Most, probably, are at least turned on by the prospect of being versatile. Nonetheless, many gay men—in spite of encouragement in the gay media and conditioning in gay erotica to see anal fucking as the high point of homosexual behavior—do not find themselves interested at all. The essence of homosexuality is expressing affection, touching, and generating a state of consciousness of sexual arousal, of deep bodily intimacy. Anality is only incidental.

## *Tantra and Kundalini Yoga*

In the etheric physiology of kundalini yoga, the anus is associated with the first chakra, the *muladhara* ("root"), which controls the experience of embodiment and the related issues of survival ability and groundedness. The first chakra is what you sit on in the lotus position of yoga. When you fold your legs, you bring your first chakra in contact with the earth. The rich, fertile soil of that earth is fed by the rotting of plant matter, animal waste, and dead bodies. What is excrement to one creature is food to another. What is death to one creature is sustenance for another. Life lives on life.

The function of the first chakra is only incidentally excretion and more specifically coping with existence on the material plane. This means being a creature that has to eat and metabolize food (of which excretion is an intrinsic element), and that means killing other life-forms. Mortality is a primary issue of the first chakra.

The anus is connected with the whole complex of autonomic functions—what is going on inside us beyond our conscious control or awareness. Because the anus is directly attached to the brain through the spinal cord and is rich with nerve-endings and scent glands that exude pheromones, it functions as a sexual organ, an organ of connection. And because in the male the prostate gland (associated with the second, sexual chakra) is positioned at the top of the rectum, anal penetration activates both the first and second of these nerve centers.

The symbolic system of the chakras was part of a tradition that developed in both Hinduism and Buddhism. It was an ancient psychology for dealing with the flesh called Tantra.[5] The two most important notions that have entered modern culture from Tantric tradition are the chakras and of the kundalini. The chakras are the seven "wheels" or centers in the mind-body-spirit that correlate with psychological states and physiological nerve plexuses. Each chakra represents an elemental human desire: to possess, to copulate, to achieve, to love, to communicate, to understand, and to ascend to God.

The kundalini is the psycho-sexual energy, symbolized as a serpent, that rises through the spine and the chakras to energize the process of consciousness. This etheric anatomy is an aid for visualizing, in the mind's eye, the flow of energy and personality dynamics as a system of the body (the "etheric body" or "spirit body").

The third chakra, in the solar plexus, is associated with aggression and bravery, "guts." The fourth chakra, in the heart, with love and generosity. The fifth, in the throat, is associated with teaching and self-discipline. The sixth, in the "third eye," with the world-creating power of consciousness. And the seventh, just above the crown of the head, with spiritual stability and vitality; this is the "uplink" with God. In Tibetan Buddhism, the soul exits the body in death through the crown chakra, called the "thousand-petalled lotus."

The "higher chakras" mirror the lower, reflected and transformed through the heart: Third chakra aggression is transformed by compassion into speech and self-discipline; second chakra biological creation is transformed into spiritual creation by which consciousness assembles a world in the mind; and first chakra survival anxiety is transformed into security in knowing your oneness with God.

In Tantric practice, one wants to be a little sexually aroused in meditation—not totally distracted with sexual fantasies, of course, but turned on in the sense of getting the kundalini to stir in the loins and then fill the body to connect the first and seventh chakras. Going through the induction of visualizing the chakras in sequence wakes up this flow. It turns on the etheric body like exercise or sexual arousal turns on the circulatory system, sending blood and vitality throughout the physical body.

That there is a link between the second and sixth chakras is evident in males in our enjoyment of the sight of other bodies. Men's sexual arousal is as much in the eyes as in the genitals. The interior eye, the "third eye" of the *ajna* chakra, can create whole worlds in fantasy and recreate past experiences for renewed enjoyment.

That there is a link between the first and seventh chakras is evident in the intense pleasure and feelings of fulfillment and justification (perhaps even in the orthodox Protestant sense) that come with being bottom in anal intercourse. The stimulation of first chakra with second chakra—of penis in anus—triggers kundalini energy to ascend the spinal cord and stimulate the crown chakra.

## Tiresias the Seer

It is told in Greek myth that Tiresias, the blinded seer, underwent a metamorphosis from male to female, and later back again. When asked which sex enjoyed having intercourse more, he answered female. Many gay men can attest to this assessment: Bottom is better.

Learning how to experience arousal in the first chakra enhances sex. It is a natural part of gay men's maturation. Like Tiresias, perhaps, we too are seers for having experienced both top and bottom pleasures.

This turns the whole male dominance/submission model upside down: Anally raping your enemy does not prove you are superior if you are serving him sexually. Stereotypical heterosexual male obsession with arousal in the penis, excluding other erogenous zones, especially the anus, can perhaps drive the kundalini into the third chakra without its reaching the transformation in the heart so that it produces only male sexual aggression.

## The Five M's

Tantric practice consists of complicated meditation styles that include: very detailed visualizations (of gods and goddesses, sometimes in stylized sexual intercourse, but also of monsters, demons, and graveyard scenes); ritual eating of meat and alcohol (and maybe ergot-infected grain, a psychedelic drug); performance of gestures and hand signs (that may have included fisting); use of mantras and magical incantations; and sacred sexual intercourse.

Tantra championed these as the Five Forbidden Things or "Five M's": *maithuna* (intercourse), *matsya* (fish), *mansa* (flesh), *mudra* (parched grain), and *mada* (wine). These represented various taboo violations—"abominations"—which Tantrics embraced for the sake of spiritual advancement. That is, the Tantric tradition broke with the previous body-denying, ascetical spirituality in both Hinduism and Buddhism to create a faster, more adventuresome vehicle for mystical

117

enlightenment called *Vajrayana*, the "lightning ferryboat."[6]

The most understandable of the Forbidden Things, *maithuna*, was ritualized intercourse. The object of the practice is for a male-female couple to remain in coitus, joining the sexual organs, for prolonged periods of time. Using breathing practice and meditative focus, the couple delays or prevents climax, perhaps holding indefinitely at the male's "point of ejaculatory inevitability"—when, brainwave researchers have found, the two hemispheres of the human brain are in perfect synchrony. The aim is to avoid ejaculation altogether to build sexual energy in the male, transformed by the interaction with the female, and so to induce his kundalini to rise through the chakras and bring direct experience of "God." In a more mind-blowing practice of yoga training, the male is supposed to ejaculate into the female but then draw the transformed semen back up through his penis into his body. The point of Tantra, however, isn't so much such yogic prowess as the symbolic blending of male and female energies to overcome dualistic thinking.

Tantric symbology relies strongly on the metaphor of male-female dualism. Gay men can participate in this blending of male and female since we can experience a difference in our own bodies of masculinity and femininity. But because we do not live in the heterosexual dualistic mind-set, the symbol of man and woman blending in *maithuna* does not speak to us directly.

The duality that gay people do experience is the two-fold division of the human nervous system into sympathetic and parasympathetic, and of the brain into left and right hemispheres. But the functions of the voluntary and autonomic nervous systems and of the left and right sides of the body, controlled by the opposite brain hemispheres, do not demonstrate duality. There is no misunderstanding by the stomach of what the legs are doing. There is no conflict between the right hand and the left. The bifurcated systems of the body work together smoothly.

Gay men and lesbians can practice *maithuna* with same-sex partners, of course. We can even utilize the sexual metaphors—though this is probably most easily accomplished with mutual genital massage than with penetration of one partner by the other in quasi-coitus. But, in truth, we're not balancing male and female; we're balancing left and right, conscious and unconscious.

Indeed, the reason Tantric symbolism uses male-female metaphors and calls heterosexuals to identify one side of the body as male and the other as female is to demonstrate how the polarities are actually supposed to work together. The experience of being in the body—which is what Tantra is about—is of everything working in harmony. This is the glory of health, a demonstration of proper ecology, and an example of androgyny.

Gay people do not have to experience the world dualistically. We can experience androgyny directly. We do not have to get caught in the polarities of masculinity and femininity. Indeed, we seem to enjoy playing with these, not taking them seriously, making fun of the deadly seriousness with which straight people, especially straight men, take them. We do not have to force our oppositely sexed traits into our unconscious. In Jungian terms, a gay man's anima—that is, the symbol of the source of unconscious compulsions—is not a woman, but another gay man.

*Maithuna* or protracted genital massage shifts the focus of sexual arousal away from achieving orgasm and ejaculation to containing and intensifying sexual energy in the body. One aspect of this practice is referred to as sex magick (spelled with archaic flair). Focusing intention sometimes allows us to influence how our lives will unfold: We can do "magic." Building up sexual energy adds power to intention.

## *Flesh Ages*

Another attribute of flesh that has to be reckoned with is aging. We naturally get older and our bodies change. Skin becomes less flexible, muscle tissue wears down, the skeleton gets creaky, testosterone levels drop. From the point of view of youth, aging seems disastrous and unfair. But the fact is most people experience that life gets better even if the flesh gets stale. Priorities change. Self and ego become less important. Moods moderate. You grow wiser in the sense that you learn your limitations and are not bothered by things as easily. Aging elevates the experience of life into the mind and soul.

Spiritual wisdom tells us to accept aging gracefully, since there is nothing we can do about it except die. Recognizing that life goes through stages helps. The most important realization is that we do not stay the same person throughout our whole lives—a reminder of impermanence. In fact, in modern life, we seem to have to live several personalities and several careers in a single lifetime. How wonderful and how taxing!

For gay men, aging presents certain obvious problems: The sex culture is focused on youth. How would it be otherwise? The flowers in the florist's window are fresh and still dewy. The wilted flowers are thrown away. But we human beings live long past our first wilting. The mistake is to think we are the bloom and not the whole plant. If the plant has not been plucked and sent to the florist's, a lot more goes on after the flower wilts and falls off. In the same way, we may lose our youthful bloom, but there is a lot more going on. We do not stop being sexual. In fact, we may learn to appreciate sex more, with fewer worries.

One of the curious discoveries of age is that youth becomes beautiful in itself. When we were younger the differences between men stood out: Some were attractive, some were not. There were many levels of sexiness. As we get older the differences fade away. It gets easier to see that everybody is attractive in his own way.

Aging allows a reverencing of our lives. We can remember the wonderful people, the inspiring experiences, the hot sex, the deeply satisfying emotional relationships as part of honoring and validating our life. Relishing memories is a great joy. It bestows mystical vision. From the perspective of age, we can see the patterns in our life as though they had been planned and chosen by some intelligent consciousness (mythologized as God) who is really us.

## Our Mind's Conception of Itself

We experience our placement in the universal process as our bodies. Our flesh is our minds' conception of itself. Flesh is subject to outside forces; flesh is subject to aging and death. But flesh is also capable of exaltation and ecstasy and transcendence. In living beings, flesh has become sentient; in human beings, flesh has become self-reflexively conscious and intelligent. In the evolution of flesh, the universe has incorporated consciousness and woven a new factor of existence into the fabric of reality.

Flesh, therefore, has responsibility for determining how it conceives itself and how it continues to transform itself at the level of consciousness. These are issues of spirituality and religion. And that is why new perspectives—like the perspective gay identity bestows—challenge conventional religious models.

# Chapter 13

## ADAPTIVE VIRTUES: ANDROGYNY AND WONDER

The modern world calls for different virtues from the old world in which the various religions developed. We are not peasants working an agrarian economy, living in little rural villages, raising a brood of happy, obedient children who will follow in our footsteps by working for the feudal lord and tithing to the bishop. Our urban lives, especially our sexual lives, call out for different virtues.

Some traits are basic to social harmony. We all have to cooperate with certain basic agreements: We cannot kill; we cannot steal. But virtues like daring, courage, paternal authoritarianism, rugged individualism, patriotism, and righteousness take on different meaning in mass society. Gay people exemplify certain virtues, especially regarding sex, that are adaptive to modern, urban society.

The archetype/stereotype of the gay man blends masculinity and femininity. He is the lover of beauty, the sensitive soul who perceives things in a larger context and appreciates art and nature. Such blending of masculine and feminine qualities produces an attractive personality. Extremely masculine men and extremely feminine women are sometimes idolized, but they are just as often ridiculed. A potent blending of male strength and competence and of female sensitivity and feeling makes for a more interesting human being with a more complex and fascinating personality. The gentle man and, in a somewhat different way, the self-sufficient woman are appealing characters.

This androgyny manifests the ability of consciousness to incorporate, and thereby overcome, opposites. As the Renaissance Platonist mystic, Nicholas of Cusa, said, "The walls of Paradise are constituted of the coincidence of opposites." The reason we cannot see that we are living in a Paradise is that we are blinded by the clashing of the dualities.

## Spiritual Androgyny

Gay people demonstrate what can be called spiritual androgyny. What it means to be spiritually androgynous is to see the world from both a woman's perspective and a man's perspective, to be good at traditional male activities (handiwork, reasoning, taking charge, and getting things done) and to be good at traditional female activities (caring about other people, noticing other people's feelings, being concerned about the big picture, and being uncomfortable with competition).

That is not to claim that androgynous people are unburdened with dualities. The world is full of dualities: wet/dry, hot/cold, desirable/repulsive, right/wrong, male/female. We are immersed in them all the time. It is a blessing to be reminded not to take them too seriously. Androgyny—in the whole range of ways it shows up in homosexuality—is such a reminder.

It is interesting that lavender is the "gay color." Lavender (or violet as it is called in physics) is formed by blending opposites: red and blue, the opposite ends of the spectrum or, better said, the turning back of the spectrum on itself—like the *ouroboros*, the snake eating its own tail. When we close the spectrum into a circle we get violet.

In the Lüscher Color Test, a psychometric tool that links color preferences to personality traits and transient mood states, preference for violet is a sign of having overcome polarized, dialectical thinking. It is considered an indicator of homosexual tendencies. At least in theory, the links are based on cellular, neural connections rather than learned social conventions.

## *A Simple Grammatical Technique*

Overcoming opposites—discovering we are still in Paradise—is practiced in a simple grammatical technique of replacing "but" with "and" whenever possible. The conjunction "but" predicates opposition and exclusivity; "and" acknowledges connection. "I want to go to the beach today but I have work to do" is a perfect example. The use of "but" restricts us to either one or the other; it manifests the belief we cannot do both and even suggests that one is desirable, the other undesirable. It makes us resent our work. If, instead, we say, "I want to go to the beach today and I have work to do," we see we can set up our day's agenda so we can do both. The contrariness disappears.

Nondualistic thinking frees us from right and wrong. Compassion and integrity, not desire for righteousness and avoidance of punishment, become the basis for decision making. "Right and wrong" do not equate to "correct and incorrect," "good and evil," "light and dark." Right and wrong is about relations between people and a judgment one side makes against the other—and always in one direction only.

## *Wonder*

Adopting the basic spiritual attitude of wonder allows us to overcome judgment and evaluation. Wonder is a complex set of ideas, attitudes, and feelings. It is an experience of joy, appreciation, and awe. It is also an experience of curiosity and of beauty. Sexual attraction and erotic arousal are aspects of wonder.

One of the first significant wonder moments in a gay man's life is the realization: "I'm a homosexual." It is terrifying to realize that you are in a tiny minority of the human race, unlike most other people (including your parents), and saddled with sensibilities those other people find repugnant. With maturity, that wonder changes from fear to jubilation as you realize what advantages your homosexual orientation offers you—among them, the heightened capability of experiencing wonder and joy at the beauty of creation. According to stereotype, we are more sensitive, insightful, and aware of beauty, rhythm, symmetry, and harmony. We know how to dance. We make good decorators and designers. We create beauty.

At a more spiritual level, we experience wonder and a sense of the poignancy of life in the realization of the whole process. Because we are self-trained to rise above the everyday assumptions of what things are and what they are for, we are able to see how much bigger the universe is than most people perceive. Doing so, however witting or unwitting, is participation in the planetary mind's evolution into "God."

Life is wonderful even when we do not understand it. Wonder is what human life is for and the propelling force behind evolution. Feeling wonder puts out good vibes.

Wonder is a practice as well as an inspiration. We practice wonder when we focus our mind on things that cannot quite be thought, like the nature of heaven or the appearance of the face of God. The epitome of such practices are Zen *koans*, thought puzzles like "the sound of one hand clapping," that are held in meditation to push the meditator beyond ordinary reasoning.

## Meditation as a Practice of Wonder

Meditation, of course, is the fundamental spiritual practice of feeling wonder. Meditation, sitting quietly and unmoving, focusing consciousness on the rhythm of the breath, is the major tool of spiritual awareness and introspection. The ritualized turning inward and pulling away from the distractions of the outside world allows us to see what is going on in our interior life. At its simplest, meditation is like closing the curtains of a bright, sun-lit room so we can see the flickering play of candlelight on the walls. Meditation is taking time to see things differently, to shift our focus from the immediate and transitory to the transcendent and eternal. Meditation is holding a thought in mind, perhaps remembering with genuine joy a mystical experience that seemed to explain the reason for our life. Meditation is watching ourself breathe as an exercise in being still. Meditation can be an ongoing practice of a state of receptive joy and fearlessness in the preparation for death.

When our ego is turned on and busy, it dominates consciousness. Meditation puts the ego functions on hold so the larger Self can be glimpsed out of the corner of our "spiritual eye." By allowing all distractions to subside, meditation is an awakening to who we really are.

Wonder includes a sense of insignificance. We feel wonder when we behold a mountain range or a thundering waterfall or when we stand beneath the immensity of the night sky or try to conceive the scope of cosmic time. How little each of us is! With that insignificance comes a paradoxical sense of magnificence and magnanimity: Because I am so little and insignificant, there is nothing to cling to in being me separate from the immensity of space and the depth of time. I am part of it all.

# Chapter 14

## ADAPTIVE VIRTUES: LOVE AND ADVENTURE

Love is an experience of wonder. We feel pleasure and joy and love of life when we behold someone we love. Deep emotional surges are triggered by the thought and, especially, the sight and touch of him. His flesh is beautiful to us, the line of his muscles exciting, the shape of his body pleasing.

Life looks better—more wonderful—when we love someone. Therefore we naturally feel good intentions for our beloved. We want things to go well for him—even, sometimes, at our own expense. Indeed, self-sacrifice for him is pleasurable because it is *for him*. Love is putting another's welfare above our own or, better said, as our own, because it is pleasurable to us that he is happy.

### Love Is an Experience of Affirmation

Anything and everything we love gives us an experience of being alive. This holds true from the love we feel for a work of art or a souvenir we have collected, to the love of our home and immediate surroundings, to the love of pets that respond with affection, to the love of friends, to the love of a sexual partner, to the love of God, to the love of truth.

Long-term committed relationships provide a pervasive feeling of love and security, along with the familiar and deep sexual contact.

Monogamy, in the literal sense of "one marriage," offers great sexual and emotional joys. Medical studies show that people in stable, committed relationships enjoy better health and psychological well-being.

Sudden, unexpected, maybe even anonymous sexual coupling, though, can provide novelty and intensity. And sexual drive is conditioned by ancient forces. Our perceptions of beauty and attractiveness derive from evolutionary imperatives. The physical traits we are attracted to—bright eyes, strong muscles, good teeth, broad shoulders—were determined by the practical needs of our ancestors: the traits of alpha males that make them good hunters, good fathers, and good protectors of women. Evolutionary biologists tell us that males have a built-in drive for novelty that is based in the reproductive strategy of spreading seed as widely as possible to ensure survival, and even dominance, of one's contribution to the gene pool.

Hygiene concerns taught to us by the AIDS crisis set certain strictures about just how we can enjoy intense, novel sex with a variety of partners. Spiritual admonitions about not getting caught in other people's karma, about practicing moderation, and about delaying gratification also impose strictures. Still we can find ways to keep saying yes.

For all that some people understandably object to such a characterization, the fact is that gay male culture is based on this biological imperative for novelty. Concerns about preserving the integrity of gene lines, making sure inheritance goes to the right offspring, and protecting women from abuse and exploitation do not apply to males playing with sex. The point of our finding in one another a reflection of our own motivations and attitudes is that, as men, we like sex and we like variety in sex. Being gay, for most men, means having had a goodly number of sexual partners. And that is a cause for celebration.

The first time, or first several times, we have sex with somebody is very special. The coupling is particularly passionate, the sexplay delectable and prolonged, the unconscious material unleashed is intense and dramatic, the sense of vitality profound. Many people go through strings of relationships so they can keep repeating this dazzling experience of falling in love and being swept away. This can be a problem, and some people's lives are ruined by their insatiable hunger for new sex so that no intimate relationship can ever grow beyond that first burst of emotion.

This string of relationships can also be a growth process, and for most it probably is. With each romance we enter, we learn something about other people and something about ourselves. In young adulthood we probably need to go through a variety of experiences in order to find ourselves. Each new boyfriend stirs different emotions, helps us to see in the other traits we like or do not like in ourselves. Each new boyfriend promises to reveal to us a different world with new people and interests, new excitements and adventures.

## Projection and the Shadow

Experiencing such a range of relationships and going through the pain of multiple breakups forces us toward psychological maturity. We have to confront the psychological mechanism of projection, that is, we have to see that in our initial fascination with a new person we are not really seeing him at all. Instead we are seeing a set of idealized characteristics overlaid on him by our subjective vision. It is an important lesson to learn. And it is important to learn how to withdraw the projections and find them in ourselves. This is how we come to understand what traits we seek in a partner.

Our relationships also allow us to confront the phenomenon of the shadow. That is, we see that the things that compulsively bother us about other people are traits we have learned to repress in ourselves. What we most dislike in other people are qualities in ourselves that we struggle to deny.

Learning such lessons about ourselves and about the dynamics of human consciousness and interaction prepare us in early adulthood for stable, mature relationships later on.

There is a caveat to be remembered in all this: In the blinding flash of infatuation and new love, when projection and shadow dynamics are running full blast, we might forget the lessons we have been taught about hygiene and about maintaining detached awareness of what we are doing. We might feel such emotion that we would die for our lover, for instance, that we would think it a sign of love to risk HIV infection. If we have such thoughts, it is a sign we have not yet mastered the notion of projection and do not realize our beloved is a separate individual with his own life path.

## Long-Term Stable Relationships

An aspect of the transformation of gay culture brought on by AIDS was a championing of long-term stable relationships. This was probably happening anyway, a consequence of the first generation of liberated gay men—those who were coming of age sexually around the time of Stonewall and the declaration of gay liberation—reaching the time in life when they were ready to settle down. This transformation has resulted in highlighting the success of gay relationships and debunking the pre-liberated stereotype of the mature gay man as sexually frustrated and lonely.

Many gay men—because of, and not in spite of, the string of serial relationships they have enjoyed—form serious, stable, and enduring partnerships. There are strains on these relationships from without. But there are also strong forces within that hold these couplings together. There are freedoms and pleasures and intimacies and adventures that gay couples can enjoy that married heterosexuals cannot because of the dualistic aspects of their pairing.

Because gay partners can agree that recreational sex is fun or that a potential third party is appealing to both, for instance, styles of sexual recreation are open to us in the context of committed long-term relationship that are not available to most heterosexuals. In enjoying the adventurous side of sex while maintaining the stabilizing force of relationship, we discover one of the glories of being unconventional. We also encounter risky business. It takes maturity, open communication, compassion, understanding, boundary-setting, and integrity to make such arrangements work.

There are certainly practical factors that support gay (and non-gay) couples: good fortune, financial resources, families that honor the partnership. But the big issues are always the interpersonal and intrapersonal emotional states that make up the relationship.

Psychotherapy and couples-counseling teach techniques, even when they can be written off as "psycho-babble," that strengthen relationships, often by providing a common vocabulary for difficult-to-discuss issues. These can work like Dumbo feathers. (Remember, Dumbo's feather did not really possess any power, but because he believed in it, he was empowered.) They create "safe space" in which to discuss issues. "I don't mean to make you wrong and I need to share..." is a nonthreatening initiation for a serious talk that does not begin with an argument. The technique of using "and" instead of "but" as discussed earlier prevents many disagreements from ever getting started. One partner's wishes do not have to seem contradictory to the other's if they are linked by "and" rather than "but." Understanding the emotions and the intrapsychic dynamics of love can greatly enhance our experience of relationship and coupling.

The truth is we can have a relationship with anybody. Love is a decision, not just an emotion. The magic is not in the other person. It is in the willingness to communicate and work through problems and take responsibility for our emotions.

Sexual attraction and some amount of psychological harmony are important, too. Human beings have "types" they are attracted to, and we have to honor this unconscious drive. It is linked with both the phenomena of projection and of karmic resonance. It is what gets infatuation started in the first place. But inevitably infatuation fades and decision takes over.

One of the important decisions is to keep romance alive by being openly affectionate and considerate with one another. Men, as men, are socialized not to express feelings. Gay men have a gift in being more emotional and less guarded with feelings. Mobilizing these skills keeps a relationship romantic and affectionate.

The "sacrament" of love is saying: "I love you" as many times a day as we can find occasion for. A sacrament is something that brings about what it signifies. Repeating our feelings, using the potent "magic words," keeps us in love and helps us manage the day-to-day problems and upsets of living closely with another human being.

## More About Projection

The basis of crisis intervention therapy and, indeed, the theory of suffering and causation behind Buddhism, is that people are never upset for the reason they think. Their upset is actually the recurrence of a pattern learned in childhood, old memories, a rough day at work, a bad experience at the gym, etc. When one member of a couple gets stressed out, for instance, who else is there to blame but the other? The ability to step outside the upset of the moment and see that it is not the other's fault can be a saving grace in a relationship.

Understanding that present experience is always interpreted through associations with previous experience, chaining all the way back to infancy, is also the explanation of infatuation and the foundation of the dynamic of projection. The theory says that if, for instance, when you were a toddler you played with a neighbor's auburn cocker spaniel one day and fell in love with the dog, 15 years later, you might experience that a man with long, wavy red hair seems uncannily beautiful to you. You fall in love with him. You feel like you know him intimately. You think you know everything about him. You even believe you know how he loves you.

The infatuation and the whole complex of sexual and psychological attraction was initially sparked by the preconscious association with the cocker spaniel. That is what inspired the desire to connect with this man. This is not an altogether bad thing: It gets people started. It creates the sexual drive to choose another person as partner. On the other hand, of course, if you expect your beloved to behave always with the enthusiasm and loyalty of a cocker spaniel, you will certainly be disappointed.

As you develop intimacy—through spending time together, talking with one another, and experiencing orgasm together—you let go of your projections onto your beloved in order to discover who he really is, just as he drops his projections to discover who you are. This is what true intimacy is about.

## Jesus's Golden Rule

To intend for the other what we want for ourselves is, of course, the basis of Jesus's Golden Rule. And, if there is a message we should have all learned from the sexual revolution, this is it.

It is important to wish for our partners the breadth of experience, sexual and otherwise, that we have achieved for ourselves. It is critical for both parties to balance their stock of experience. Like keeping a joint checking account, it amounts to a shared investment in life. Often this means being liberal about sexual rules (though not about hygiene) and, especially, pursuing ways to share sexual adventures together. "Monogamy," after all, means "one relationship," not poverty of experience. Sometimes this is easy; sometimes it is difficult. What is important is the attitude of wanting for each other what we want for ourselves.

Too often lovers define their commitment around what they cannot do, rather than what they can and will do for each other. This seems based in the heterosexist, patriarchal double standard in which men control women's behavior for the sake of certainty over their offsprings' genetic makeup. That model does not make sense for gay men. The resistance to allowing our lovers their own lives is the weight of the projections we impose. We resist allowing our lover experience separate from ours because to do so reminds us he is not just a projection of our past associations; he is not really the cocker spaniel.

Of course, sexual exclusivity is something lovers might want to give one another. Certainly during the first few years of a relationship, exclusivity naturally follows the emotional and sexual absorption in one another of young love. And always in a serious relationship, partners have to agree not to be cruising for another lover or looking for a different relationship. The important issue is not hurting each other and honoring the relationship—whatever the rules you agree to. Both monogamy and non-monogamy can cause hurt. The necessary balm is communication.

## Love Does Not Make Sex Okay

In Christianity, marriage and the commitment of monogamy are thought to make acceptable, even holy, what is otherwise lustful, animalistic, and sinful. This notion appears in a watered-down way in today's liberal culture that deems it okay to have illicit sex if you "love" each other.

In fact, there is little difference between the joy and arousal and pleasure of sex in committed relationships and in one-night stands. The beauty of the other man's body, the electricity of his touch, the contact of erogenous zones, and the alteration of consciousness are the same. "Being in love" with somebody usually means, at least in part, being sexually turned on by them.

Since the Middle Ages, Western society has generally believed we should "be in love" to have sex; and we should not have to have sex with somebody we are not "in love" with. This is especially true in modern America where soap operas and modern media show passionate sex, even adultery, as okay so long as it is consensual and emotional. It is now sex as "conjugal duty" that is considered suspect.

"Loving" someone is different from "being in love." Love, in this sense, does not necessarily entail sexual attraction. We speak of love in this way in regard to parental and filial affection, to long friendships, to deep psychological bonds that form with people in our lives, and to sexual partners. Ideally, we would like to "love" the people we are "in love" with. And we would like the love to keep the sexual connection alive.

We fall in love because we are looking for a companion and because we are sexually motivated to find someone with whom to share this particular, and sometimes difficult to get, physical experience. Falling in love is the start of building a loving and lasting relationship.

But love does not make sex okay. Sex is okay. Sex does not need justification. Being sexually motivated is being human. The reason for building a lasting relationship is for the companionship. And the best companionship includes being sexually available to each other. This solves the gnawing need to seek out sexual partners. And it allows a deep bonding to occur. Loving a sexual partner and making love with him gives us security and confidence, and connects us to each other at a soul level.

Sexual exclusivity confirms our commitment, allays our anxieties, and saves us from distractions. For some couples, sharing sexual adventures or delighting in each other's separate adventures enhances their commitment by validating their sexuality and demonstrating that their bond is deeper than mere sexual desire.

After years of a relationship, sex usually is not hot and hungry every night. Still most of the time partners can pleasure themselves and each other, perhaps with the aid of the VCR and skinflicks. It is important to make sure we regularly experience sexual arousal with each other. In that altered state of consciousness, we can connect with the primal and transpersonal in human consciousness. We can merge our individual spirit and karmic selves in the intimate bonding of coming to orgasm together.

## Getting in Sync

A certain sort of "telepathy" develops in long-term relationships, gay and straight. People get in sync with each other so that they find themselves thinking about the same thing, making the same associations, being reminded of the same memories—almost as if they are reading each other's minds. In a way they are. They are resonating with one another's vibes. A very similar thing happens when they get in sync in sex, so that the coming to orgasm of one triggers the orgasm of the other. Like tuning forks resonating to a common vibration, the pleasure of one spills over to sustain and build the pleasure of the other. Sex is a way of getting in sync.

There is a saying that moves this experience up to a mystical level: "To love another person is to see the Face of God."

God is the vitality of the planet that "wills" all beings to love life. Since that experience manifests itself as flesh, God becomes the face of our beloved. Love is being "God" to the other's "God."

## The Solitary Life

While celebrating gay relationships—especially in this time of political strategy focused on marriage rights for homosexuals—we also have to see that many gay men are single and like being single.

They can be adventurers. They live out the theme of the wandering hero. Going from relationship to relationship, or just trick to trick, they interact with other men and potentially enrich each other's lives. They are the solitaries; they find in their lives, perhaps, resonances with the wandering monks, hermits, and jungle sadhus—Hindu ascetics—of old.

Some gay men are cast into solitary life unwittingly. They lose a relationship they had counted on or they just never find the right partner. They may indeed end up unhappy and lonely. But being single has a place in modern, urban society. There have always been men who have forsworn marriage and family to be sailors and soldiers, cowboys and trailblazers. No doubt many of them were homosexual.

In fact, gay men and lesbians, especially singles, ought to be welcomed into all the hazardous professions. It is an irony that police, fire fighting, and the military have excluded homosexuals in the notion these dangerous jobs require macho heterosexual men. Actually, the jobs require people who do not have familial responsibilities, who are unencumbered. It is especially heartrending to hear of a policeman or firefighter killed in the line of duty who leaves behind a large family. We have to ask what a man with children is doing in such a dangerous profession. It is irresponsible. The hazardous professions should be happy to employ singles. And society should recognize and honor single people for the specific contributions they make because of their freedom and "expendability."

The existence of openly gay people in society challenges the assumptions that everybody is in a heterosexual nuclear family, or else desperately unhappy. We are changing the great thoughts of the planet about what a good life is.

## Experiments on the Part of Nature

As an important part of our function of forcing open the conventions of sexuality, we are experimenting with different styles of relating. We tread the top of a precipitous wall.

As scouts of cultural advance, as sentinels upon the world's far frontiers, we are experiments on the part of nature in the creation of the human. We are, therefore, like the canaries in the mine. We run the risk of being injured while we show humankind the way. Pioneers who demonstrate by their disappearance that on certain paths there are dragons make just as important a contribution as those who return with news of a successful route. It is all part of breaking new ground.

Gay men are adventurers in consciousness, experimenting with a variety of styles of living—some of them extreme and dangerous—for the sake of assisting the human race in learning how to live and how to shape conscious evolution. We test new possibilities of behavior to see if they are adaptive and if we survive.

The AIDS epidemic demonstrated possible consequences of the change in sexual mores in the twentieth century. Globalization in the wake of the two World Wars and the development of effective contraceptives changed the rules of sex. Coming as a surprise to many, AIDS demonstrated that sexual hygiene is demanded even in these times of modern medicine. It revealed that unprotected penetrative sex spreads diseases we had never before imagined. On a personal level, the health crisis showed that people can change their sexual behavior. On a scientific level, it showed that medicine needs to change its focus from developing antibiotics that kill microbes to understanding and supplementing the immune system's ability to establish equilibrium with microorganisms and render them innocuous.

In part because of ease of travel and in part because of increase in population and population density, modernization and globalization have allowed the spread of diseases outside their ecological niche and driven the evolution of new diseases and virulent forms of previously benign microorganisms. AIDS has been but one of the plagues that face the earth as more and more microbes become resistant to antibiotics in a dazzling but horrific demonstration of the truth of the Theory of Evolution. AIDS is not just a medical crisis, it is an ecological crisis—one that dramatizes the dynamics of planetary ecology.

## *Teaching the Lessons of Our Adventure*

The evolutionary model of life on Earth that is generally embraced by modern consciousness parallels the developmental model of ego-psychology in the individual: As we grow, we go through stages. Primitive religions ritualized these life-stages with "rites of passage." The most important of these is the celebration of puberty and the start of adult life.

The awareness that people grow through developmental stages— especially around sex and love—reminds us that what is appropriate behavior for people depends on where they are in their life evolution. While "elders" certainly possess important wisdom, these days they cannot give very good advice to the young about youth. By the time they have learned their lessons about life, the culture has changed.

It does no good for 60-year-old men to tell 20-year-olds, for instance, that love is more important than sex, that they ought to settle down and be responsible, that monogamy is better than promiscuity, that they should not take chances with their lives because they are not invulnerable. The 20-year-olds will discover these lessons on their own, and they cannot learn them until they have lived long enough for the lessons to make sense. Too many rules in society are made by elders and forced on the young "for their own good." This causes rebelliousness and widens the generation gap. Still, elders can be models. Many 20-year-olds do look up to elders. Many, in fact, would prefer relationships with older men because they are less fraught with turmoil than relationships with peers.

The issues of age difference arise in gay culture around AIDS prevention and safe-sex training. Some of the elders of gay liberation, now in their fifties or older, want to tell the young they ought to avoid perpetuation of a gay sex subculture that turned out to be unhygienic and inadvertently lethal. The youth are not apt to listen. They do not experience the fragility of life. And somebody else's experience does not prove it.

This is a serious problem for safe-sex education. The young—the sexual rebels—have a right to their own mistakes. The older, more experienced of us, no matter how grieved and bereaved we might be, cannot impose our wisdom on the young—at least not through shame and wrong-making. Unfortunately, AIDS and the speed of change in the modern world does not allow for leisurely learning. It is one thing to make a few mistakes about matters of the heart. It is quite another to get infected with an incurable virus.

Perhaps the best motive for safe-sex practice and good hygiene is the realization of the spiritual meaning of one's life *right now*. The fact is, young people may not be as careful about situations of danger as older adults, but in some ways they are more idealistic and spiritually minded. Maybe it is love of life and participation in changing morphogenetic fields around sexual behavior, not fear of danger, that would make sense to them.

In general, it is the belief that we have an important role in life and are worthy, contributing, participating, beloved members of our community—more than fear—that can motivate us to love and care for ourselves and each other. This lesson may be the most important reason for the whole enterprise of finding spiritual significance in our sexualities.

# Chapter 15

## ADAPTIVE VIRTUES: INNOCENCE AND TRANSPARENCY

The sight of a man stretching his abdomen to impel his sexual thrust and the surge of energy and affirmation that spreads through his body is a joy to behold. The thrust that energizes his nervous system and opens his consciousness sends thrills to heaven. Don't we all experience this? Isn't it obvious? And isn't it innocent?

Innocence and transparency are essentially gay virtues—by which we tell the truth and realize we can tell the truth because we are not guilty of fundamental sin. Our homosexuality does not hurt anybody. That is what innocence means: not causing harm. Such innocence, not naïveté or stupidity or ditziness, but rather a basic orientation to goodness, is a marvelous trait. Its related trait is transparency, being without guile. Transparency manifests as genuine concern, and innocence as "eternal boyishness."

### Puer Aeternus

Gay boyishness, part of the positive stereotype, is an interesting phenomenon. Becoming a parent creates transformation at all levels of the personality. With the birth of a child, men and women change. They begin to identify with their own parents. In their children's development, they re-experience their own childhood. This transformation appears in their bodies and their faces and their ways of being. They look older.

People who do not become parents do not undergo this transformation. Gay men, as gay men, usually do not become parents, and so they maintain a youthfulness. And gay men who do become parents often resist the tendency to drop sexual identity and refocus on fatherhood. Even though they have children, they are still not evolving into their father's life. Homosexuality retards aging.

Gay youthfulness has only partly to do with maintaining physical beauty, though because we are concerned about our attractiveness we likely use moisturizers and skin creams. It is more about how we feel in our bodies. Gay men stay playful. We cuddle kitty cats. We sit on the floor, like children, not like adults. We skip down the path in the park.

There are pitfalls. Not parenting costs us the important healing experience of observing our children and reliving our own development vicariously. Furthermore, struggling to stay young and sexy-looking can become an all-consuming, ultimately hopeless obsession.

But there are achievements that come with not shifting self-image from youth to parent. These are the powers of Peter Pan, the eternal boy whose innocence and good will are infectious—and redemptive. The eternal boy saves the day. In fairy tales, this is accomplished by fairy magic, quick wits, and determination. In religion, it is accomplished by being an unblemished, pleasing sacrifice, like Jesus, "a eunuch for the sake of the kingdom." In day-to-day reality, it is accomplished by being kind and truthful and concerned. We save the day by being good guys.

Goodness, openness, and willingness to delay judgment and take risks is exemplified in the Tarot card of The Fool. The *fol* or *fool* in medieval French lore was a bisexual male. The carefree and innocent Fool is an expression of the Jungian archetype of the *puer aeternus*, the "eternal boy."

A variation of the Fool is the Trickster, the archetypal figure that reminds people of spiritual truth by trickery, playfulness, and irony. The medieval Mattachines were tricksters.

Native American traditions have lots of Tricksters. The most familiar is Coyote. One of his tricks is seducing handsome men by pretending to be a beautiful woman. Some Indian wisepeople assume the role of contrary-walkers; they do everything backwards. Like the jesters of European courts, Tricksters can speak the truth that others dare not say.

## Eunuchs for the Sake of the Kingdom

The closest Jesus ever got to speaking about sexual variance is the mysterious comment: "Some men are made eunuchs by men, some by God, and some make themselves eunuchs for the sake of the kingdom. Him who can take it, let him take it" (Matthew 19:12).

Eunuchs were castrated men, usually castrated so they could serve as attendants to the King's collection of wives: Because they could not produce sperm, they would not accidentally father a child that could be mistaken for royal lineage. Some eunuchs were temple prostitutes, i.e., priests, like the *galli* of Cybele, who participated in sacred sex rituals with worshippers. They were castrated to keep them from impregnating women, but more importantly to make them boyish and androgynous, since most of the worshippers seeking their blessing would have been male. "The Persian Boy," Bagoas, lover of Alexander the Great, was such a eunuch. *Hijras*, eunuchs in traditional India, were—and are—transgendered men, many of whom work in show business. Eunuchs were not men who did not have sex. They were men who did not reproduce.

When Jesus praised "eunuchs for the kingdom," wasn't he talking about men who abjured marriage and family for the sake of an experience of life beyond normalcy and convention? Many gay men can rightly be thought of as eunuchs for the kingdom, because we have responded to an irresistible vocation and turned our lives away from normalcy for something more wonderful, more innocent, and more immediate. Eunuchs live for the here and now, not for some future generation. Mystical vision is not concerned with the future. Now is the point. Now is God.

## Innocence

Innocence is purity of heart, holding good intentions with no malice. Of course, not all gay men are good guys and not all good guys are gay. But it is the common joke that women, especially urban women, complain that it is so hard to find a considerate, attractive man because they have all already found each other.

We challenge the macho stereotype that men are hard and competitive, ill-tempered, crude, and arrogant. It was said that gay men in the military endanger unit cohesion. The general public thought that was because of the dangers of dropping the soap in the showers (incorrectly attributing to gay men the urge that straight men apparently experience to force sex on vulnerable partners). But didn't it really mean that gay men are peacemakers, cool heads whose presence calms the macho posturing, one-upsmanship, and sexual rivalry that bonds men in collective belligerency? Don't you think gay men are threatening to conventional society because we represent cooperative males who are looking for ways to work together? Don't you think we are threatening because we demonstrate the virtue of love and kindness that is so praised in theory but so little manifested in practice and so detrimental to male dominance and hierarchy?

A caricature of gay men is the malicious bitchy queen. However, like all the elements of camp—exaggeration, archness, irreverence, impropriety, ridiculousness—the point of the humor is always satirical. These traits are feigned to make fun of people who might really be like that. The negative traits are pretended precisely to eschew them. Everybody is supposed to understand the joke. In fact, the myth of the bitch queen is that he has the proverbial heart of gold.

## Have Faith

An aspect of innocence demonstrated in gay men's sexually-liberated culture is what might be called "having faith." The admonition "have faith" does not mean to believe in a set of doctrines or opinions. Rather it means to be optimistic and persevering, to trust life and trust others. Being open to new sexual experiences is almost always an act of faith. We never know what might happen. Tricking is dangerous. We are called upon to trust our intuitions about another person and to trust that that person is presenting enough of the truth about himself for our intuition and reason to make an assessment.

To have faith also means to expect a positive outcome, to believe we will be able to overcome obstacles and adversities and that we will benefit from having done so. To have faith is to intend that things get better, to not become dispirited and cynical. It is to see the world through the eyes of innocence.

## What Is Wrong With Gay Life?

We have been raised to think of ourselves as anything but innocent. Indeed, we make a game of reveling in our badness. We revile the good, "normal" people and play at being wicked. Sometimes we actually become wicked out of society's self-fulfilling prophecy for us. Sometimes, out of the sense of being damned anyway, gay men behave horribly to one another. We adopt "attitude" out of self-defense and fear. We become looksist snobs, rejecting other gay men who do not fit our idealizations of physical beauty and sophistication. We obsess over our looks, getting snared in ego like Brer Rabbit in the Tar-Baby.

Embracing our innocence, relaxing our fears and unrealistic demands might go a long way toward solving practical difficulties that beset gay community. We have not discussed the problems much. There are other commentators who are doing that. We do not need another book about what is wrong with gay life. If, indeed, we demonstrate revolution through consciousness change, then let us solve our problems by changing how we think about ourselves. Certainly spiritual gay men should not be acting like mainstream religious people figuring out who is to blame.

Of course, there are problems. Drug addiction and sexual compulsion, the inability to form lasting relationships, self-inflicted anger and bitchiness and selfishness, almost suicidal disregard for the consequences of actions, acquisitiveness, and greed—these afflict some gay men. Not all of us are saints and reincarnated bodhisattvas. We are human, after all. But perceiving sex as innocent and our love and desire for one another as holy would change the trappings of modern gay subculture.

## Integrity and Transparency

Gay identification witnesses to essential integrity. The reason for coming out and acknowledging ourselves as gay is because it is true. And because to live some other way would be untrue to our experience of life. People do not become gay because they are morally lazy. We commit ourselves to the truth of our feelings because we experience compunction and moral commitment. We see that we have to rise above caring what other people think because we consider our integrity more demanding.

Transparency is saying the hardest thing. This is a principle in psychoanalysis: In telling your therapist about your life, whenever you see you have a choice about what to tell and how to tell it, you should always choose the harder thing to say. This brings repressed feelings and denied memories into consciousness. This is the major healing tool of psychotherapy.

To live transparently is to open ourselves to remembering the hard memories and acknowledging the embarrassing truths, denying nothing, releasing the patterns of repression that cause neurosis. Being transparent is not letting our ego get in the way of our experience, not worrying what other people will think.

Studies have shown that gay people are generally more psychologically healthy than the general population. Isn't this because our very experience of bringing our homosexuality into consciousness—the hardest thing of all to discover and tell the truth about—is itself psychotherapeutic and growth-producing?

Choosing to say the hardest thing is transcending the polarities of easy and hard. It discharges the pent-up energy around realities and truths we fear. It is choosing to suffer in order to not suffer. We overcome the suffering involved in the polarities by embracing both poles. We experience liberation from the obligations and compulsions of masculinity by embracing and relishing our femininity.

Transparency is an important step in the evolution of a planetary mind and a harmonious urban mass society. In order to cooperate, we have to negotiate our needs and wants by openly declaring them. A hallmark of neurotic living is trying to get what you want by subterfuge and manipulation, seeming to renounce your goals in the hopes of making somebody else so guilty he or she will give you what you want in spite of yourself. A hallmark of healthy living is honestly stating your needs and then learning to want what you get.

## Compassion and Caring

From innocence and transparency come compassion and caring for others. When we do not feel guilty or threatened, we can look beyond ourselves. We can acknowledge and cultivate our innate sensitivity to others. It is said homosexuals develop hypersensitivity to other people's nonverbal communications out of self-defense. Once we see we do not have to keep the secret, our sensitivity can flower.

# Chapter 16

## ADAPTIVE VIRTUES: SELFLESSNESS AND GENEROSITY

There is a selflessness in letting go of the biological imperatives of gene dominance. The gay (and celibate) choice to renounce reproduction and propagation of our genes is a dramatic act of disidentification with ego. We do not pretend we're going to live our lives over or achieve immortality through having offspring.

From compassion, caring, and love of life come celebration and generosity. We all experience joy, gratification, and fulfillment of longings when somebody wants to have sex with us—especially when he is somebody we want to have sex with, too. Should we not always want that joy for other people? And want it so that there are no undesirable consequences for them: no disease, no unwanted pregnancy, no unequal or neurotic relationship in the aftermath?

### Transforming Sexual Culture

A sex-positive attitude transforms sexual culture. Pornography, for example, is maligned in mainstream culture. But if we understand it as sexually accomplished young men vicariously sharing their beauty, it is an act of generosity. Erotic photographs and videos offer both casual sexual playmates and long-term lovers opportunities to enjoy a common experience of celebrating male beauty together. Erotica is like a meditation focus, concentrating the mind on the single point of awareness of incarnation.

Prostitution can be understood as patronage of beauty and recompense for achievement of sexual skills, just as athletes are recompensed for physical achievements. Youth and beauty are highly valued, but little paid. Young people should not have to depend on their looks and sexual prowess to provide them a living. These things fade. But neither should the onus of dishonor be laid on the exchange of money for sex. Understanding prostitution in a better light would help alleviate the problems that exist in the red-light world.

Many of these problems arise out of heterosexual duality and power imbalance. Men pimping women has nothing to do with valuing youth and beauty. It is about men's ownership of women. These dynamics are much less present in the gay world.

What is impugned as gay men's agenda to "recruit" more homosexuals is really our desire to share the gift we've discovered. When we see an attractive man, a man who glows in our eyes, we feel an upwelling of·emotion. It is, in part, sexual arousal and, in part, spiritual exaltation. It is joy that such beauty exists, evidence that the incarnate world is wonderful and worthy.

With that emotion come intentions. We hope the attractive man is gay and, therefore, in theory, available, and that he'll find us attractive. But underlying these feelings is an even more general and selfless hope that he is gay, knows he's gay, and knows what a treasure that is—purely for *his* sake. We want others to be gay because we want them to be as lucky as we are.

"Recruiting" is our concern that others not suffer the same confusion we did. It is, especially, a parental concern for the well-being of the next generation of gay people. Independent of AIDS and the activism the health crisis has spawned, most of the effort of the gay movement has been to improve the world for future homosexuals and to reach out to conflicted homosexuals with the news that they're not alone.

The function of the organized gay rights movement is not only to educate straight people and accomplish change in the law, it is to reach young gay people with the news that they can change their attitude toward their sexual feelings and that, by embracing their truth, they can discover that what they have been told was a curse is, in fact, a blessing of great magnitude. By this act of transformation, they can recreate their world.

## Sexual Generosity

A certain generosity with sexual experience shows up in gay relationships. There is a natural symmetry of sexual feelings. My lover and I can both be attracted to the same man. I can understand my lover's attraction. I can affirm it out of love for him. I can, in fact, share it with him.

Heterosexuals generally do not experience this symmetry or generosity. Hence, violation of the rules of monogamy threaten, and destroy, their relationships. Perhaps if Arthur and Guenevere had been able to invite Lancelot to their marriage bed, Camelot might be alive today.

Whether three-ways appeal to you or not, the point is we can finally tell the truth about our feelings. In fact, in a way, we have to. We do not have rules for our relationships. We stand outside the framework of appropriate sex roles and legally enforceable conventions about how two people with an emotional and sexual bond should relate to each other and the outside world. We have to make up our own rules. We have to negotiate agreements for how we live and love together.

Sexual generosity flows from the feeling of the wonder of life. It is good to give other people pleasure. It is a gift to show someone that we find him attractive. It is virtuous to satisfy another's curiosity about our bodies. It is generous to find occasions to shed our clothes in an affirmation of human beauty. The practice of such generosity improves our own self-esteem and helps us stay in shape.

Between men and women there are power imbalances and misperceptions of intention that make generosity with the beauty of their bodies dangerous. Men assault women who too easily show themselves as attractive, saying they are "asking for it." Women are modest because they have to protect themselves.

Gay men do not need to protect themselves that way. We seldom force ourselves on each other. Often we are so insecure that we let opportunities pass us by because we fear we have misread the cues. Too many gay men are "modest" because they are ashamed of their bodies and conflicted about how they look to others. It is a contribution all around for us to let others see our bodies and for us to discover our own beauty in the appreciation of others. In general, gay men have a sensible and admirable attitude toward nudity. It is part of our affirmation of incarnation and an expression of generosity.

Sexual generosity does not necessarily mean having sex with everybody. That creates another set of behaviors that are not always virtuous. As a group we need to learn to show our appreciation for other men's beauty and allure without being demanding. It is the fear that somebody I am not attracted to will come on to me that prevents me from accepting others' appreciation.

We get caught in webs of karma—wanting attention from some men but not from others, giving attention to some but not to others. If we all want to get picked up by someone more attractive than ourselves, no one will never connect. We get rejected by the men we want because we reject the men who want us. Gay men sometimes behave badly toward one another in anonymous, especially group, situations. We become defensive and adopt attitude to protect ourselves. Our kindness and sensitivity get scrambled by the overwhelming experience of being around so many other men.

We would all feel better if we learned to say no appropriately, to take no graciously, and to find more varied and wonderful ways to say yes. Wonder is always about saying yes. We cannot say yes to every proposition put to us. But we can avoid saying no in ways that hurt other people and that make us feel small.

## Demonstrating Solutions

Gay relationships, especially these days when legal recognition is in the public consciousness, can demonstrate modern solutions to outmoded but deeply ingrained patterns of bonding.

Certainly we can demonstrate that a simple act of "infidelity" is not a reason to destroy a marriage and break up a family. There is an odd notion perpetuated by the people who intend to strengthen families and promote family values that any violation of the rule of sexual exclusivity calls for dissolution of the relationship.

Paradoxically, efforts to enforce family values by encouraging draconian reactions have the effect of destabilizing families. Demanding that homosexuals suppress their sexuality in order to marry and have children requires them to suppress natural urges, and sets them up for divorce.

What would more effectively strengthen the family would be clear encouragement for everyone who even slightly questions their sexual orientation or doubts their parental urges or capabilities to opt out of the heterosexual lifestyle—early before there are children to endanger.

The believers in family values support large families with many children. Some straight people make wonderful parents and should raise whole broods. (Perhaps society should license and subsidize them.) The self-enclosed nuclear family of two adults and one or two children may be a cause of the breakdown of society. Children are not socialized and taught cooperation at home. They compete with their parents, not their peers, for attention. At any rate, for there to be large families, there need to be fewer of them. For the idealized version of family dreamed about by family values advocates to be realized, fewer people can reproduce.

Gay lifestyles demonstrate that people can live successful, fulfilling, and contributing lives without reproducing.

## Political Correctness

What has come to be derided under the rubric political correctness—an idea that permeates the lesbian and gay civil rights struggle—is the ethical imperative that we consider the consequences of our actions on the lives of other people.

A problem with the old morality, based in foreign and antiquated cultures' notions of cleanliness, hygiene, and taboo, is that it focuses on acts rather than consequences. This is one of the points Jesus got in trouble for with the religious authorities. He insisted that compassion, even compassion for a donkey trapped in a hole, superseded the Law about what one could and could not do on the Sabbath.

The struggle to be politically correct is ridiculed for being so concerned with terminology that it sounds like its own kind of legalism and rigidity. The notion of political correctness means we have to pay attention to the effects our behavior has on other people and on the ecological environment. We have to use words that do not hurt others. We must not perpetuate attitudes that cause hurt.

Because politicized lesbians have been so instrumental in creating the gay movement, the feminist and New Left notion of political correctness has permeated gay community organizing. At times it has hobbled action. But by and large, the effort to be politically correct and to be concerned about all social issues and causes of oppression must be seen as one of the glories of the Movement.

Other minorities often take a more single focus; they are concerned about their own grievances. Gay organizers have always felt—though almost always argued the issue endlessly—that the gay cause must include all other causes, even those that have been content to leave gay grievances out of their purview of concern. This has not been for political expedience. It is a matter of principle. And it demonstrates the basic religious orientation of the Movement and its countercultural commitment to changing the status quo.

At least as it functions in gay and lesbian thinking, political correctness involves the creation and cultivation of community. In fact, we change one of the central notions in mainstream society: For us, the building block of society is not family, but community. Because of political realities, our fortunes are tied to the larger community. *By virtue of our gay identity* we become part of an abstract collectivity. This is a spiritual relationship with other gay people, not at all unlike the Buddhist notion of the *sanga* or the Christian notion of the church as the Mystical Body of Christ.

A corollary of political correctness is ecological correctness. In other words, paying attention to the consequences of our actions necessarily includes paying attention to the effects we have on our environment and our ecological niche. This is part of being a global citizen. Though the gay movement has little association with the environmental movement, politicized gay people are likely to support environmental causes because it is the responsible thing to do.

## Drugs and Sex

With a definite countercultural bent, gay people are generally more generous with issues of drug use, partly because we see that drug laws are more concerned with social control and big-money interests than with human welfare, and partly because we're able to be more adventuresome in our own lives. When you do not have children to be responsible for, you are more free to take risks with your life.

Drugs have always played a part in religion, because they alter consciousness and therefore render one more aware of what consciousness is. The shamans and medicine men of old, often homosexual, used mind-altering herbs and plants.

There are dangers with such substances, especially in the highly refined forms in which some now appear. Not all drugs are the same. A particular problem with drug use exists in the gay community because so many gay men think of themselves as outlaws, then fulfill that prophecy by violating laws—even those of good sense, just to break the law and be contrary.

There are also benefits in mind-altering substances, especially those nature offers. The trick is to use these substances to expand consciousness, to open the mind and the personality, not to anesthetize pain and close down the experience of life. The real test—the adventure—is knowing the difference.

Drugs and alcohol are indeed problems for some homosexuals. In fact, their abuse is the most common manifestation of the razor's edge that living at the forefront of cultural evolution incurs. To be true to our sexuality and to escape to the gay enclave, we abandon the rules and shibboleths of conventional society. Significant ego-strength is demanded of those who forge their own way through life, often without role-models or guides. There are casualties among those who make their lives an adventure.

Sex itself can be a problem for some homosexuals. Deep, unconscious material is tied up with sex and the pursuit of sex. When powerful boosts—and blows—to self-esteem collide with karmic chaos, it is not surprising that some people get dazzled, make poor judgments, and get themselves in trouble. The presence of a sexually transmitted virus in our midst creates a whole new level of trouble we can get ourselves (and other people) into. Awareness of the problem some men have with sexual addiction and compulsive behavior has—appropriately, adaptively—dampened the adventuresomeness of gay society. But that does not have to result in sex-negativity.

Transforming attitudes about sex and drugs can help resolve the problems. Following in the traditions of the past, perhaps gay people are supposed to be the dispensers of drugs for sacred use, understanding their power for good and for ill. It is part of our effort at virtue to demonstrate the pitfalls and glories of alternative styles of living.

The straight world is not likely to take our advice on these matters. But they have an uncanny knack for following our lead while denying that is what they are doing. The real effects of our experimentations and our cultivation of adaptive virtues show up in the vibes we put out into the collective mind. We help change the world by changing ourselves.

## Longing for Justice

Gay people's interest in justice and making the world better for future generations is a matter of principle. We have no vested interest in the future. We are not making the world better for our children, we are making it better for all children.

We feel ourselves the innocent victims of undeserved injustice. As children, we were excluded for our difference without being told what was really going on. Living in gay society, we have heard stories of unbelievable atrocities committed against us. As a consequence, a central feature of our personality is a deep yearning for a better world and a discomfort with the blind stupidity of the masses around us. We long for a world in which there is no injustice, in which the law of love is followed gladly and nobody tries to make anybody else wrong for being themselves.

Such longing for a better world may not be enough in itself. It may need to be complemented with contributions of time, money, and participation in political demonstrations and community organizing efforts. But this longing is the origin of good intentions for the world.

The longing participates in the whole world's yearning, which is the driving force of evolution. It is God's good will that the world gets better. Because we feel this yearning we can forgive the blind, stupid masses. In fact, we can love them and say yes to their struggle, because that is what it takes for all of us to reach the heaven on earth we long for.

## Ecological Ways to Live

Affluence and gay sensitivity have led some people to collect art, surround themselves with beauty, and accumulate wealth. It is certainly true that some gay men, because they do not have children and because they're talented—and perhaps lucky—have lots of disposable income. Some gay men are rich. This adds its own set of problems to their lives.

In reality, however, the vast majority of gay people are no better off financially than anybody else. But they may live better. Gay taste and conscientiousness teach some people how to live simply and economically with beauty, order, and symmetry. A meager income, like that of many gay men who have moved to urban gay meccas and accepted "downward mobility" as the price for living there, does not have to mean living in squalor. We might call this style genteel poverty, i.e., living in clean, tastefully if inexpensively decorated surroundings, using money not to collect objects, but to gather experience. It is an important adaptation to modern living.

We all have to share the world's available resources, and we mustn't deplete them thoughtlessly. The human race needs to achieve an ecological balance with the organism of the planet, lest we be to it like a microbe that's gotten out of ecological balance and become virulent. We certainly do not want Gaia's immune system to mobilize against us.

Simplicity of life and a certain parsimony with energy use demonstrate sensible, ecological ways to live. A paucity of possessions and responsibilities frees our resources for adventures and our wherewithal for taking risks. These are the things that give texture to life and offer the opportunity for greatness.

The cultural stereotype is that gay men are selfish and spoiled. This accusation comes out of the fact that most of us do not have children, as though having children were an unselfish thing to do. For people who'll make good parents and raise emotionally healthy children, creating a family can be a major contribution to the life of the planet. It demonstrates admirable generosity and selflessness. Parents put aside their own satisfaction for the sake of their children. On the other hand, reproducing just for the sake of duplicating oneself, or having a baby so somebody will love you and then take care of you in later life, or having a child just because it happened is incredibly selfish.

The AIDS crisis demonstrated that gay men and lesbians are enormously generous. Huge amounts of money and uncountable donations of time and energy have poured into the effort to comfort the afflicted and to stop the spread of AIDS. There is no way to know how much of that money and concern might otherwise have been donated to other gay causes or to other efforts to ease suffering around the world. There is no record of how generous gay people have been to the United Way, Save the Children, and the Red Cross. No way to tell how generous they've been with friends and family. The generosity demonstrated regarding AIDS causes—while certainly "self-serving"—suggests caring and compassion are strong in the gay heart.

Fund-raisers for gay political action groups complain they're underfunded. And that is probably true. However, they do a marvelous job at their primary function of creating enough media presence that young homosexuals realize they're not alone. Even if none of the goals of the political movement are achieved, in the process of striving for them important work is being done.

We should be generous with AIDS and gay-related charities. We should support our political activists. And we should spend money in the gay community to support the community infrastructure. Money spent in businesses that cater specifically to gay people ends up as advertising revenue for the gay media and donations to community causes.

One of the problems of modern capitalism is that we have lost touch with the old notion of *noblesse oblige*: the obligation of honorable, generous, and responsible behavior associated with high rank or birth. To the extent that we recognize what a gift we have in our homosexuality and what opportunities and wealth we have been accorded—especially by not having children—we see we have obligations to give of ourselves and our largesse. Sharing our money is participation in the ecology of earth.

## The Measure of the Good Life

The anthem for gay youth, quoted in full earlier, identifies the measure of the good life.

Don't be rattled by names,
By taunts or games,
       but seek out spirits true.

If you give your friends the best part of yourself,
       they will give the same back to you...

And the only measure of your words and your deeds
Will be the love you leave behind when you're gone.[1]

# PART II

## Seek Out Spirits True

Though there are crooks and disturbed characters among the homosexual population, the experience of most of us is that we can trust other gay men. Their spirits are true. We share something in common. We are motivated by the world's oppression to offer one another the best parts of ourselves. We can be friends. What we want from one another is love, friendship, and shelter from the storm of the straight world. We seek—and we create—community. This communal movement, loosely called gay spirituality, is concerned with finding kindred spirits.

## Chapter 17

## THEMES IN GAY SPIRITUALITY: CIRCLE-MAKERS

Circle-making is concerned with creating community, bringing like-minded people together to unite common intentions and get things done. The building of community and a sense of connectedness and loyalty to other gay people is the heart of gay liberation and gay identity development.

Circle-maker themes are: 1) Faerie consciousness, 2) gay therapy and self-help/personal transformation programs, 3) gay wild man gatherings, 4) bear identification, 5) pilgrimage and adventure-seeking, 6) 12-step programs, and 7) Native American *berdache* tradition.

### Faerie Consciousness

The Radical Faerie movement and aligned groups of progressed hippies and counterculturalists constitute the most visible group of gay men consciously working to create a specifically gay spiritual tradition.

The Faeries developed out of the hippie amalgam of idealized Christianity, Eastern religions, Western esoterica, and New Age optimism. "Fairy" was a term gay hippies embraced for themselves, a term of derision turned positive, like "queer" for a later generation. Fairy resonated with the vibes of "flower power" and with the mainstream meaning of "gay" as happy-go-lucky and whimsical. Fairies,

*165*

like brownies, which homosexuals were also called but with less wholesome associations, do good deeds, help people, and make things pretty.

Fairy, as a gay community-appropriated term, had its spelling changed and was given a kind of archaic—and arcane—medieval grandeur. It became "faery" and then "faerie." It was institutionalized in 1979 in the grassroots, loosely organized Radical Faerie movement when a wilderness gathering in the Arizona desert brought a large response and inspired a segment of fairy-identified cultural activists to promote a new kind of gay lifestyle.

This gathering was instigated by Harry Hay, titular founder of the gay rights movement in America. In 1951, Hay had established the Mattachine Society. He took the name from a medieval society of troubadours in the south of France, a group not unlike a modern-day New Orleans Mardi Gras krewe. The original Mattachines may well have been the medieval equivalent of drag queens doing guerrilla theater, carrying news and politics across the countryside and parodying established religion—just like the modern gay Faeries.

The Faeries mock gender roles. They costume themselves in outrageous outfits that employ elements of drag and cross-dressing, but seldom in serious female impersonation. This gender-fuck drag is often a protest of how women in male-dominated society are objectified and hobbled by the demands of fashion and attractiveness. It is also a demonstration, and sacramentalization, of gay men's liberation from society's obsession with appropriate sex-role behavior.

Cross-dressing shows up in gay culture with a variety of meanings. For some, wearing women's clothing is a sexual turn-on; for others, it is satisfaction of a compulsion to be a different person. For some prostitutes, it is a work-required uniform; for some stage performers, it is a costume. For some men, it is a problem; for others, a liberation. The fact that gay men can don women's clothes at all is a sign of freedom from social taboos and conventions. Cross-dressing is a staple of comedy, but outside the permissiveness of show business it makes most people anxious. To some radical activists and Faeries, this last might be the best reason for doing it.

Faeries, like monks and nuns of old, often take new names—pseudonyms to symbolize the transformation of character and the choice of who one is. Faerie names often sound hippie, American Indian, or campy: Hyperion, Crazy Owl, or Sister Missionary Position.

There are Faerie sanctuaries and intentional communities around the country, mostly in rural areas, which regularly organize gatherings of like-minded men. Faerie gatherings are generally unstructured in a way that allows spontaneous events to unfold. Participants are encouraged to create rituals and celebrations that run from the silly and camp to the reverent and profound. Almost always part of the agenda are no-talent talent shows, costume pageants, and serious heart circles where men talk openly about their lives in a kind of self-guided group therapy. Also part of the spirit of the gathering is a certain liberality with sex. Radical Faerie gatherings are a chance for men to respond spontaneously to one another in joyous celebration of gay sexuality.

In spite of the silliness, camp, and friendly camaraderie, Faerie spirituality belongs to an ancient tradition that worships life and nature. Yet it is also forward-looking. It demonstrates the modern perspective on religion. It is based in the understanding that we create rituals not so much for the pleasure of the gods, but for our own edification. Among the Faeries, there is no orthodoxy. Anybody's god or ritual is as good as anybody else's. There is a genuine appreciation for the arbitrariness and interchangeability of religious symbols.

Faerie consciousness includes a fascination with magic and witchly powers. In part because of gay liberation's Aquarian "New Age" origins, and in part because of a campy gay interest in gypsy-like women with Earth Goddess powers, many gay men are fascinated with Tarot cards and fortune-telling. Some of this fascination is cultural fad, and some is resonance with the homosexual men before us who were shamans and seers, witchdoctors and medicine men, wizards and mystics, wandering monks and hermits, who lived outside normal society. These men could see, and foresee, things normal people could not.

## Gay Therapy and Self-Help/Personal Transformation Programs

Paralleling the Fairies as creators of community, but appealing to a different group of gay men, are the various encounter and therapy groups run by openly gay therapists.

At approximately the same time that Stonewall gave rise to a gay political identity, homosexuality was removed from the American Psychiatric Association's list of mental illnesses, opening the field to gay-positive psychotherapy. Peer counseling organizations, gay rap groups, and various forms of psychotherapy began to address gay people's need to change their interior lives, just as the political groups of the day had set out to change external governmental and societal oppression.

One of the most organized of all such quasi-psychotherapeutic trainings, The Advocate Experience, focused the technologies of personal transformation on the gay issues of coming out and letting go of homophobia. The Advocate Experience was, and is, a training in how to transform negative, unconscious assumptions into positive intentions for how to live your life. Originally a gay spin-off of *est*, it proposed the mythical, mystical notion that each person is responsible for everything that happens to him or her in this lifetime: You are God in your own universe. In other words, the way to change how the world deals with homosexuality is to transform your own way of dealing with it.

Important to The Advocate Experience and other forms of gay-oriented psychotherapy was the exercise of writing a long and detailed coming-out letter to your parents. You did not have to send it, though you could. In this way you could be honest and open about childhood pain, especially around your being gay or not feeling normal. Disclosure, to oneself and to others, is an important part of transforming the experience of homosexuality. Researchers of journal-writing as a psychotherapeutic tool have found that writing about one's life, especially about traumatic events and interior upsets, for as little as 20 minutes per day for three or four consecutive days can reduce not only mental health difficulties, but also symptoms of asthma and arthritis. It can also improve immune function. As such, the writing exercise in The Advocate Experience was often profoundly healing.

## Gay Wild Man Gatherings

Similar to the Faeries, and overlapping in membership, are gay offshoots of the mainstream men's movement that started in the 1980s. The men's movement appealed to people who wanted to change their lives. It proposed to extend to men the kind of group identity and support the women's movement and feminism bestowed on women, proclaiming that men had personal issues that could only be dealt with in manly ways.

Organizers of men's gatherings designed meetings in the wilderness to help men discover and honor "the wild man within." This discovery was often accomplished through screaming, crying, and expressing affection to other men—things not allowed in mainstream society. These actions released pent-up feelings and alleviated the stress of living in urban, mass society.

Gay and bisexual men who attended these events found them affirming of themselves as feeling and emotional persons, and also as gay men. Many of the men's events made a ritual of honoring gay men in attendance as a way of releasing the fear of homosexuality straight men recognized as stress-provoking and restricting in their lives.

Gay men organized spin-offs to share the good experience with other gay men. They realized that some of the men's movement events were shot through with homophobia, even when the straight men thought they were being accepting. These spin-offs centered the discussion on gay issues and the expression of gay camaraderie, rather than on the repressions straight men suffer.

Men's events tended to be serious, usually focused on experiences of personal failure. Many of the participants were recovering from addictions like alcoholism, cocaine dependency, or workaholism. Many had suffered physical, emotional, or sexual abuse as children, and many had conflicted feelings about their fathers. The work at the gatherings, founded on a therapy model, was intense and structured.

The gay spin-offs have tended to interpret personal failure as being outside the individual and rooted in the homophobia of society. The basic idea is that gay men are flawed and neurotic and need to recover, but not from something of their own doing.

Because some of the men who attend these gay groups have deep intrapsychic issues based in sexual abuse, these gatherings tend to be less sexually liberal than Faerie gatherings. A rule of no sex is often imposed to free the men from the pressures of cruising and seeking comfort in transient sex.

Both the Radical Faeries and the Wild Man spin-offs are part of the back-to-nature dream of urban hippies. They each share an interest in Native American traditions: Much of the costume and ritual derive from American Indian culture; being ritually cleansed in a sweat lodge and dancing around a blazing fire while beating on drums in magical time and sacred space are common practices.

Another aspect of Men's and Faerie gatherings that is founded in American Indian culture is regard for ancestors and community elders. In indigenous society, elders were bringers of initiation into manhood, holders of wisdom, and mentors who could speak of, with, and for the spiritual realm. By remembering the past, they placed issues of the present in larger context. With Wild Men and Faeries there is a deliberate effort to reverse the ageism and disrespect for old-fangled people in modern society. Elders are ritually honored and accorded reverence and, most importantly, asked for their sage advice.

## Bear Identification

Another movement born out of an acknowledgment of aging and back-to-nature sentiments is the "bear" culture. Bears are burly, hairy, heavy-set gay men. For some, the term is a physical description, like "swimmer's build." For others, it represents a real identity. Because these men often had to overcome childhood and young adult fears of being fat, there is an element of transformation in embracing bear identity. The bear metaphor implies an inner spirit of rustic manliness, strength, complementary gentleness, cuddly lovableness, and sensitivity to nature. Some bears are circle-makers, some are loners. Certainly part of the image of the wild man in the woods suggests magnificent isolation and lusty self-sufficiency.

## *Pilgrimage and Adventure-Seeking*

Also aligned with circle-maker practices are pilgrimage and travel to sacred places. Traveling with a band of gay men provides security, eliminates the stress of worrying what other tourists think, and creates community and camaraderie for an adventure. In an age-old tradition, some gay tour operators focus on the spiritual side of travel.

In all likelihood, some of the original Mattachines of medieval France were "tour operators." The troubadours likely organized fans to travel with the troupe to local festivals and holiday events, and to visit historic and sacred sites. These pilgrimages would have also offered the travelers sexual opportunities not available at home.

## *12-Step Programs*

Gay-specific 12-step programs also fall into the circle-maker classification. The strength of 12-step programs is the rigidity of the 12-steps, the group support, and the quasi-religious faith in the god of higher power. An especially gay-centered aspect of such programs was the application of 12-step ideas to sexual activity and behavior change in the wake of AIDS.

12-step programs excel at changing difficult-to-change behavior through group support and personal conditioning. This model helped profoundly sexually active men adjust to the realities of the health crisis. Unfortunately, the parallel of substance abuse with sex popularized a notion of sexual compulsivity. However true and in need of correction this was in some men's lives, this parallel laid a pall over mystical sexuality.

## *Native American Berdache Tradition*

Native American traditions have contributed one of the basic ideas of gay spirituality, the notion of the *berdache*, or Two-Spirit

Person, believed to be powerful and magical because of his gender variance. *Berdache* was a term used by French trappers and traders in early America for the cross-dressing and sometimes obviously homosexual characters they encountered in indigenous cultures. Not understanding the sacred functions these *berdache* played in the tribal religion and culture, the Frenchmen used a term of derogation to describe them. *Berdache* derives from the same source as "buggery" and implies acceptance of the dishonored role of bottom in anal sex.

Among the Navajo, such characters were called *nadlehee*, "changing ones," because in choosing cross-sexed styles they had undergone a transformation from normalcy to sacredness. The native Two-Spirits were often community builders. They told the stories of the past and organized the rituals and celebrations that united their people. They were good communicators; they had style and tact. They were often the diplomats and peace-makers, the emissaries to other tribes.

Modern gay Native Americans have called for use of the term Two-Spirit, from the Anishinabe/Ojibway term, *nizh manitoag*, which emphasizes that androgyny means to possess both a male and a female spirit.

Though not uniformly honored among all Indian cultures, the Two-Spirits represent an example of sexual variance as a sign of divine election that is close enough to us in time and space to provide a precedent for American culture. The Two-Spirit phenomenon is especially appealing to gay spiritual activists because it is tied into religion, healing, and ecstatic mysticism in a way other historical manifestations of homosexuality are not. That modern gay men can trace spiritual roots to American aboriginal cultures is an example of the arbitrary nature of religion. We select the metaphors and stories that speak to us.

The Two-Spirit tradition does not have an institutional existence in mainstream gay culture, though some independent groups of spiritual gay men have adopted names for themselves like Berdache and Two Spirit, and gay and queer-identified Native Americans have formed groups in the Two-Spirit tradition.

An important aspect of Native American spirituality is reverence for nature and a generalized belief that the world is alive. Gay men drawn to the androgynous shamanic characters can participate in the myth through modern "spiritual disciplines," such as recycling, conserving energy and water, and reducing pollution, as well as by adopting elements of Indian art and clothing. To be *berdache* or Two-Spirited is to seek harmony with nature, to live aware of the life cycles of Gaia.

# Chapter 18

## THEMES IN GAY SPIRITUALITY: ECSTATIC REVELERS

Intense emotional and physical exercises can bring ecstatic experience. The quest for ecstasy represents another theme in gay spirituality. Ecstatic reveler themes are: 1) Tantric sex, 2) enlightened masturbation, and 3) leather spirituality.

### Tantric Sex

Tantric sex, as discussed above, is a technique developed out of the basically matriarchal, tribal traditions of India using yogic exercises to include and sublimate sexual arousal. It became popularized in the days of the sexual revolution with the idea a man and woman could remain in coitus without reaching orgasm for extended periods of time.

The practice of genital massage without orgasm was promoted by sex therapists to alleviate performance anxiety, erectile difficulties, and premature ejaculation.

In the gay world, Tantric tradition has been revived to use intentional breathing and genital massage to expand sexual experience and generate mystical states. The most notable example is The Body Electric School of Massage, created by former Jesuit Joseph Kramer. In workshops called Celebrating the Body Erotic, Body Electric teachers show men a different way to experience sexual arousal.

Appealing to gay men's fantasies of group masturbation, the weekend trainings show the participants how to experience nudity, touching, and arousal without anxiety or compulsion for intercourse and orgasm. Many men attend thinking they're going to a circle jerk and discover instead that through disciplined breathing and bodily stimulation they can "see God."

The breathing exercises, leading to mild hyperventilation, alter the chemistry of the body enough to prevent ejaculation so that sexual energy builds in the body. Instead of experiencing sex as squeezing this energy tighter and tighter, like blowing up a balloon, until it "pops" in orgasm, participants are taught to relax and allow the energy to suffuse through their body. The penis is likened to a "magic wand" which can generate and store a sexual charge, like a glass rod stroked with fur. Instead of reaching orgasm and ejaculating, the men complete the exercise by clenching the whole body and then abruptly releasing. This "big draw" throws consciousness into a transcendent experience—an orgasm in the etheric body, a climax in the soul and psyche instead of the seminal vesicles and urethra. The training gives a vivid demonstration of sexual arousal as an induction of mystical consciousness.

As the amalgam of Tantra and modern sexology appeared in gay culture, it shifted to structured groups. It is quite remarkable that gay men have evolved this kind of sexual/spiritual blend. Though there are now versions of the trainings aimed at women and heterosexual men, most straight people couldn't imagine what goes on in a Body Electric workshop. They'd be confused by the merging of sex and spirit and repelled by the group setting, thinking sexual arousal is only supposed to happen between two people, paired and alone. That is the model offered by dualistic patriarchal religion.

Patriarchal traditions teach that the desire for sex and sensation is a hindrance to spirituality and mystical awareness. They urge rejection of desire and shame at the body. They are probably right that some people's lives have been ruined by their pursuit of sex, but their reactionary anti-sex attitudes only instill negativity and resistance, and further the problem.

On the other hand, matriarchal religions, as imagined by feminist anthropologists, delighted in the physical, sensual world. No escape into disembodied spirit or mysticism was called for. The evidence of the Great Mother's fertility and generosity was visible everywhere.

The Body Electric and similar Tantra-based workshops offer a real alternative to the usual sex-negative tendency of religion. They can alter the experience of embodiment, demonstrating the potential for ecstatic transcendence in the flesh.

## Enlightened Masturbation

A practical reality of men's lives is that most of our sexual experience is solitary masturbation, sexual induction without attachment to interpersonal feelings and dependencies—sexual pleasure for its own sake.

One of the strengths of gay men's relationships is that couples can masturbate together—a different pattern from making love—sharing this personal experience and acknowledging sexual arousal as a joy to be sought in itself. Heterosexuals have a harder time with mutual masturbation because men and women have different attitudes toward sex and different patterns of arousal. Furthermore, their conventions about sex denigrate, and even condemn, sexual arousal separate from coitus.

But usually masturbation is neither a failure to find a partner nor a sign of psychological weakness. It is making love with yourself. Joseph Kramer coined the term "soloing" to convey this meaning: solo loving. With such a positive attitude, masturbation can be a rich, meditative experience.

To love yourself is to love your experience, to say yes to the intersection of the world's phenomena—cultural, genetic, karmic—that result in you. Making love to yourself, soloing, enables you to make love to life.

## Leather Spirituality

Leather spirituality has a mystical and transcendent layer underlying the athletic and fetishistic style of sexplay associated with S/M.

Leather spirituality is less orchestrated than the Body Electric training, but uses some of the same power of prolonged sexual arousal to
generate mystical consciousness.

Leathersex, so-called because of the association of extreme forms
of sex with black leather, interweaves desire and fear to generate
intensity. In general, leathersex is highly ritualized. Indeed, for some
men it is primarily ritual: a set of protocols about how prospective
partners are attracted, how they approach one another, how sex is
negotiated (usually playing off familiar male stereotypes and subcul-
tural jargon), and how it is finally played out—with each partner following strict rules of role-playing throughout the process.

Among the activities that may be negotiated are dominance and
submission, bondage, feigned violence, and prodigious anal penetration with toys or fists. For men with a spiritual bent and an interest
in such styles, these activities can be profoundly evocative. While different activities produce different experiences, at the heart of all of
them are two factors: intensity and trust.

Because S/M activities involve at least the threat and possibility of bodily injury, even death, they stir deep emotions. Masculine
stereotypes trigger associations of violence and psychological
abuse. Bondage creates dependence. Spanking, light whipping, or
anal penetration further energizes the body, stimulating endor-
phins, creating anxiety and arousal. All of this must then be contained in a space of trust.

There is an element of infantile regression, a recapitulating of primal fears about bodily survival and of feelings of trust and dependence on parental love. The fetishes and styles of sexual arousal act as
stepping stones to deep, preconscious states, taking one beyond ego-
personality.

A theme in leather sexuality is dominance and submission, acting
out the roles of master and slave. In part, this is just playing with
(and for some people succumbing to) patriarchal hierarchy. But it is
also participating in a long tradition of ascetical training. For some,
the master/slave relationship reverberates with the spiritual relationship of teacher/disciple, guru/student.

Being a master is taking responsibility for another person's training. Being a slave is seeking guidance and practicing patience and equanimity. The various rituals of dominance and humiliation are, on one level, concerned with teaching the slave/disciple self-control and detachment from ego. Commands to keep one's eyes downcast, for instance, or to avoid eye contact in a sign of subordination, trains the will to calm and manage the emotions.

Humiliation and nonsense commands were common stock in monastic formation and military boot camp, designed to teach obedience and to calm resistance and ego. Custody of the eyes (keeping the gaze downcast and avoiding meeting others' glances) was an important practice in ascetical training. While presented in a sex-negative way and focused on preventing "particular friendships" (the monastic euphemism for sexual infatuation), custody of the eyes is an exercise in brainwave control, just like the meditative practice of sitting unmoving and mindful in a relaxed but rigid posture. Biofeedback research shows that keeping the eyes down-turned, or up-turned, and slightly unfocused causes the brain to shift into the relaxed, ego-detached alpha rhythm.

Extreme physical states can produce extreme mental states. Threat, feigned or real, can push a person against his limits, forcing him to relax his fears and to let go the need to be in control. Pain and pleasure have a way of looking indistinguishable, an explanation of how the association of sex and torture got started in the first place. A person, humiliated, stripped of clothing and writhing in pain, looks very much like a naked body delighting in the throes of orgasm.

Nonetheless, it is surprising to the uninitiated that black leather or an executioner's mask would seem sexy; that the appearance of pain would stir a sexual urge; that the elements of torture, which should horrify and repel us, could inspire reverence and ecstasy.

The most immediate explanation, based in armchair psychoanalysis, is that the leather experience acts out internalized homophobia, self-hate, and a compulsion to punish oneself. Another explanation, from evolutionary biology, is that throughout the animal world, and in the human world until recently, males contended with one another for the right to have sex with the females. Such competition has bred anger, hostility, rivalry, and high emotion into the sexual urge, thus explaining the sexual link to hostility, aggressiveness, jealousy, and envy.

But why the torture? Using the popular mythology of reincarnation, we can speculate that for people who were martyrs for the faith in previous incarnations or victims of religious and ecclesiastical persecution, their most exalted and spiritual moment came as they died under torture. Perhaps the *autos-da-fe* of religious history have created karmic resonances so that those very intense emotions reverberate down through time and alter present perceptions. Perhaps leathersex—and the mime of torture—is spiritual because it is evocative of exalted, holy death.

Certainly there is an element of purgation in S/M styles. The notion of purgation is that ecstasy follows the overcoming of ego. An aspect of overcoming ego is facing and accepting our own shadow, recognizing things about ourselves that society has taught us to disapprove of and be embarrassed by, like our homosexuality. S/M can be a practice of confronting the shadow.

Some gay men embrace the underworld style of homosexuality—the black leather, the sexual athleticism and yogic-like discipline of pain—and experience it as spiritual. They may choose suffering as a sacrifice in expiation of guilt. Others view S/M sex as a challenge to their endurance and force of will. Whether for sexual turn-on, religious practice, or a combination of both, the embrace of pain is a test of self-control and a practice in the experience of letting go.

There is an important lesson here for all of us. By relaxing into pain—and the general suffering of life—we can learn to transcend pain and suffering.

According to Gnostic tradition, after the Last Supper Jesus led the Apostles in a circle dance and sang a song that told his disciples to "learn to suffer so you will not have to suffer." When you can experience pain without resistance, it is not suffering.

## *The Disco Ball*

Aligned with this theme of ecstatic revelry through excess and intensity are intentional or accidental achievement of altered, mystical states through drugs, dancing, and physical exhaustion. You would probably be surprised (or not!) to know how many gay men have raised their eyes to a disco ball twirling overhead and seen God.

# Chapter 19

## THEMES IN GAY SPIRITUALITY: SUPERNATURAL SEEKERS

Mainstream religion is the most common outlet for the spiritual impulses of gay people. American Christianity and popular religion in general have an underlying mystical layer. Indeed, mysticism is at the core of the religious urge. Because of AIDS, gay people have discovered another access to the mystical and supernatural in familiarity with death and the experience of grieving.

The supernatural seeker themes are: 1) gay church membership and religious practice, and 2) AIDS-based spiritualities and interest in healing and miracles.

### Gay Church Membership

The churches are full of homosexuals with deep religious feelings: bishops, priests, ministers, rabbis, organists, deacons, parishioners. Especially since the rise of gay liberation, these people, however closeted they be, have necessarily found ways of making accommodation for their homosexuality in their doctrine. Even devout believers have learned to take doctrine with the proverbial grain of salt.

Gay Christians can understand that the anti-gay bias in their religion is a man-made thing, not contained in the revelations that form their faith. Gay-oriented Biblical studies, for example, offer alternative interpretations to the supposedly anti-gay passages in the

Scriptures. Gay-sensitive research, like that of classics scholar John Boswell, suggests the anti-homosexual bias in Christianity developed late in the history of the faith and has nothing to do with the message of Jesus.

The Metropolitan Community Church—and affinity groups within the mainstream churches, like the gay Catholic Dignity, the Episcopalian Integrity, Methodist Affirmation, Presbyterian More Light, Mormon Affirmation, Unitarian Universalist Interweave, and openly gay synagogues—are gay incarnations of the religious impulse. Members of these groups probably sense they are more accurately living up to the teachings of their religion than mainstream believers who act with hostility to gay issues.

Founded in Los Angeles in 1968 by Reverend Troy Perry, the Universal Fellowship of Metropolitan Community Churches, referred to as MCC, has become a worldwide gay community institution. In the U.S., it is one of the few—if not the only—national gay institutions that owns property. MCCs provide meeting rooms and sometimes office space for a variety of grassroots groups. Called non-denominational, MCC is, in fact, a full-fledged Protestant denomination with seminaries, Boards of Elders, annual conventions, and big budgets. Yet the Church has a very open theology. There is hardly anything one has to believe in to be a member of the MCC, though all individual churches offer training to become a member. Most ministers maintain a biblical, almost evangelical, stance, though they are quick to argue, in the orthodox Protestant tradition of private interpretation, that what the Bible means is what it means to you.

MCC services are relatively high-church, with vestments and candles, sometimes even incense. The services consist of the basic Catholic Mass, with consecration and communion as regular sacraments, along with a Protestant-style sermon and a mix of traditional American hymns from a variety of Christian sects. The idea is to appeal to as many gay people as possible, offering them an opportunity to worship in Christian style in ways that feel familiar and comfortable.

For many gay men and lesbians, MCC offers traditional religion blended with positive spiritual attitudes, free of the anti-gay bias of most mainstream churches. The fact that MCC, while orthodox Christian, can be laissez-faire with doctrine and eclectic with liturgy and sacrament is evidence of a modern, enlightened understanding of religion.

There is a possibly apocryphal, but certainly perspicacious, story told in the Metropolitan Community Church: Even while the National Council of Churches was denying membership to MCC, its theologians were encouraging MCC's ministers to develop theologies of sex, saying, in effect, "If you don't do it, who will?"

Specifically because it is a gay religion—and therefore an outsider—MCC is in a position to address, and demonstrate, the transformation of all Christian religions.

## Inverse Religiousness

There are gay men and lesbians who reject MCC along with all the Christian churches, dismissing religion as oppressive and antiquated. Often there is an inverse religiousness in their intense anticlericalism. Many homosexuals are outraged at the Church's history of persecution of women and homosexuals. For many, it is because they are committed to the message of love and compassion that they shun institutionalized religion.

## Variety of Religious Practice

Also in the tradition of gay participation in mainstream religion are gay Buddhists, gay yogis, gay Sufis, and various other utopian and self-help movements. There are gay monasteries and ashrams and utopian colonies around the country. All of these call for certain kinds of discipline and commitment to a transcendent purpose.

Remarkable states can be achieved through discipline and practice. Meditation is a powerful tool for altering consciousness. The practice of voluntary simplicity and/or the choice of austerity—fasting, denying comforts, pleasures, and even sex—can dramatically change our perceptions. Such practices concentrate the mind and focus attention on things beyond the surface. Dietary restrictions, avoidance of intoxicants, fasting, etc., are spiritual less because God likes human suffering and self-sacrifice than because they alter brain chemistry and produce states of exaltation.

Some people enter Zen monasteries and practice rigid disciplines. Following your bliss this way and responding to karmic patterns that point in such directions can be a wonderful training in enlightenment. For many people, such practices are the meat of spirituality.

Such a choice may be admirable, but it is not necessarily the point of spirituality. Indeed, the rejection of the world that often goes with monastic and meditative disciplines of the past is inconsistent with the love of life and incarnation of the modern paradigm.

But the world is a vast place. There is room for everybody and for many styles of enlightenment. The trick for those who follow their bliss into austerity is to do so, not in rejection of the world, but in embrace of it. Then such a choice adds to the fullness of consciousness.

Buddhist and modern-day monasticism differs from the conventional style of Roman Catholic monasticism in which lifelong commitment was demanded. Buddhist monasteries and meditation centers accept practitioners for however long or short a time they want to stay.

## *AIDS-Based Spiritualities*

The second category of supernatural seekers arose with the health crisis. Because of AIDS, a whole strain of beliefs developed in gay culture about healing and dying. Gay men have become precociously aware of death and the transitory nature of life. Exposure to death and dying have a way of changing priorities, turning attention to things beyond.

Being with a person who is dying can have a profound effect on consciousness. When the tunnel of light opens for the dying person, a certain amount of what Tibetan Buddhism calls the "Clear Light" sometimes radiates into the souls of everybody around, allowing them to glimpse through the doorway into God.

The health crisis brought out a new kind of gay activist, the volunteer who helps others endure disease. Part of enduring disease is finding ways of healing or at least ameliorating the symptoms and discomfort. Spiritual healing—which includes acknowledgment, acceptance, and a sense of meaning for the suffering—can relieve discomfort.

## *Spiritual Healing*

Spiritual healing is a mystery to science. There is evidence that prayer works. Miracles do happen. Although these events cannot be predicted or controlled, they hint at powers in consciousness that we have not evolved far enough to use with certainty.

Healing is most easily explained as the result of self-fulfilling prophecy, though some experiments with prayer specifically rule out this possibility by not telling patients they are being focused on for healing or by experimenting with animals or plants that would not be affected by such a self-reflexive mechanism. Self-fulfilling prophecy and human intention may be more powerful forces than we know.

It is telling, for instance, that the so-called placebo effect actually demonstrates that some people can get all the benefits of a drug without any of the chemicals. In fact, it appears that one of the unexpected by-products of drug experimentation in double-blind studies is cures by placebo. The luckiest people in a double-blind experiment are the ones who get the sugar pills and also get healed.

Self-fulfilling prophecy certainly explains healing of disorders brought on by imbalances and dysfunctions in the body. Positive expectation, especially when magnified by faith and spiritual belief, can help people change their bodily processes. Healing of the damage caused by outside invaders, on the other hand, seems much less susceptible to such explanations.

No one has ever come up with the magic incantation that can be uttered over people to cure them of HIV infection. But participation in healing rituals and exercises in realizing one is loved and lovable and healed of homophobia have helped delay onset of symptoms and alleviated discomfort. And sometimes it has brought about real miracles.

## *Forgiveness*

Central to the notion of spiritual healing is the practice of forgiveness. Illness, misfortune, and unhappiness, healers say, come from unresolved guilt and grudges. Healing comes from forgiving ourselves and forgiving others, holding nothing against other people, feeling no guilt or resentment about our own life. Forgiveness is letting go, forgetting the past, letting the past be over and done with. Forgiveness is accepting things the way they are. Right now, when it matters.

An often neglected aspect of forgiveness is forgiving God. If we believe God can answer prayers, then we also have to believe God can decide to not answer them. The failure of prayers to be answered brings some people to resent God. Many gay people have prayed for their homosexuality to disappear; this prayer is seldom answered.

Forgiveness of God includes a loving embrace of life as expression of "Divine Will," of God's greater plan, even if that plan includes misfortune. Even God, after all, cannot change the realities of life. We must not take it personally.

The biggest step in forgiveness—especially for gay people who have been raised to feel guilty about their sexual orientation—is to forgive yourself, to let go of your feelings of unworthiness. The most important forgiveness of all is of life itself. We must not hold a grudge against life lest, in turn, we find that life holds a grudge against us.

## *Looking in the Rearview Mirror*

*A Course in Miracles*, the spiritually dictated text that has become so influential in the New Age Movement, says that sickness and misfortune happen when the natural and miraculous processes of life are suppressed. What causes this suppression is anger and resentment. And what causes anger and resentment is the unconscious association of events in the present with unresolved events in the past. This is also a basic notion of psychotherapy.

People automatically, if inadvertently and erroneously, judge everything based on past experience. We are always looking in the rearview mirror, as it were, as we try to direct our path in the present. The chain of associations works itself back to infancy when every concern seemed like a threat to survival and we felt powerless to protect ourselves. Hence, every threat in the present gets overblown and taken as an actual threat to survival. We project our desperation onto other people. The solution *A Course in Miracles* suggests is to recognize that all the meaning of all the things in our lives comes from us—it is not "out there," it is "in here," in the mind. The corollary to this is that the sins we think other people commit against us never really happen. They, too, are all in our minds. The conscious practice of that insight is forgiveness and acceptance.

When AIDS first appeared and there were virtually no medical treatments, notions like those in *A Course in Miracles* caught on big among gay men. They were not particularly helpful in eliminating viral infections, but they were emotionally and spiritually comforting.

## The Problem With Spiritual Healing

The problem with spiritual healing is that it is usually sought after the fact, when it is too late. The ideas are good. People should not feel guilty about being who they are. People should not project their bad feelings onto other people. People ought to understand the dynamics of unconscious association. But these understandings do not help after the damage is done.

Suppose a fellow feels guilty and worthless after being fired from a job. He goes out to the bars one night hoping to get laid in order to change his unhappy state. Instead, he gets drunk, runs off the road driving home, and breaks his neck. It is certainly true that the bad feelings about losing the job (which create legitimate, if exaggerated, concerns about ending up homeless) were a direct cause of the broken neck. But coming to grips with his feelings about the job while he is recovering in the hospital will not affect his neck much. This fellow needed to heal spiritually before the disability.

On the other hand, if the symptom of this fellow's distress is asthma attacks, shingles, or heart palpitations and panic—all understood to be stress-related, although perhaps also associated with microorganisms like herpes zoster—then practicing forgiveness and seeing through infantile anxieties will very likely bring relief. And if, as was the case with many of Sigmund Freud's female patients, the symptoms are hysterically induced, like neurotic malingering or odd forms of paralysis, then a psychological transformation will bring a complete cure.

## The Case of AIDS

AIDS presented an interesting case for the gay community. If the currently accepted model of causation by a virus that attacks one important mechanism in immune function is correct, then the disease is infection by that virus. But the problems and symptoms that follow come from the damage done to the immune system, not from the disease. Because the AIDS diagnosis is so understandably anxiety-producing, stress-related symptoms are bound to follow, even if they have nothing to do with the immune system damage.

As with the broken neck example above, psychologically based healing probably does not have much effect on the original viral infection. It may, however, have a tremendous effect on the progress of the infection and on secondary symptoms, especially the emotionally induced ones.

The popularity of healing modalities among gay men faded as the disease was better understood. The expectations of miracles faded as scores of men died despite their spiritual transformation. Nonetheless important lessons were learned about psychological dynamics and disease processes, and many lives were changed. Healing is not the same thing as cure. Talking about a cure is talking about a disease; talking about healing is talking about a life.

## True Miracle-Working

There is yet another kind of spiritual healing that has little to do with a patient's psychological state or mental dynamics. This is what is considered true miracle-working. Prayer is the common experience of this process.

Evidence, anecdotal and scientifically controlled double-blind studies, show that sometimes prayer and miracle-working bring about change. Healers, using the power of their intention, can influence how seeds grow. The Catholic Church has for years rigorously investigated cures as part of its process of canonizing saints. The church does not accept most miracle claims, but it has found some that defy any other explanation.

Some healers seem able to diagnose physical problems by intuition, sometimes at a distance. They can be given the name and location of a person unknown to them and, after a moment of meditation, describe what the person's symptoms are, what the underlying cause is, and what remedies will work for him or her. Other healers, especially working in groups, send forth "healing energies" to people, either in their presence or far away, intending their health to improve. Sometimes it works. A major problem, of course, is that these modalities are not predictable: You cannot tell when it's going to work and when it's not.

That it works at all is mind-boggling. It certainly supports the argument that our conventional model of reality is inadequate. Healing power and efficacy of prayer demonstrate the "creative" abilities of the human spirit which are conceived as the power of God. Intentions do radiate from us. Our thoughts and actions and mental states do create ripples in the spirit field and alter the course of events.

Spiritual healers and miracle workers have not proven to be the answer to AIDS. Even if such modalities can work to activate a patient's immune system to fight off a disease, an infection like AIDS that is resistant to immune response will evade cure. But spiritual healing does raise people's minds beyond the surface of life, pointing to a mystical reality.

As tragic as AIDS has been, it has resulted in spiritual salvation for many individuals. It has helped some people regain control of their lives, reminded them not to get caught in the traps of compulsive sex, excessive drinking and drugging, and living without regard for consequences. Some people have said it was the best thing that ever happened to them because it reminded them to live in the present and smell the roses.

## Spiritual Lessons

AIDS has caused major psychological trauma and value reassessment in the gay community. The self-observation and self-critique that has resulted can be thought of as spiritual. Moving our perspective beyond day-to-day concerns makes us question the assumptions of conventional society: Is it bad to die childless? Is it bad to die young?

In some ways, AIDS is a fulfillment of the youth-culture dictum: Live fast, die young. While this heedless sentiment is usually ridiculed, at times it has been taken as a demonstration of religious piety. The teenage saints so many Catholic youth were taught to emulate—Therese of Lisieux, Gabriel of Our Lady of Sorrows, Aloysius Gonzaga—lived intensely and died young (usually of tuberculosis) as a demonstration of their zeal.

There is a lesson here. Who is to say a long life is desirable? Especially if punctuated at the end by Alzheimer's disease or debility. Especially in a world whose resources are already overtaxed. Who is to say a short life is wasted?

We do not want our opportunities for experience and joy snuffed out prematurely—especially before we have made our contribution to the life of the planet. We have built into us a will to live, and we do not want to die. But perhaps our emphasis on the preservation of our egos blinds us to what we really are and to what time and existence really are.

Theoretical physics tells us time is just another dimension like height or depth. The passage of time, though absolute and inescapable, is more a function of psychology and perspective than a physical reality. Things seem to occur in sequence and to only move in one direction because we cannot see from a perspective beyond the physical dimensions.

What if, in fact, from a higher point of view, we could see that all time exists simultaneously? That every one of us lives through all the time there is? From our limited perspective, the entire history of the universe is squeezed into the years of our lives and projected onto the screen of our experience. If we really are just a manifestation of consciousness experiencing itself as the universe, then perhaps we experience the entire universe in our span of years, however many or few, as it appears from our perspective.

The notion of afterlife is the most widespread mythological teaching to ease our fear of death. Whether it makes sense to the rational mind or not, it is a comforting and even thrilling thought that human consciousness transcends death. All the metaphors of religion offer reassurance in facing mortality. It is okay, the myths tell us, to die. It is an awakening to another consciousness. Whatever death is, for our own good, we should not fear it. The fear sours life.

AIDS can teach us how to not resist mortality. As our notions of spiritual meaning shift away from the stories of pie-in-the-sky, the message behind the metaphors must not be lost.

The arguments about avoiding disease and practicing safe sex are common sense. The fact that some people scorn such common sense may be a manifestation of the intuition that it is okay to die. Ego is an illusion that can be dropped and transcended by letting go of who you are. We can accept death as a natural phase of life and our self as a momentary intersection of events in the greater consciousness of planet Earth.

These are mystical notions that do not address the heartbreak of losing a loved one or the feelings of being cheated by the prognosis of a premature death. But they help us raise our vision. Accepting death as a necessary part of life eases our clinging to the illusion of ego—which is the source of most of our suffering and frustration.

This is not to diminish death. Death is a serious subject. But the mystical notions help us to find the Clear Light in our present experience. The reality of death is a reminder to find your bliss now.

## Voluntary Redemptive Suffering

The horror of AIDS is that it kills so slowly and uncertainly; the course of the disease is unpredictable. Most of us would probably opt—at least in theory—for a death that has no symptoms until 30 minutes before death. Indeed, many of us would probably agree to a shortened life span in exchange for a guarantee of that kind of passing.

But that is not how it works in reality. None of us is a Bette Davis character. We often die painfully and slowly. A theoretical embrace of an early death in exchange for a brilliant, if short, life free of disfigurement and physical pain and discomfort is easily lost when we actually face death. None of us wants to die. Life itself urges us to go on.

An irony of modern medicine is that technology allows us to delay death, but often with a reduced quality of life. As technology continues to accelerate social change, the long, long lives that futurists predict seem potentially unbearable. Age saps the life out of a person. People tire of always keeping up with change. Death can cease to be an enemy.

For some, the notion of voluntary redemptive suffering justifies their continuing to live with reduced quality. They shift the purpose of life from enjoyment of health and freedom to acceptance of pain and suffering for a higher purpose. For instance, they might participate in drug trials, serving as a guinea pig for the sake of others. Or they might trust that their voluntary suffering puts out good vibes for the benefit of humankind.

## Benefits of AIDS

There have been dramatic social benefits that have resulted from AIDS. The most practical is that medical science began investigating the immune system. This is likely to result in cures for all sorts of disorders and new drugs to combat the potential plagues of antibiotic-resistant organisms. The cure for cancer is likely to come out of AIDS-related research; there is even evidence that one piece of the HIV genome itself kills cancer cells. Gay responses to AIDS have strengthened the hospice movement and emboldened health activists of all stripes. FDA procedures have been simplified. There are new attitudes toward death in gay society and in mainstream society. Death and dying—and certainly condoms—are not the taboo subjects they were 30 years ago.

Maybe more than anything else there has been a transformation in how gay people are perceived. At first the epidemic resulted in shock and dismay at the prodigious numbers of partners some gay men had. But now much of the public views gay men as selfless care-givers and noble victims.

Efforts to find spiritual meaning in AIDS are not intended to diminish the horror and tragedy of the epidemic. But it is not enough to mourn. We must create positive attitudes—karmic reso-nances—in order to demonstrate that we are in the business of evolv-ing a better world by transforming horror into bliss through our enlightened vision.

## Transcending All the Themes of Gay Spirituality

Beyond all the specific practices that can be identified with trends in modern gay culture as a manifestation of spirituality, there is the gay personality itself. Gay men glow. There is a sweetness and light that surrounds us—not all, not always, and it is perhaps visible more in youth than in age. But there is something in the aura of gay men that identifies us to one another and that makes straight people like us as individuals, even when, paradoxically, they do not like homo-sexuals in general. There is a cultural stereotype of the gay man as a loving and unexpected saint.

An ongoing practical problem, however, in the gay men's spir-itual movement is that there are too many chiefs and not enough Indians. Many gay people have their own notions of what is true and how things ought to be, and they are unwilling to give up these notions. The history of gay liberation is cluttered with dead organizations and failed initiatives because one faction did not like what another was doing. It is often not so much that one person or group thought the others were wrong, as much as that they thought they had a better idea. And so off they went with their followers—until one of them had yet a better idea. Most of us who have been involved with gay community organizing have experi-enced the irony that there is enormous strife in a movement that is founded around ending strife and accepting differences.

While this multiplicity of ideas and goals creates organizing nightmares, it is consistent with the basic tenets of the gay movement. According to the new religious paradigm, everybody has to create his or her own mythology. Thus, nobody is supposed to be a follower. Religious organizations have always encouraged the concept of leaders and followers. In a spirituality without specific content, while there can be teachers and helpers, nobody is a leader.

# PART III

## Walking the World's Weird Wall

For some people, homosexuality is a genuine spiritual vocation, a religion in itself. But it has no set doctrine, no explanation of God or the Divine Plan.

The author of this book believes the insights and observations he's gleaned about God and the nature of religion flow from his homosexual orientation. This is so if only because by being a gay man and therefore a religious renegade, he's been able to think outside the box of traditional doctrine.

The ideas and interpretations of the meaning of religion that follow offer an example of how each of us creates our own mystical vision in order to evoke vitality and beauty in our lives. But these are just the author's ideas. They are true only insofar as they inspire readers to find similar ideas for themselves. These are meditations, not statements of fact. What matters is not having the right ideas, but being a loving person. How we behave, and not what we believe, is what counts. (In this, the orthodox Protestants with their notion of salvation by faith alone have it exactly backwards.)

So let's look together to see what we can discover about the meaning of religion.

# Chapter 20

## WISDOM: HEROES AND SHADOWS

Our perspective from over and above religion allows us to investigate and reinterpret traditional myths with a certain freedom, levity, and poetic license. Understanding the nature of mythology helps us see the messages in the lives of the world saviors. In these messages are clues to understanding our lives and to helping human consciousness evolve.

### The Hero Cycle

The basic pattern of all myths is the "hero cycle." The main character of the story encounters some sort of problem. In the effort to solve it, he or she becomes increasingly involved and, perhaps, personally threatened. Leaving the familiar world, the hero encounters obstacles to accomplishing the task. When everything seems at its most threatening, the hero, through his or her skill and mastery, resolves the problem, accomplishing the task and saving the day. He or she then returns to the familiar world bringing benefits for other people—good news, treasure, a change in the social order—which the hero gained through solving the problem.

This is also the basic plot of every TV drama. In fact, one of the curious things about our modern culture is that we are overexposed to meaningful myths and accounts of heroic adventures. We get a new hero every 60 minutes, every night on TV. One moving and inspiring story is replaced by another every time we push the remote's channel button. A myth about the cosmic battle between good and evil, like *Star Wars*, appears, becomes popular, attracts fans, sweeps the public imagination, and then becomes trite and stale or simply out of fashion. Until recently, most people were exposed to only a few such heroic stories in their lives. They could base their entire existence on a particular inspiration.

Saviors, heroes, and heroines—Jesus, Buddha, Mohammed, Krishna, King Arthur, Hercules, Mithras, Osiris, Begochidi, Coyote, Astarte, Diana, etc.—are symbolic of our deepest selves. People project their experience of self onto the heroes. We learn about human nature from their stories. And we project our present experience of what it is to be human onto them. Some of these figures are historical in the sense they are based on actual living people; others are imaginary. All have been so completely absorbed into the myth-making mind that they are more figures of metaphor than of history.

## *Historical Authenticity*

The claim of historical authenticity is itself a myth, a metaphorical way of giving authority to a particular story. More importantly, it is an expression of the particular tradition's notion of metaphysics. Hinduism and Buddhism, its major spin-off, both imagine the world as thought. Matter is a thought-form for experiencing higher level thoughts. Judaism, Christianity, and Islam understand the world as matter. Thought is a phenomenon that influences matter. Eastern religions have little concern with historical authenticity; Western religions seem burdened by it.

The Christian claim of historical authenticity is an affirmation of incarnation. If God became flesh, then the flesh and the activities of the flesh must interest him. For all that Christianity makes claims to historical validity, this was not a concern of the evangelists. The authors of the New Testament did not seem concerned about agreement of witnesses, which is the evidence required for historical truth: Observers must all agree that the same thing happened.

Even with something as central to the mythology as the events surrounding Jesus's resurrection, the gospel accounts agree on practically none of the details of what the witnesses saw. The one common report is that the tomb was empty on Easter morning when the disciples returned to finish embalming Jesus's body, and that afterward the disciples had various—but sometimes conflicting or inconsistent—experiences of the presence of a mystical Jesus.

The evangelists were concerned with presenting, symbolically and mythically, the intense experience they'd had of Jesus. The historical claim is the metaphor for the importance of Jesus's life and teaching—and for the proclamation of the glory of fleshly incarnation.

That is the meaning of the metaphor: God is in the flesh. The events of the supernatural order are manifest in the lives of people and are understood by the stories the people tell each other in their culture.

The major stories and legends of the religions, then, were about heroes, people who broke with the status quo, left the village compound, and did marvelous deeds for the benefit of everybody. This basic pattern applies to backwoods strongmen and world saviors alike. When most of us grew up, we were not taught that our religion was a manifestation of universal themes. This is a new paradigm. We did not hear Jesus spoken of as a hero. The mythological heroes we heard about were characters such as Hercules, King Arthur, and Beowulf.

## Beowulf and Grendel

*Beowulf*, for example, is the story of a brave, strong man who battles a monster called Grendel, a great man-beast like a Himalayan *yeti*, that is terrorizing the tribe. Beowulf saves the clan when he pursues Grendel into his underworld lair and slays both Grendel and its mother. And so saves his clan. Though later Beowulf is killed while slaying a dragon, his legacy is the memory of his heroic deeds celebrated in legend.

A function of the hero legend was to provide a model for warriors. Men, alone in the woods hunting or exploring, could remember the story. Perhaps they memorized the epic and sang or chanted it to themselves. The story would bolster their courage and challenge them to excellence in the manly art of surviving in the wilderness. And it would also give meaning to their exploits when they risked their lives. Perhaps one of them would come upon a monster and slay it like Beowulf slew Grendel, and so bring good fortune to his people and create for himself a place in the memory of the tribe.

In some ways, Beowulf is just a big, strong brute obsessed with his accomplishments. Grendel is the more interesting character in the story. He reveals something about the nature of evil and the phenomenon of the shadow. He has an important role in human society.

Grendel is the character lesbians and gay men can find meaning in. In the modern novel *Grendel* by John Gardner, which retells the Beowulf legend from the opponent's point of view, Grendel calls himself a "shadow-shooter, earth-rim-roamer, walker of the world's weird wall."

Grendel sees what the townsfolk cannot see. He sees that he is an imaginary projection of their fears. Because he walks the wall around the world he can see what is on both sides. Grendel shows people what to be afraid of so they know what not to be afraid of. As a "shadow-shooter," he understands that people need to believe there are monsters in the forest that leap from shadow to shadow. The knowledge of the presence of monsters makes the townsfolk feel safe inside the city walls.

Walls and stockades and fences separate and protect. The wall around the city tells everyone where civilization and safety ends and the forest begins. Monsters lurk beyond the wall: lions and tigers and bears.

In the modern world, gay men and lesbians are earth-rim-roamers, walkers of the world's weird wall. We live at the margins of society. Our culture's fears about sexuality are projected onto us. We live in the shadow of normal society. We inhabit a world invisible to most people. They cannot see our world because it is obscured by their shadows. They cannot understand who we are because they are blinded by their need for the security of the wall.

## *Wall Walkers and Gatekeepers*

From our perspective on top of the wall we can see things others do not. We can see both sides of the wall. We can pass from one side to the other.

African Dagara religion considers sexually variant men and women "gatekeepers," mediators between the genders, because they have a "higher vibrational level." Gatekeepers can move between sides of the wall. Modern gay spiritual writers use expressions like "openers of old gates," "in-between people," and "walkers between worlds" to describe our spiritual identity.

There is a certain jeopardy that goes with wall walking. You can suffer vertigo. You can lose your balance and fall off. You can see too much.

Most people want to be left alone to live happily inside their walls, unbothered by the monsters that lurk at the margins of the world and in their unconscious minds. Yet most people also want to believe the monsters are out there—somewhere far away, beyond the walls.

Grendel calls the wall around the world "weird" in the original meaning of this word. In Old English *wyrd* meant fateful, something pertaining to supernatural destiny. Wyrds were oracles or soothsayers who lived outside the normal world, beyond the wall, and were able to see what regular people could not. Oracles and soothsayers and seers, we now understand, were often sexually variant individuals: homosexuals, cross-dressers, transsexuals, bisexuals, pansexuals.

Many gay men grew up being weird, as well as queer, wanting to be different for the sake of being different, not wanting to be like the other boys on the playground. ("Please, God, please, don't let me be normal!") We have scaled the wall.

Some people occasionally hear the siren songs from beyond the wall. They see signs in the sky or hear the whispers of the gods or listen to the call of duty. They feel compelled to leave the village compound, to go into the forest to prove their mettle and save the people. They respond to the call to adventure. They try to be heroes. Many gay men are among them.

## *Heroes Are Called*

As we said, the hero cycle in myth, as in life, is predictable. A knight, for instance, leaves his castle in search of the Holy Grail. He has adventures. He fights an ogre, avoids a whirlpool, or runs into a wise old man who tells him what direction he should go. Soon he hears of a damsel in distress about to be eaten by a dragon. By going to save her and risking his life, he becomes a hero. He must go into the "underworld" of the dragon's lair, where in the very deepest chamber he meets and vanquishes his foe in pitched battle. He is then rewarded by being given the vision of the Grail he had been seeking, perhaps while he is in a delirium recovering from his wounds. When the knight returns the damsel to her father's castle, the people rejoice. The knight marries the girl, and everybody lives happily ever after.

Heroes frequently have sidekicks: Achilles and Patroclus, Arthur and Lancelot, Quixote and Sancho Panza, The Lone Ranger and Tonto, Batman and Robin, the Buddha and Ananda, Jesus and St. John. The knights of the Round Table had their squires, the holy men and hermits of China and Japan a servant or disciple, the wizards an apprentice, the wandering monks of Europe a traveling companion. Sometimes the hero gets the girl, but often he and his buddy ride off into the sunset together to look for another heroic quest. In myth and in Hollywood, the buddy story of—presumed non-sexual—same-sex love and affection is a major archetypal theme.

An essential element in the hero cycle is that the future hero is *called*. He does not so much choose to be a hero as he finds himself compelled to be in order to address his problem. He cannot help but respond. The hero sees that a transformation of the world is demanded and knows it is his destiny to bring that about.

For many of us, our emerging homosexuality was interpreted as religious vocation. The love of God exceeded the love of women or the desire for a normal sexual and family life. We were called to priesthood or monasticism or spiritual herohood because we were gay.

Not all homosexuals manage to be heroes. But the opportunity is there. To change what we think sexuality is makes us a different person. Perhaps it changes the morphogenetic fields around us. To discover the "gift" of our homosexuality can bring boons to the world.

# Chapter 21

## WISDOM: JESUS AND KRISHNA

The religious myths of the world saviors are more abstract and the themes more subtle than fighting a dragon. The "dragon" that world saviors confront is the reality of evil and human suffering.

In the religions of the Bible, evil and suffering are explained as punishment for the offense the first man and woman committed against God. Human beings had been placed by a loving God in a Garden of Paradise where everything was given to them. But because they disobeyed God's command not to discover ("eat of") the distinction between good and evil, they were cast out of the Garden and condemned to suffer. A world savior was needed to appease God's anger.

In Christian mythology, Jesus Christ was that savior, and his bloody sacrifice on the cross was sufficient appeasement. But Jesus's message was actually that the cause of evil and suffering was not God's anger at Adam and Eve or his continuing anger at violations of his rules of cleanliness and ritual purity. The cause was human beings' failure to recognize their oneness with each other and to follow the Golden Rule and love one another. His death was a demonstration of such love, not a ritual sacrifice in appeasement of divine wrath.

### Jesus as Everyman

The story of Jesus is about Everyman. In the Christian world,

Jesus is the image of the Self in every man and woman. Jesus is the loving, compassionate person inside all of us whose wisdom would save the world if we only followed it. His is the story of the good person who sees through the rules and conventions of his society to the real meaning beneath. Jesus realized that the point of belief in God was not to obey rules and taboos about ritual cleanliness and ownership of property, it was to help people be kind and loving to one another.

Jesus urged people to let compassion, not obedience to the Law, determine how they would treat one another. When he revealed his beliefs, some people rejoiced, others objected. He was set upon by the powers of church and state, temple and emperor, and killed as a heretic and a troublemaker. But, because of his goodness and his willingness to accept life as it comes—"not my will, but thine"—he passed through death and returned bearing the boon of liberation for everybody.

Each of us goes through a similar cycle as we mature from childhood. As generous, well-meaning innocents, we announce to the world our discovery of what life is all about and our intention to change the world for the better. We are immediately beset by the powers of church and state. We have to behave the way other people expect us to behave. We have to learn that what they say is right. We have to learn who to mistrust and fear. We have to work. We have to pay taxes.

We have a choice between becoming a hero—like Jesus—or giving in to the demands of the world. We can choose to be good and compassionate, or we can let ourselves become cynical and resigned to being driven by cultural and economic forces. We can follow our bliss or work for The Man.

## Crucifixion, Death, and Resurrection

The trick of the world savior hero is discovering how to cope with the suffering inherent in life. Jesus saved the world by his crucifixion, death, and resurrection. He was nailed to a cross. The cross symbolizes the four directions of the compass, that is, earthly existence in the three dimensional world. He was wounded in five places. The wounds symbolize the five senses that have to be transformed so that earthly existence can be perceived as heavenly. Jesus is a hero because he accepted incarnation, and then accepted death as part of life. Thus he lived beyond death and became the symbol of mystical realization.

Jesus's teachings were obscured by the cult of the person of Jesus that followed his death. His followers developed metaphors about who he was to emphasize the importance and authority of his message. But the metaphors got in the way of the message. Jesus would probably be appalled that his legacy is a religion that proclaims him a god rather than a world in which everybody follows his advice and loves one another.

Overlaid on the story of Jesus is a set of myths in the literary genre of *midrash* about the Hebrew notion of salvation from God's anger for Adam's sin in the Garden of Eden. These myths developed in the context of a primitive culture that practiced human sacrifice. There are Christian theologians who would argue that the juridical theory of salvation by human sacrifice is not really part of church doctrine, that the Second Person of the Trinity became Man out of generous love for humankind, not out of exacting justice. Nonetheless, Christianity is shot through with the imagery of torture, suffering, blood-spilling, and cruel death.

The good sense of Jesus's teaching is confused by the notion that he was sent to be the perfect oblation. Jesus does not have to be a god born of a virgin for his teaching about love of neighbor to make sense. Jesus's restatement of the Commandments—"One commandment I give you: that you love one another"—has nothing to do with whether he was the Second Person of the Blessed Trinity, consubstantial with the Father.

Jesus's turning upside down the class hierarchy of patriarchal Judaism—"the last shall be first"—and restating values in the Beatitudes—"lucky are the poor, the meek, the merciful, the peacemakers"—are ideas that still reverberate as reminders of how we ought to live. But we do not need to belong to a church or pledge allegiance to the Pope or proclaim Jesus is God to embrace the wisdom of his message.

The mythological images are powerful if we understand them as symbols and metaphors. But they don't make sense if we try to understand them as scientific facts. And people who try to do so often end up fighting with one another over what the facts mean, and therefore violate the message.

## Jesus as God

The belief that "Jesus is God" really means that in each human being consciousness has taken on flesh; in each of us there is a spark of divinity, what is called the abiding presence of sanctifying grace. Saint Paul expressed this in the words: "I live, no longer I, but Christ who lives in me." (Galatians 2:20)

"Jesus is God" means "God is in flesh." As we will see, it means the same thing as "The jewel is in the lotus." This statement, "Jesus is God," is not about the historical personage of Jesus of Nazareth. It is about human consciousness *now*. Jesus's teaching about love makes the most sense when we understand that we're all one, all cells of Gaia, all organs of the Mystical Body.

This is a mystical vision. But it has nothing to do with religion and institutions. It may have something to do with ritual and storytelling and communal singing, but not with Christian dogma or the authority of the church. Christ is not the Founder and CEO of Christianity. Christ symbolizes the life force of the planet, the web of life, the vast ecological system of Earth that is his Mystical Body.

## Rejecting Jesus to Follow Jesus

In our Christian American culture, the rules the hero is called to violate—like Jesus dismissing the Law and preaching love—are communicated through the story of Jesus. But Jesus's message is that we have to get the *lesson* in the myth, not just agree with the symbol. In a paradoxical way then, the disciple of Jesus must see through the trappings of religion and leave the church, rejecting Jesus to follow Jesus's example. The heretics who were burned at the stake for disagreeing with official doctrine or questioning the authority of church leaders were more like Jesus than the faithful who agreed with the leaders and didn't rock the boat.

A parallel experience of rejecting religion in order to pursue the meaning of religion—of walking atop a wall—is coming out. It is an event in a person's life of mythological proportions. It often means leaving the village compound, rejecting authority and tradition, abandoning one life in search of another, and taking a leap into the unknown—a leap, potentially, into hell. Jesus's taking up the Cross out of integrity symbolizes such a leap.

For many people, their entry into gay life results in suffering and loss. They give up notions of self-respect, place in society and family, sometimes even their career. All of us have faced the threatening questions about our attractiveness to other men, looked in the mirror and wondered if we were good enough, suffered through rejections and disappointments, stood in smoky bars hoping to catch an attractive man's eye, only to go home alone and desolate. These are our spiritual tests. We are called to be true to ourselves, in spite of what the authorities say. And then we are called to transform our experience of what gay life is.

The ostracism from normal society is the call to the gay hero to leave the village compound, to live as an outlaw, to embrace the desires and drives that normal society denies and represses into the cultural shadow. It is a stage of transformation that, for some, opens the way to light and life, to fulfillment and sexual joy. But, for others, the failure to accomplish this transformation leads to a life of loneliness, debauchery, and dissipation.

Coming out is a call to herohood and a challenge to correct the self-fulfilling prophecies in society that produce the real problems of the "gay lifestyle." The boon the gay hero must return with is the affirmation of life, through compassion, beyond the rules and conventions, beyond religion. This is how we save our world.

## *Krishna*

A Hindu world savior who, if only for one remarkable miracle, should appeal to gay men's sensibilities is Krishna. This semi-historical figure is best known as a character in the Hindu epic, the *Bhagavad-Gita*.

Hindu tales sometimes portray Krishna as the mouthpiece of Divine Omnipotence, as when he manifests himself (as Shiva the Destroyer of Worlds) to Arjuna on the field of battle. There he explains the nature of war and declares the great spiritual principle: "Renounce the fruits of action."

Krishna is also portrayed as a lovable but callow and mischievous boy, and as a randy and propriety-flouting youth. He is a goatherd and plays the flute, not unlike Pan. He is said to lure wives away from their sleeping husbands by his piping and to lead them in mystic dance in the woods.

It is told that on one occasion when all of the girl goatherds in the countryside had come to hear him perform and to dance with him, Krishna multiplied himself so that he could take each of the girls simultaneously into the bushes to play. In addition to having a long-term mistress, Krishna is reputed to have had some 16,000 "tricks." Krishna's message as world savior, at least on this level, is to relish life and live in the present moment: "renounce the fruits," follow your bliss.

The stories of these world saviors, because they have been preserved through history and told over and over again, give us clues to who we really are and what our lives are about. But they are only symbols. The real truth is our own experience of who we are and how we heroically pursue our lives.

# Chapter 22

## WISDOM: BUDDHA AND AVALOKITESHVARA

The story of the Buddha, though not as familiar to most of us as that of Jesus, is worth looking at because Buddhism is more than just another story about a mythological hero. Buddhism is about the nature of mythology. It is not a religion as much as a method of analyzing religion. It provides an example of a religious tradition that understands myth as symbol and metaphor.

Though the Buddhist attitude of detachment and resignation discourages technology and scientific advance, in practice, Buddhism has beneficial effects in society. In countries with fundamentally Buddhist cultures like Thailand and Tibet, the people are friendly and helpful. There is very little destitution, though nearly everybody lives simply by Western standards. There is little violence, and attitudes toward sex and pleasure are loose. Buddhists may be strict and abstemious, but they're seldom judgmental. Buddhism is perhaps the one religion that has never been spread through violence. While there have certainly been martyred Buddhists, no one has ever been murdered in the name of Buddha.

The way to understand the meaning of Christianity, especially mystical Christianity, is to view it through the lens of Buddhism. Consider it a metaphor about how to live a good life, not as a statement about historical events that give authority for societal rules and institutions. The Buddhist view of religion as myth exemplifies the modern paradigm we have been discussing.

Buddhism should be of special interest to gay men, because its view from over and above the content of religious mythology parallels the perspective of critical distance on social conventions and assumptions in which gay people are inadvertently trained.

Besides, Buddhism tells the charming story of Avalokiteshvara, a mythological character who displays what today we see as gay personality traits. His story may resonate especially strongly in the souls of contemporary gay men for several reasons.

## Prince Gautama the Buddha

The Buddha's story is of the good person who, through his own diligence, confronts suffering and the human condition. He discovers that the cause of evil and suffering is fear, desire, and resistance to change. His boon to humankind is the announcement that the way to escape suffering is to follow the path of moderation.

Prince Siddhartha Gautama Sakyamuni, the historical person who started Buddhism, was born around 563 B.C. to a powerful king in northern India. When it was prophesied that he would be either a political ruler or a religious savior, his father decreed that young Gautama should not be exposed to religious asceticism or the problems that gave rise to it. No yogis around the Prince. No news of misfortune. No old people or poor people or even ugly people. All the young prince was to see were riches, extravagances, and worldly pleasures.

Because he was so overprotected, Gautama began to wonder about the world beyond the walls of the palace. He could sense there was something they were not telling him. Gautama was not a mere boy. By this time he had already married and had a son. But he was inexperienced, having seen only one side of life. He was shocked to learn that being born meant being subject to the vagaries of life and, most importantly, condemned to old age and death. Thus he abandoned his father's palace and became a monk to confront the reality of suffering that had been hidden from him.

Gautama joined a colony of yogis practicing asceticism and self-mortification in the forest. He performed rituals to the various gods of polytheistic Hinduism and prayed for deliverance. He meditated, fasted, and punished his flesh for seven years. It is said he became so emaciated he could grasp his spine from the front. But nothing happened. This is not the way, he realized. Neither luxury nor privation nor worship are the means to conquer suffering.

Rejecting what he had learned both from his father and from his religious teachers, that is, from temporal and spiritual authorities, he sat down beneath a tree—the Bo Tree—to investigate *his own experience*. He vowed to remain beneath the tree until he achieved his goal of understanding the causes of suffering and death. After seven days, he was enlightened.

## All Things in Moderation

The Buddha's enlightenment is summarized in what are called the Four Noble Truths: all life is suffering; the cause of suffering is resistance to reality, experienced as fear and desire; there is a solution to suffering; the solution is moderation, according to the Eightfold Path, expressed as right view, right purpose, right speech, right action, right livelihood, right effort, right mindfulness, and right concentration. Luxury is not satisfying; asceticism is not satisfying. There is a "Middle Way."

In the modern world, each of us discovers—or at least is supposed to discover—this same wisdom about suffering when we are teenagers and learning to cope with disappointment. We discover that we should not allow ourselves to expect too much because we might be disappointed. We discover that we should not be too attached to outcomes. The successful accomplishment of this lesson is to avoid despair, to keep on living, accepting that life is just the way it is.

This is also the lesson of moderation and of delaying gratification. It is a mistake to think if one drink is good, two drinks are better. The fact is one drink, or one toke, or one ride on the roller coaster gets you high and makes the world seem wonderful, but two or three or four make you sleepy, zonked, or dizzy.

## Suffering, Impermanence, and Non-Ego

The Buddha's enlightenment is also summarized in three key-words that describe phenomenal existence: suffering, impermanence, and non-ego. The first refers to the discovery that suffering and rebirth arise from desire and that we all live in ignorance of this basic dynamic of life. The second refers to the realization that all things change, nothing remains the same. The third refers to the conclusion that since everything is always changing, there really is no human soul, no ego, no self.

What we are is a series of passing events, the coincidence of ephemeral phenomena, caught in suffering because we cling to the illusion that we exist as solid, everlasting selves. We are unable or unwilling to accept things the way they are without resistance. We fear things as they are and desire that they be some other way. It is this resistance to impermanence, Buddha said, that creates the karmic patterns that result in the illusion of ego and the pain of suffering.

If there were no resistance, we would disappear into nonexistence. That is the Buddhist notion of salvation, *nirvana*, which means extinguished, like a fire that has burned up all its fuel.

Buddhism, especially the Tibetan tradition, assumes reincarnation. But what it teaches, unlike the popular notion in the West, is not that a soul or personality survives from one lifetime to another, but that karmic patterns from one life reverberate in future lives. What is reincarnated is the karma, not the soul. The goal of spiritual practice is to release all resistance so that no karma is accumulated and the cycle of reincarnation ends.

## Buddhism as a Religion

After achieving Enlightenment, Gautama was faced with a question: Now what? One logical answer was to find a little hut, settle down, and practice moderation until he died and moved on to some higher level of consciousness. Part of his realization was that everybody is on his own; we can only save ourselves. Since Gautama had saved himself, what more was there to do? If he had chosen that route, of course, nobody would have ever heard of him.

Instead Gautama decided to return to the world and teach others what he had discovered. Thus he became a hero. He went on to live a long, full life teaching the Noble Truths and organizing an order of monks to spread the teaching. He died of food-poisoning, a very old man.

His monks went on spreading his ideas, telling his story and embellishing it with religious imagery. Soon a religion developed.

As a popular religion, Buddhism organizes rituals and teaches prayers. But the core of Buddhist practice is solitary meditation. Like Gautama, each person can only achieve enlightenment and liberation from suffering by sitting down, quieting the mind, and getting a perspective on his or her life. We can only achieve critical distance from our ego by learning detachment, mindfulness, and concentration. This is what meditation is concerned with.

Buddha means one who has awakened. Meditation is the means of waking up. Ordinary life is like sleep. Living on the surface of sensations, moved by opinions and fads, unaware of and unconcerned about the patterns that move through life, most people are blind to meaning and significance, unaware of the big picture, driven only by societal conventions and the worry of what other people will think. Through meditation, we become mindful. We become aware of what is going on from a higher perspective. We can be conscious of dynamics and motives, appropriately skeptical of popular beliefs and religious doctrines, and conscientious about the consequences of our actions. With practice, we can detach ourselves from ego and recognize ourselves simply as consciousness interpreting itself to itself.

Buddhism takes an instructive approach to morality and behavior. Instead of declaring Commandments, Buddhism urges followers to voluntarily adopt certain Precepts. While all Buddhists are expected to follow precepts against killing and stealing, the precepts regarding sexual morality, lying, gossiping, the use of intoxicants, and general lifestyle are up to the individual to choose to follow or not. The issue is not so much the rightness or wrongness of the actions as their effect on mindfulness and meditation practice. The Buddha did not give commandments. He gave good advice. There is no threat of punishment for failing to follow that advice.

In one of his sermons, the Buddha likened the state of human suffering to the plight of a man who has been shot with an arrow. It would be foolish, he said, for the man to stop the physician from removing the arrow until he had first determined who shot the arrow, how the arrow was constructed, where the archer came from, and why he shot him—all the various questions that could be asked. The point is to remove the arrow. Just so, the point of life is to end suffering and achieve happiness and fulfillment. It is foolish to worry about the gods, or why there is evil, or what started it all, or who is to blame. Pull out the arrow.

## The Gods Are Not Real

Gautama taught that the gods of his culture were not real. They were (and are) symbols for the different factors that comprise experience. They are real in the sense that what they symbolize is real. But they do not exist as independent entities, nor can they help with the quest for salvation. That is something we each must achieve on our own.

Thus Buddhism is said to be nontheistic, that is, unconcerned with God and the gods. Buddhism is concerned with waking up. Over time, as it evolved into a popular religion, Buddhism developed an elaborate mythology. As a folk religion, Buddhism has a huge pantheon of supernatural characters and a tradition of superstitions. Even so, the mythology was never believed literally.

Throughout its history, Buddhist tradition has held the metaphorical nature of myth. This has been its greatest strength and its major contribution to the spiritual heritage of the earth. Twenty-five hundred years ago Buddhists were teaching the kind of awareness of the nature of myth that the West is only now beginning to recognize. Thus a Buddhist analysis helps us understand Christianity and the broader religious urge human beings feel.

## The Two Worldviews Are Intermixing

Curiously, the states of consciousness that the Eastern religions urge their followers to overcome—fear and desire—are the driving forces that Western religions use to motivate followers to obey religious injunctions: fear of hell and desire for everlasting happiness in heaven. Christianity and Islam, at least on one level, teach resistance to life: They promise salvation beyond life. They have inspired industrial development and technology and changed the face of the earth. Hinduism and Buddhism teach acceptance and resignation. They promise escape as salvation. They have resulted in profound spiritual insight, but in a society that has remained industrially and technologically underdeveloped.

As we enter the modern "global village," the two worldviews are intermixing: Perhaps the West needs to do a little less meddling with nature and the East needs to take more responsibility for the life of its people. This is happening. Industrialization is bringing modernization and improved living conditions to the East. The coming of Buddhism—and the whole pantheon of Eastern religions—to the West is transforming the world's understanding of religion.

Just as children are supposed to learn the lesson of moderation, all of us today are expected to learn aspects of Buddhist wisdom. Modern stress reduction programs and studies of psychoimmunology show that people are healthier and happier if they learn to stay mindful, practice relaxation, and be kind. This does not have much to do with being a Buddhist. This is common sense. Buddhism has developed techniques for training people in such skills.

Although Buddhism is just another mythological tradition, it contains a core of wisdom that is adaptive to the modern world, free of the superstitions of popular religion.

Buddha taught that every man is on his own (early Buddhism, some 2,500 years ago, ignored women), with no help from gods or religious rituals or superstitious practices. This was a step in the evolution of individual consciousness. The Buddha both denied individual ego—in seeing that ego is really just a sequence of transitory events—and affirmed individual personhood—in seeing that each human being is personally responsible for overcoming suffering on his or her own.

Gautama would probably be surprised that he has been remembered 2,500 years later, that the world is full of statues of him, and that his followers pray to him as though he were a god. He only wanted to teach the message that human beings could overcome fear and desire, live moderately, and stop suffering.

## The Two Ferryboats

Besides Buddha, there is another world savior in Buddhism. Connected with him is the Buddhists' affirmation of the phenomenal world. The mythological, non-historical character of the Bodhisattva Avalokiteshvara appeared during a reformation in Buddhism, as the religion shifted from a purely monastic practice to a popular religion.

Early Buddhism taught that escape from suffering and disappointment could be achieved by living a life of simplicity, moderation, and discipline in the search for nirvana, the extinction of desire and escape from the cycle of reincarnation. This escape was limited to males living as monks. The best that women and lay people could hope for was, by dint of good karma they incurred by giving alms to monks, to be reincarnated in a future life as a monk. Then they would be able to avail themselves of the Buddha's wisdom about achieving enlightenment through meditation. This "way of the elders" (Theravada Buddhism) came to be called "the little ferryboat" (Hinayana), because only a few could cross over into nirvana.

The popular religion, called Mahayana, "the big ferryboat," developed around the same time as Jesus's reform of Judaism. There are questions in the study of comparative religion about which might have influenced which, or whether the two reformations appeared simultaneously because of a change in the collective unconscious. Just as Jesus taught that love is the one commandment superseding all the elaborate rules of ritual cleanliness that comprised the Pharisaic Judaism of his day, the Mahayanists taught that compassion for others is the saving attitude that leads to enlightenment, not solitary meditation on philosophical abstractions.

## *The Lord Looking Down in Pity*

The Mahayana myth of the Bodhisattva Avalokiteshvara is pure metaphor. There is no suggestion that Avalokiteshvara was a historical figure. The story was devised by the Mahayana sages to dramatize the message of compassion.

The story goes that a man had worked his way through countless incarnations to become a bodhisattva, a stage of development just before becoming a buddha. In what promised to be his final incarnation, he was the beautiful, kind, gentle, and androgynous Avalokiteshvara, whose name means "The Lord Looking Down in Pity."

In a culture that revered age, and out of a mythology that imagined him to be countless lifetimes old, Avalokiteshvara is usually portrayed as a youth. Perhaps this was to suggest vitality and a certain sexiness. Openness to experience, innocence, good will, vivacity—all are conveyed in the image of youth.

As Avalokiteshvara entered his final meditation and was about to achieve his goal of lifetimes beyond number, he heard a groan from all around him. He came out of his meditation and asked, "What's this about? I was about to achieve nirvana. Why the groan?"

All of nature answered in a single voice, "Oh Avalokiteshvara, we are happy for you that you are about to enter nirvana, but we are sad for ourselves. Life is hard and full of suffering. What's kept us going was the thought of you. You are so kind and lovely. You've been a source of strength and inspiration. Now you are about to leave us, and so we groan."

Rapt with compassion, the saint responded, "Then I won't leave you. I shall renounce my nirvana until all sentient beings are likewise enlightened." He went on to say, "It would be better for one to suffer than for all. Therefore I vow to take upon myself all the karma and all the suffering of all sentient beings. I shall remain in the cycles of reincarnation until the end of time bestowing grace and mercy for the good of all."

Avalokiteshvara is one of the most worshipped gods on Earth. All the prayer flags and prayer wheels throughout the Buddhist world vibrate with his mantra: *Om mani padme hum*, "The jewel is in the lotus." Yet the name of Avalokiteshvara is little known in America. One artistic representation of him, however, is strikingly familiar. In the form of the goddess of compassion, Kuan Yin, the "Madonna of the Orient," his statue is available in virtually every garden store around the country. Chinese artists, unfamiliar with the Hindu notion of androgynous, bisexual gods, mistook his effeminate appearance and reproduced him as a female goddess.

As Kuan Yin, the bodhisattva is usually standing, clearly a woman, sometimes holding a water bottle. As Avalokiteshvara, he is usually sitting in a relaxed pose with his right knee up and his left leg folded under him or hanging over a wall. His right hand rests languidly on his knee. Often broad-shouldered and slim-waisted, he is usually shown either barechested or wearing a sarong with a scarf thrown over his shoulders, and he has flowers in his hair. Sometimes he wears women's beads so that he is dressed (like the Native American berdache medicine men) in sexually ambiguous attire. He is always shown in peaceful reverie, as though sitting in a garden enjoying the quiet of the afternoon.

## The Lord Who Is Seen Within

In institutionalized Buddhism, the story of Avalokiteshvara's ongoing reincarnation is interpreted as explaining the mystical identity of certain religious leaders. The myth is understood to mean that somewhere in the world the bodhisattva is incarnating to do good works, usually as leader of the particular Buddhist sect. The Dalai Lama, for instance, is believed to be a direct incarnation of this bodhisattva, and elaborate tests are performed to determine the lineage of a prospective Dalai Lama to make sure it is the incarnation of Avalokiteshvara who is given the office.

According to another interpretation of the myth, however, when Avalokiteshvara made his great vow, all other sentient beings were at that moment ushered into nirvana, leaving Avalokiteshvara to live out their karma for them. This androgynous being, then, is the only being who is incarnating. Though we think of ourselves as separate individuals—all fighting, struggling, conquering, or succumbing to the demands of our unique karmas—we are actually simultaneous incarnations of Avalokiteshvara. We live out the vow and discover that nirvana is not the renunciation of the world, but the loving, compassionate embrace of all possible human experience. The name Avolokiteshvara also means "The Lord Who is Seen Within."

This Buddhist myth from the first or second century is not about homosexuality and gay identity as we know them in the twentieth century. But the character in the myth displays what are thought of as gay traits. Avalokiteshvara's sensitivity and generosity, his lovableness and sweetness, his attractiveness, vitality, and pluckiness reflect qualities that shine forth from many gay men. The appearance of such traits justifies our speaking about "gay men's spirituality."

The Bodhisattva Vows, the wording slightly changed for this context, are: "However countless sentient beings, I vow to save them. However inexhaustible the resistance, I vow to relinquish it. However many the doors of incarnation, I vow to enter them all. However incomparable the highest perspective, I vow to attain it."

## Jesus as Bodhisattva

Avalokiteshvara's mantra, "The jewel is in the lotus," means that enlightenment and salvation are found in the here-and-now, in physical reality. The lotus is a waterlily that floats on the surface of ponds, symbolizing the beauty of spiritual unfolding. Most of the plant's roots and stalk are underwater. They grow up from the mud and muck at the bottom of the pond. The meaning of the image is that spiritual beauty is rooted in the reality of fleshly existence and the round of birth and death. This is the same meaning as "The Word has become flesh" or "Jesus is Lord."

Jesus became a world savior by willingly dying to expiate the sins of the world. He was the perfect human sacrifice, the ultimate scapegoat for the sin Adam committed against God. The Mahayana character, Avalokiteshvara, became a world savior by delaying his entry into nirvana out of compassion for all sentient beings.

Within the mythic worldview of each, it seems Avalokiteshvara's saving act was more effective than Jesus's. The Christian savior's self-sacrifice to appease his Father's anger did not change anything. People still hate. People still suffer. The Gates of Heaven have been opened by Jesus's saving acts, but each individual still has to face trial before an exacting judge. There is no guarantee of getting through the gate.

According to Buddhist myth, however, when Avalokiteshvara took upon himself the suffering of the world, *all* the sentient beings entered nirvana and none are suffering anymore, just Avalokiteshvara. Every sentient being went through the gate.

Jesus's saving act makes more sense in the Buddhist context than in the Hebrew. In the Gnostic-like, mystical images of the Gospel of Saint John, Jesus declares: "I am the vine, you are the branches." (John 15:5) He prays, "That they all may be One, as you, Father, in me and I in you. That they all may be One in us." (John 17:21) Jesus makes more sense as the Christ-energy in everybody than as sacrifice to appease God's wrath.

In his resurrection into a glorified body, Jesus transcended death and individuality. He became one with his disciples, signified by the sacramental eating of his flesh. In the story of the encounter on the Emmaus road (Luke 24: 13-35), two of the disciples recognize Jesus's mystical presence in a stranger they meet along the road when they share a meal with him. It is said that the way to follow Christian ethics is to see Jesus in every person we meet.

In the metaphors discussed above, we could say the vibes from Jesus's death resonated through the whole complex of morphogenetic fields, etheric holograms, and archetypes of the collective unconscious that comprise the mind of Earth. Clearly that is so. His life and death changed human consciousness as much as any event in human history.

## Ripples in the Spirit Field

To address the question of the simultaneous origins of Christianity and Mahayana, perhaps it was from the karmic resonances of Jesus that the pure metaphor of Avalokiteshvara arose in the meditations of the Mahayana sages who devised the story of the Bodhisattva. Though perhaps this resonance started even before Jesus or the Mahayana sages.

Modern chaos theory gives us the image of the butterfly in Australia whose flapping wings start a ripple in the air that becomes a hurricane in the South Atlantic. Perhaps it was the life, the sacred lovemaking, and solitary meditation and deep sensitivity to suffering of some Two-Spirited shaman somewhere in the world that started a ripple in the spirit field that ended up resonating around the world as the message of love and compassion taught by both Buddhism and Christianity.

Whatever the original source, this ripple, reinforced by the Christian and the Mahayana myths, still resonates. Most gay men live like Jesus: unmarried, without children, striving for beauty, looking for love and friendship, building community, and speaking truth. Occasionally we even get crucified. But we always rise again.

One of the ways homosexuality differs from race is that bigots and dictators can succeed in annihilating a race by killing all the members of that race. But even if they manage to kill off all the homosexuals in the world, in the next generation there will be just as many as there were before. This surely is resurrection from the dead.

# Chapter 23

## WISDOM: GOD

God is the central focus of religion and spirituality in the West. For most of us, the major way we talk about spiritual issues is to define and explain God and the reality he inhabits: heaven and hell and eternity. How we conceive of such transcendental issues is how we think about the meaning of life. We are constantly involved in refining and redefining our notions of the divine.

Because of our estrangement from organized churches, our perspective of critical distance, our fundamental trans-dual vision, and our detachment from the practical issues of child-rearing, gay people are blessed with the ability to rethink God.

God, after all, is not just another thing in a universe of things. God is an elusive idea. God refers to the whole process of the cosmos evolving life and consciousness. God is a name for nature and the way things are. God is also a question: "What is consciousness?" Thinking about God creates the world.

### The Sun Is God

According to the scientific, realistic modern worldview, God is the Sun, the star of our solar system. In his autobiography, Carl Jung told the story of talking once with an American Indian wise man during a visit to the United States. Jung said he was explaining the

Western notion of the invisible, transcendent God. The Indian stood, walked to the edge of the verandah, pointed up, and said, "The sun is God. Everyone can see that." Jung said his philosophical argument fell flat in the face of that obvious truth. Clearly, the sun is God.

It was in the corpses of stars that lived and died through unimaginable aeons that the atomic elements were formed that make up the world we live in. Our star is the source of the energy that caused those elements to combine into molecules and develop until they came to life and evolved intelligence as us. We are literally made of star-stuff.

The human mind's tendency to tell stories, contrive metaphors, and project human traits into the phenomena of the world results in the image of a personal God. Today the anthropomorphic notion of a personal God who is a demanding despot doling out punishment for offenses against his notions of cleanliness does not make sense. God as the ground—and evolutionary goal—of consciousness and the matter of planetary ecology is likely to make more sense to the contemporary mind. Such a concept is consistent with the way we see the world. It is the current myth.

This God is beyond personality because it exists at a totally different order of being and magnitude. In modern terminology, God is the constants of space-time, the rules that determine how the Big Bang unfolded, and the way the universe operates.

This is a God we participate in, and which we can literally see. At the rising and the setting of the sun and moon, we can observe the magnificence of the modern universe. We can hold in mind the model of the vast cosmos science has discovered. We can envision the motion of these huge objects in three-dimensional astronomical space.

To see the moon rising over the horizon as the earth turns away from the sun at twilight fills us with awe and wonder and gladness, even as it makes us quiver with trepidation and insignificance.

When we look at the expanse of stars and galaxies modern scientific instruments have allowed us to see, we are necessarily awed. The space we are looking into, extending at least 32 billion light-years, is beyond anything ever attributed to any god ever worshipped by human beings. The modern universe, as modeled by science, though probably just the surface of a multi-dimensional reality, is truly a source of religious feeling. It is a direct experience of cosmic reality that does not depend on metaphor or anthropomorphism. (Though it is certainly okay to layer the anthropomorphic metaphors about the personal God on top of this direct experience; it is a poetic way to conceive the interconnectedness of all things that the evolutionary, ecological model reveals to us.)

In our reverie, we might realize that the function of the universe is to convert nuclear energy in stars to spiritual energy in intelligent beings. Just as a rose flowers, the universe peoples. All of evolution is about the sun's growing a planet on which consciousness can occur. Evolution of life on earth is the growth of a mind for the sun. We are the sun's consciousness. We are God's incarnation in the physical world.

In the ecological worldview, we are part of a complex web of life, organs of the biosphere of Earth. Human beings are the organs of consciousness, just as in an individual human being the brain is the organ of consciousness. Indeed, following that same metaphor, individual human beings are to the planetary mind as individual neurons are to the brain.

Just as we are not aware of the functioning of our individual neurons, the planet's consciousness is not aware of us as individual persons. That is a problem with the traditional mythology: Whatever God is, by all the attributes of omniscience and omnipresence, he would not be bothering himself over minor events in the lives of individual human beings. In fact, he would not see us.

## The Personal God

The personality of such a god is not entirely lost. Indeed, it exists in each individual person who imagines God and projects his or her own personality into the cosmos. Where the sun is getting personality is in the evolution of intelligence on planet Earth.

God is a personal being because he is a human idea. The idea of God we cultivate in ourselves is powerful. It influences everything we think about life. Perhaps we have an innate moral responsibility to choose a life-affirming, loving, generous God.

God is personal in the vision of personal beings. The medieval aphorism (attributed to the fourteenth century German mystic Meister Eckhart) says: "The eye with which I see God is the eye with which God sees me." God sees me as a person by my seeing God as a person. The eye with which God watches my life is *my* eye. There is no watcher outside us, no cosmic accountant that keeps track of our failings. Nobody is watching us but ourselves. The personality of God comes from our projections.

In the best and worse sense, the traditional image of the personal God is like Santa Claus. The metaphor of the wise, generous, jolly old man conveys a lesson about life, especially to children. As people grow up, they learn there is no actual Santa. This is a kind of enlightenment. As they continue to grow, they have the opportunity to come to the next realization: "Yes, Virginia, there is a Santa Claus. He exists as certainly as love and generosity and devotion exist."

This is the realization of what the metaphor means. This is a higher enlightenment. The three stages of progression is expressed in the Zen saying: "First there is a mountain, then there is no mountain, then there is."

"Before I studied Zen," the Master said, "I thought there were mountains and trees. Then I studied Zen and learned that these are all illusion, just thought-forms in the mind. Then I was enlightened. And there were mountains and trees again." The understanding of the metaphor is a higher truth.

If God is beyond conception, then to believe in nothing is the highest belief. Such belief recognizes that we cannot know anything absolutely because we can always rise to a higher perspective from which to understand things more comprehensively. We can never know the absolute truth about God. We can only entertain metaphors. The highest thought is the thought beyond content— the sense of wonder at something incomprehensible.

The sun doesn't care what we think about it or how many rituals we perform to greet its risings. Religion is for us, not God.

## God as Creator

God's most characteristic act is to create the universe. Creation myths are a metaphor about our responsibility for our experience. God the Creator is, as Freud pointed out, a projection of human fatherhood. On a more subtle level, God the Creator is a symbol of the mechanism by which each of us creates our own world by assembling and making sense of the vast amount of sensory data we absorb every moment.

Somewhere inside our head the whole world we live in is being generated as an image in our mind. That image is then projected back into experience as the world around us. We see the world "out there," but it is really "in here," in the churning neurotransmitters in our brain.

Creating our own world proceeds on a variety of levels. The most obvious way we create our own world is by making choices. Where we live, what we do, how we spend our time, who we befriend, what we do with our money—all this determines what goes on in our experience. We are constantly building a world.

We are also constantly expected to affirm the world of people around us. So much of human discourse concerns agreement that we are all having similar experience. That is partly why people talk so much about the weather. We create our own worlds, but always in the context of society, history, and social milieu. And almost always with other people.

Everything around us is comprised of the experience of people building their worlds. The chair you are sitting in was created from the experience of woodcutters, carpenters, upholsterers, fabric dyers, designers, even truckers, salesmen, and office clerks. All of their experience went into that chair. If they had not had those experiences you would not be sitting in that chair. The bread you ate at breakfast was made of the experience of bakers, and before them of millers and farmers. And before that, of grain ripening in the warm sunlight. Everything around us is created by life. And everything we do participates in creating the world of future experience for others and for ourselves.

## Us as Creators

The mechanical, neurological process by which we see or hear something generates an image in our mind. This is a creative act. The cognitive process by which we recognize what the thing is, based on previous experience of similar things, is a creative act. The next step is to find meaning in the thing by defining our relationship to it. This too is a creative act.

These sensory, cognitive processes are passive activities. We do not control what our senses perceive or how we recognize and give meaning to our perceptions. Nonetheless there is a complex and active process by which all this happens. This is what our brains do all day long.

We have more control over the process than we recognize. Of course, we cannot choose what we experience. The things around us are what they are. But our past experience and our self-identity determine how we value and prioritize them.

What we experience is often what we expect to experience. People necessarily interpret the strange in terms of the familiar—the queer in terms of the normal. We sometimes miss what is going on because we were expecting something else. We sometimes bring about what we were expecting—or dreading—by our attitudes and expectations. This is the mechanism of the self-fulfilling prophecy.

This means we each create the universe of our own experience. But because we have so little control of the process (even though we are participating in it every moment), we project this creative power out onto a Creator. The personality we attribute to this projection goes a long way toward determining what gets created in our experience. Imagining a loving, forgiving God, for instance, will likely make us loving and forgiving people and cause us to be surrounded by generous people who like most everybody they know. Imagining a just and vengeful God will likely make us stiff-necked and rigid, surrounded by people who think others are always trying to take advantage of them.

We cannot control individual events, but we can control the context in which we hold all events.

## Karmic Intentions

There is a higher level of creation from which we sometimes are able to influence the course of outside events by our intentions. This level can be called karmic. Examples of this are the practices of creative visualization and prayer of petition. These work primarily by self-fulfilling prophecy: When we expect something to happen, we are likely to bring it about, however indirectly or unconsciously. But sometimes there seems to be an even deeper mechanism at work: self-fulfilling prophecy at the level of destiny. What we wish for we might really get. Coincidences just might happen. Luck might be with us.[7]

## God Is a Metaphor

God the Creator is a metaphor for these elusive processes. God is the thought form we hold to try to understand how time unfolds. God is the personification of destiny we beseech for favorable outcomes, thereby creating powerful intentions and self-fulfilling prophecies for our benefit and the benefit of those in the world we affect.

How we define God for ourselves—or choose not to define God—determines how we think about our lives, how we use our creative powers, and how we relate to the world we share with others.

# Chapter 24

## WISDOM: THE WORLD

One of the powerful metaphors about God is God's sex. Attributing sex to a noncorporeal being is clearly metaphorical. But it is a metaphor that determines the whole tenor of a religion. It is more about the nature of the world than about God.

Some feminist anthropologists, citing the discoveries of Marija Gimbutas, hypothesize that early human beings imagined God as a Great Mother. Life was seen as participation in her joy and pleasure. With the rise of the patriarchy and the development of agrarian economies, the collective metaphors for God and nature shifted from images of a generous and provident Mother to a belligerent and demanding Father.

Around the year 500 B.C., at the time of Pythagoras in Greece, Buddha in India, and Jeremiah in Israel, religious imagery changed. Instead of a paradise of divine benevolence, the world came to be seen as a fiery vortex of delusion, desire, violence, and death—a shift Joseph Campbell called "the Great Reversal."

To this day, western religions remain patriarchal. In the last few decades, however, since feminist theologians promoted the notion that the sex we imagine for God is a personal choice and God can possess both male and female traits, we have begun to hear God called Mother as well as Father.

There is a different flavor, feeling, and tone to each. The widespread embrace of God as feminine is evidence of the acceptance that the figures of myth are metaphors that change through time and circumstance.

## The Blessed Virgin Mary

Catholic tradition has long kept a feminine aspect for God in the person of the Blessed Virgin Mary. One of the great cultural trends of history is the cult of Mary in the Middle Ages that resulted in the building of the Gothic cathedrals. The Blessed Mother provides a clear image of God as generous and caring, giving a softer face to the rigid God of Catholic theology.

The identity of Mary as virgin and sexless mother has had a sex-negative effect in Christianity. But that is not the real meaning of the metaphor. The image of the Virgin Mother is not about sex or the lack of it; it is about the coincidence of opposites: To be mother and non-mother simultaneously calls for rising above contradiction.

In Hebrew, the word "virgin" did not mean a woman who had not had sex, but rather a woman who had not yet given birth to a child. Jewish culture at the time of Jesus did not honor virginity as such: Women were supposed to have offspring to make the descendants of Abraham as numerous as the stars in the sky. A virgin was not fulfilling her proper purpose. The religious cult of virginity as we know it is a Greek concept that got attached to Christianity several hundred years after the time of Jesus. The first Christians would not have understood it at all. And they probably would not have understood the sex-negative implications Christian tradition has drawn from it.

As the story of Mary's virginity is told in St. Matthew's Gospel, it was a sign of scandal, not purity. It meant Jesus was conceived out of wedlock. Joseph, Mary's fiancé, suspected her of adultery and would have put her out as a sinful woman but for a dream in which an angel explained the miracle to him. The good religious people would have considered Mary worthy of stoning—just like a homosexual.

The myth of virgin birth is not about Mary. It is about Jesus. The point of the virgin birth—of both Jesus and Buddha—is twofold. The first is that there was something remarkable about their birth that foreshadows their significance. The second is that they came into the world directly from the unitary Absolute, not through the world of dualities. The virginity of Mary and of Queen Maya, mother of Prince Gautama, represents the goodness and purity of nature unsullied by involvement with the clashing duality of male and female. The Saviors save the world by overcoming the polarities.

## The Saviors

Savior myths are about how we should fulfill our responsibilities for the creation of the world. The stories generally begin with the notion that the world is not working correctly. Something has gone wrong and the world needs saving.

Because people do not put out consistent and harmonious intentions, their creative power is misapplied. And so a savior is needed, somebody who can see both sides and judge what is best for all, somebody who walks walls.

The notion that I have a savior both comforts me when I experience the hardships of life and calls me to participate personally in saving the world by rising above my own conflicting intentions.

According to the Christian savior myth, God, or especially Jesus, is a Cosmic Friend and cosufferer. One of the functions of such a God is to be the listener to our self-talk. We need to articulate what is going on in our lives. Sometimes there are other people—friends, lovers, colleagues—we can talk to; sometimes we pay therapists to listen. In order to think through things, we often need to externalize our thoughts by putting them into words.

This is an important aspect of intimacy and relationship: In order to experience some things, we need to share the experience. A sunset is more beautiful when we can show it to someone else. An event in our lives is more wonderful or more bearable if there is someone beside us to experience the joy or the trauma with us.

The shared experience is more real than the solitary. This is, therefore, an argument for validating gay relationship. Human beings need companionship to realize their experience. Gay people need other gay people to bring their universe into full reality. This is how we save one another.

When there is no other person, or when the issues are too personal, too shameful, or too urgent to share with others, God is there. This God is not the Lord God Almighty, creator of the starry hosts, Judge and Ruler of the Universe. He/She is a part of mental functioning, an imaginary friend, the other side of our interior voice.

This personal comfort is one of the most important functions of God in our lives because it is the source of our sense of having a place in the world and of being loved and lovable. We create our own world by talking it over with an Other. The myth of God as friend generates a state of mind in which we can talk to ourselves. And our selves—the deeper layers of who we are—can talk back to us.

## Signs From God

This is how all divination works. Through words or symbols we talk to the universe and the universe can talk back to us. Such practices allow us to step outside rational consciousness and see what is going on at other, less conscious, levels of our mental functioning. Those deeper levels which speak to us in the voice of God reveal things we did not know we could know.

Tarot cards or the I Ching are such techniques. They provide something like a Rorschach inkblot into which we can project our hopes, fears, and psychological motivations. They sometimes truly give signs and revelations. The coincidence of the fall of the cards can be unbelievably accurate. Other arrangements would be totally inaccurate. Where do these miracles of coincidence come from?

That question is its own answer in the sense that it hints at the creative power at work in consciousness and that is conceived of as God. It is not a matter of our minds controlling the fall of the cards. If that were so we would all win at poker. Yet apparently our minds are able to synchronize with larger patterns that include both the array of the cards and our psychological states.

The miracles of divination and the coincidental signs that flow through our lives are powerful clues to the larger reality of which our ego-consciousness is but a tiny blip. The signs evoke feelings of wonder and awe and consternation in us, and they call our minds beyond the surface of things into that deeper reality we call God.

## God Shapes Our Lives

In order to stop resisting life, we can entertain the myth that God shapes our lives by the events that befall us, teaching us lessons we need to learn for spiritual maturation. We can believe we are being tested or that we are suffering to strengthen our souls and steel our resolve to love life in spite of everything. We can even believe we are God in our own universe, causing everything that happens, making us responsible for everything we experience.

There is a Sufi saying: "If the rose knew what the gardener's care would result in come spring, it would joyfully bend to the pruning knife." Gay people experience pruning in late childhood and early adulthood. We realize the truth of our orientation and have to give up familial and cultural expectations of what our lives will be. Often we experience ridicule and ostracism by schoolmates and peers, along with rejection and disapproval by parents. Even if we grow up feeling it is okay to be gay, we experience confusion and trauma because we will not follow in the path that our parents, teachers, and role models have laid before us. Later, we have to deal with the complex, contradictory, and self-defeating dynamics of the gay lifestyle. We suffer fears of inadequacy. We envy those we think have perfect bodies. We suffer rejections and the pain of rejecting others. All this pain can be understood as God/life pruning us.

Such metaphors enable us to examine our attitudes, to observe the dynamics of memory and association, to rise above the moment-to-moment collision of events, to achieve perspective, and to remember what we really are: consciousness delighting in the variety of experience. Underlying these metaphors of God is the faith that the universe is unfolding as it should and that we each have a place in that unfolding.

## Conversion

A savior myth implies the need for conversion. A savior can only save you if you are in trouble in the first place and if you allow him to come to your rescue.

Such conversion is a double-edged sword. On the one hand, it is fundamental to achieving certain mental states. Converts to a cause or religious tradition discover their lives are changed; miracles begin to appear in their lives; their karma changes; their self-fulfilling prophecies are transformed. Conversion, based in the notion there is something wrong with us that somebody else can fix, is a powerful trigger of spiritual energies. On the other hand, it is also an organizational ploy of institutions. In America, televangelists condemn popular culture and convince people they are wrong and unhappy to get them to join the church (or at least make donations).

The conversion experience is central to gay experience. Coming out is a major conversion that creates miracles and transformation of life—just like being "born again." One of the reasons the fundamentalist preachers might be so anti-gay is that we represent competition. We offer a different "answer"—an answer that leaves the preachers out.

## No Resistance

Conversion is a fundamentally dualistic notion. We can only convert from a bad state to a good one. When we see that everything is perfect—everything is God—just the way it is, conversion is not possible, and the organizational concerns of religious institutions drop away.

Curiously, having been saved means not having to do anything. This is one of the strangest moral notions in Protestant Christianity: If you have been "born again," you cannot sin, no matter what you do. (If you do sin egregiously, it is because you were not really born again.)

In fact, this notion is a statement about choosing life as it is, though that usually is not how it is interpreted by Christian preachers. But if we are not saved by our good works or our religious actions and reception of the sacraments, but because of Our Savior's death and resurrection, then everything is fine just the way it is. There is nothing to do. No resistance called for. No conversion needed.

Buddhism teaches that to attain full enlightenment we must overcome the passions. One of the bodhisattva's vows is to extinguish the passions, however inexhaustible they be. These passions are symbolically depicted in Buddhist art as a barking dog, a slithering snake, and a randy rooster: anger, envy/greed, and lust.

One way to extinguish the passions—the way of monks and yogis—is to practice self-denial, to suppress and sublimate the passions. This is the orthodox, life-denying technique of austerity and discipline, called The Right Hand Path. This developed with the Great Reversal and the intuition that life in the flesh is pain and suffering, an ordeal to be endured for the sake of spiritual life beyond.

Notice that the passions are all centered on feelings of inadequacy and deprivation: anger that our life is not the way we think we want it; envy, and subsequent greed, that other people have things we want but think we cannot have; and lust for sex because we think we are not getting enough.

So another way to extinguish the passions, the way of The Left Hand Path, is to let go of the inadequacy and deprivation: to be happy for other people, to be satisfied with our lifestyle, and to have regular sex—by ourselves, with playful strangers, or with a deeply committed lover as appropriate at different times in our life.

Intensity is born of frustration and hankering. Denial of desire, especially of sex, can force psychic energy into spiritual obsession and exaltation. But this denial does not extinguish the passions. It just displaces them. And maybe makes them worse.

A positive attitude, the affirmation of human life, is what is meant by the saviors' embrace of the human condition—even of sin, suffering, and sex.

## Overcoming the Senses

The familiar warning in religion about getting stuck in the senses is really about getting caught up and distracted by the particulars. For in the particulars of life there are good and bad, desirable and undesirable—the distractions of the polarities. Imagine looking into a crystal and watching the light being broken into a multitude of rainbows. If your eye is dazzled by an individual gleam, you miss the sight of the white light pouring through. Just so, to be trapped in the senses is to be dazzled by distractions.

Overcoming the senses is seeing the big picture. It is not accomplished by keeping our eyes downcast or living in drab environments or denying ourselves sensations and sensual pleasures. It is accomplished by expanding our consciousness. Overcoming the senses means overcoming judgment and preference for some things over other things. It means enjoying everything with loving equanimity.

Meditation practice, while temporarily confining the senses by disciplined focus of attention, enhances sense pleasure by bringing a fresh and open mind to each new experience. Zen art is an example of how simplicity intensifies beauty. Meditation research has found that adept meditators do not lose immediacy of experience the way the rest of us do. When we hear a repeated sound, for instance, like the ticking of a clock, it quickly fades into the background and our hearing stops picking it up. But, as demonstrated with brainwave and biofeedback equipment, Zen monks react at the sensory/cellular level to each tick as though it is a brand new sound. This is every meditator's experience. After prolonged practice with its inherent sensory deprivation, the world looks refreshed and renewed. The air smells sweeter; the sun shines brighter; the trees are greener and the flowers more resplendent than ever. Life is good. We are in Paradise.

## The Garden of Eden

The image of the Garden of Eden parallels the image of the Blessed Virgin Mary. Eden is a presexual state before the "original sin" of discovery of the difference of male and female. Gay identity participates in that Edenic consciousness. For all the emotional difficulties and developmental stages we experience in growing up gay, we never go through the loss of innocence that comes with the discovery of heterosexuality. We never have to shift our object of affection from our best friend with whom we share everything to a first girlfriend about whom we understand nothing.

The myth of Eden, of a Golden Age in the past, is always about the innocence and carefree state of childhood. It is also about an idealized world waiting for us in the future. The Golden World is a reward for successfully accomplishing the hero journey of a human lifetime. The Golden World is also a metaphor about how to see the world of everyday reality. Just beyond the veil of the polarities is the original perfection. The trick is to pierce the veil. That is what myths of afterlife are about.

# Chapter 25

## WISDOM: AFTERLIFE

Afterlife myths point to the levels of consciousness available to human experience through insight, understanding, and religious discipline. Afterlife is a metaphor for mystical experience, for finding the Golden World.

There is a telling parallel in the experience of high romance. When you are in love, you think and say things to your partner like: "I will love you forever," "I'll never leave you."

Terms like forever and never are slippery. They are a source of anger if the romance fades for one person and the other says, "But you promised we would be together forever." Forever and never are not about the future. Such words are really concerned with the depth of intensity in the present. "I will love you forever" means "I love you with all my heart and soul *now*."

Similarly, heaven is intense joy and vision *right now*. Hell is intense unhappiness and bad fortune *right now*.

Heaven is not somewhere else. Heaven is an attitude toward our experience. Eternity is not a long time. Eternity is *right now* with all its intensity and immediacy. If we are conscious, we can live in eternity now, free from the pain of change and loss because we can rise to a higher perspective from which we can experience our entire life as a coherent and unified whole.

Understanding what afterlife myths are about does not mean there is no survival after death any more than our analysis of the language of high romance denies that love may endure. But it does mean that the point of afterlife myths is not to displace us from the present with the promise of pie in the sky sometime in the future.

It is said that the desire for continued existence beyond death was the origin of religion in the first place. As human beings evolved enough to sense their own existence and the existence of their loved ones, they were horrified at the prospect of life's ending. They also felt guilty about the lives they took in order to live—the animals they ate and the enemies they killed. Thus they invented gods and afterlives to mute their horror.

Certainly the notion that our loved one is in heaven is a beneficial denial in the grieving process. But it is more than that. Afterlife mythology creates a context for all religious imagery. The notion of God is a layer of such mythology. A personal God residing in heaven is able to take our loved one to his bosom. In the West, where God is personal and the myths are taken literally, the model is continuation of personal existence beyond death. In the East, where God is more elemental and the myths are more lyrical than historical, the afterlife model is reincarnation, i.e. an impersonal afterlife. Life goes on, but not "you" the person.

Beyond the dynamics of grieving, afterlife myths function as maps to mystical experience. In the Gnostic Gospel of Thomas, Jesus says, "Do not ask when the Kingdom of God will come. The Kingdom does not come by expectation. The Kingdom of God is spread out across the face of the earth and men do not see it. Behold, the Kingdom of God is within you" (Logion 113).

## Going Through the Bardo

There is a notion in Tibetan Buddhism called the "Clear Light," that appears in the *Tibetan Book of the Dead*, which provides instruction for the soul undergoing the journey through the "bardo state" between one life and the next. The text is to be read to the deceased in the days following death, because, confused and uncertain, the soul in transition needs direction.

What the soul experiences in its journey includes a variety of lights—reddish lights, smoky blue lights, pale lights—that lead down paths to different possible incarnations (some of them quite unattractive: as an animal, for instance, or as a "hungry ghost" or a denizen of hell). The soul needs help in ascertaining which colored lights to avoid and which to follow.

Immediately upon leaving the body, according to this mythology, the soul sees Absolute Reality in a blinding vision of Clear Light, one with no color, not even white. If the soul realizes what it is seeing, Buddhahood is attained at that moment. But souls usually miss the experience because the light is not what they were expecting. In that case, reincarnation will occur. The expectations of what afterlife will be like are so confused they prevent us from entering afterlife when it is presented.

We cannot possibly know what happens to individual consciousness after death. Perhaps as we die, if we are sufficiently aware and not too caught up in our expectations, we can experience consciousness waking up from our individuality, as if waking from a wonderful dream, as we become part of the life force that is ever reborn in new human lives.

Or perhaps eternity is in the death experience itself. As individuality fades we might experience our whole lives in an eternal moment that goes on forever because the individual perspective that could see an ending disappears into greater consciousness.

If we are conscious enough to perceive our individuality and our placement in space and time fading into nonexistence, time might seem to stretch out forever. Our focus might widen to allow all of our life to seem as one complete experience—full of all the people we have loved and all the happiness we have generated—all existing in the eternal moment. That is heaven. If instead we cling to our ego and try to maintain selfhood and consciousness of being in a particular perspective, we may find ourself going out of existence in a state of fear, trying to stay alive because we think we have not yet experienced enough love and happiness. That is hell.

As we begin to die, we can either think "Oh, wow!" or we can think "Oh, no!"

## *Purgatory Is Becoming Conscious*

Catholic tradition adds a couple of other possible stop-offs: limbo and purgatory. Limbo was a mythical solution to an organizational problem, a place for unbaptized people who did not deserve eternal punishment just because they lived outside the influence of the Roman Church. Purgatory, on the other hand, is a more mythologically meaningful notion.

Purgatory is a way station, a stop-off on the road to heaven. In the Catholic system, purgatory is where we get punished for all the sins we got away with, but that were not serious enough to damn us to hellfire for eternity. In the mystical system, this is the time for ego and limited vision to be stripped away so we can see God.

The myth of purgatory expresses the real truth that letting go is painful; change implies purification. We can learn from our suffering to be less obsessed with ourselves and blinded by our egos that cast such broad shadows. Blurring the Roman and Tibetan metaphors into each other, we might imagine purgatory as the experience of the soul floating around in the bardo state, seeing the truth of what was really going on in its life.

This kind of awareness of truth is what is sought in psychotherapy. Discovering it can be an experience of purgation. Seeing how our own shadow traits and our projections onto other people ruined a love affair or caused us to miss out on joy is a discovery that can change our life and open our eyes. Purgatory is about becoming conscious. We should not wait for death to do that.

## *A Meditation Practice*

Holding thoughts about dying and afterlife is a meditation practice for rising above ourselves. As we meditate about waking up and popping out of our body and floating through a "tunnel of light," we can shift our consciousness beyond our ego. The image of afterlife is a practice of mystical perception.

Realizing we cannot possibly imagine afterlife allows us to understand that we cannot know what is and is not the Clear Light. Once we understand this, we can understand that we see the Clear Light right now. Such a vision, always fleeting and available only in special moments achieved through meditation or psychedelic realization, helps us overcome the limitations of ego.

If we think we are our name and looks and body and the history we remember, there will be nothing left of us when these things fall away—as they inevitably will. If we understand instead that we are just a point of view of the consciousness of the universe, then even when that particular point of view comes to an end, we go on.

When we see beyond ourselves, we can see that everybody else is also just a point of view of consciousness. Then when our ego sees other egos, it can rejoice in their joy, experiencing their joy as its own with no judgment, no disapproval, no jealousy. What a comforting meditation it is to understand that the being inside the beautiful young men you see is you! They are not separate, alien entities. You can enjoy their beauty as a sign and manifestation of your own beauty, their supple bodies as yours. This is the meditation that founds a positive experience of pornography. It is the meaning of the story of Avalokiteshvara.

The images of the myths—and the exercise of seeing into and through them—are practices in awakening consciousness now. If we have seen heaven during life, we are more apt to recognize it after life.

A real problem with afterlife mythology is that it has been used to control people's behavior; God the Judge is a moral policeman for society. It has been offered as a sop to the suffering to keep them suffering. It has been a justification for not according justice. The church has kept the poor destitute by promising them justice after death, when it is no threat to the riches of the rich and the stability of the social order. Belief in a literal heaven to which one goes after death can prevent us from going after the Clear Light now. By suggesting our ego is everlasting, it prevents us from transcending ego. What a terrible misinterpretation of the myth!

## *Karmic Patterns*

Karma is Sanskrit for "cause and effect." The myth holds that things that happen to us as if by coincidence are sometimes caused by processes we cannot perceive. In turn, the events of our lives sometimes have effects we cannot perceive. The metaphor is based on the assumption that bad things should happen to people because of bad things they have done and good things should happen because of the good they have done. Since this is not verifiable, the causative behavior must have occurred in a past life.

Karma and the myths of reincarnation are about the effects on us in the present of the behavior of those who have lived before us. The myths are a reminder of the effects our lives will have on those after us. Karmic patterns are the resonances of other lives in ours. What are called our past lives are the ripples in the spirit field, vibes, that have intersected in such a way as to produce us.

From the perspective of our new religious paradigm, we can say that karma refers to the multidimensional reality that we are part of but of which we see only hints. This is not something magical, just imperceptible.

The power of pheromones is an example of such a phenomenon. Because our cerebral cortex, where conscious thinking occurs, evolved out of the olfactory bulbs, most human beings have lost awareness of the rich universe of scents that surround us. Nonetheless we are influenced by these scents. The presence of another person in sexual arousal and exuding chemical signals may arouse us sexually. We may think it is because he or she is such a wonderful person. But it is really because of the pheromones wafting from their skin.

We resonate with the karmic vibrations from the lives before us. Like radio receivers tuned to pick up certain frequencies and not others, our minds play and replay certain patterns, like songs on the radio. These are experienced as phantom memories and innate preferences. Mythologically, they are called past lives.

## The Great Thoughts

Another way to talk about the patterns in our lives is astrology. In the West, where reincarnation has never been especially popular and the guiding myth has been one of life after death, the perennial way of talking about recurring patterns in people's lives has been to ascribe them to external influences from cosmic sources.

We could think of these patterns as the great thoughts of the planet. We can imagine that from a high enough perspective we could see patterns and themes in the evolution of the planet and the history of culture that transcend individual lives—but which necessarily show up in the lives of individuals. We see such patterns in our own lives. We can see how we have learned from things that have happened to us as we have matured. We can see how we are who we are because of critical moments that have determined our lives.

If we look at our lives, we are bound to observe patterns, some of them seemingly composed entirely of coincidences, that have made us who we are. Such patterns might be good luck in finding jobs—or bad luck in holding jobs. We might see that we have been in the right place at the right time to get credit and financial and social rewards for events we did not really have any control over. On the other hand, we might see that we have been blamed for other people's mistakes. We might see that boyfriends come around at just the times we need a helpmate with our life's project. Or we might see we keep falling for the wrong type. We might notice that we do not get what we think we want, and go through a major disappointment, only to find we got something better that we did not even know we wanted and that we would not have gotten had events gone the way we originally desired. We might find that we choose the same clothes every morning, effectively creating a religious habit for ourselves.

These can all be explained as self-fulfilling prophecies. They are. What is interesting, though, is that our self-fulfilling prophecies sometimes seem to be fulfilled by other people's actions. If being on time is one of your patterns, it probably means you are good at estimating distances and travel times. But that does not explain how traffic jams seem to open up just in time for you or how the bus arrives just when you need it. The events in your life and the events in the world around you can be seen as all of a piece.

An astrologer may show us how all these things flow out of the pattern of the stars at the time of our birth. A psychoanalyst may show us how they were set up by events in the first three years of our life or by experiences we had as a preadolescent. An Indian guru may explain how all these events are a result of karma from past lives. A priest may tell us everything is God's will. Rising above the specifics of these explanations, it seems like we are part of something bigger than ourself, something that demonstrates itself through coincidence and luck.

## Our Lives as Works of Art

One way we participate is by creating our lives as works of art that demonstrate the beauty and symmetry of the patterns we uncover. We use symbols and metaphors—most of which have come down to us from the past as myth, religion, and art—to enhance and explore these patterns.

For instance, we might face some great difficulty by drawing a parallel to the adventure of the knight-errant, Don Quixote de la Mancha. We do not want to make the mistake of actually thinking we are a knight and going to joust windmills. But we might think about Don Quixote's story and sing "The Impossible Dream" to ourselves when we are screwing up our courage to face the difficult situation.

In the early days of our gay life, that difficult situation might have been going to a gay bar or a bathhouse for the first time or attending a meeting of a gay student group. It might have been telling a friend we were in love with him. Later, it might have been coming out at work or joining a political protest. When we were in a serious relationship, it might have been bringing up feelings that were hard to talk about, saying "I love you," or, perhaps, "I'm not happy." There are many ways to be a hero, to boldly go into the place that scares us most. The story of the knight or the story of Jesus accepting his fate in the Garden of Gethsemane provides a model for how to plunge ourselves into the underworld of our fears so that, in the end, we come forth victorious.

A common way to think about all this is that the patterns we find in our lives represent lessons we are supposed to learn. There is probably no teacher developing a lesson plan, but such a metaphor reminds us to go with the patterns, to cope with things and to shape our lives according to our intuitions of what makes our lives meaningful and blissful. These lessons come from deep within us, rising up from the collective mind. They are our personal experience of the great thoughts of the planet. They are how we experience heaven now—the kingdom spread across the face of the earth.

## The Three Wonders

It is said there are Three Wonders of the Bodhisattva to meditate upon. The first is that the Bodhisattva is bisexual,[8] that is, simultaneously male and female, transcending the polarities like the Two-Spirit Persons of Native-American tradition. Sometimes Avalokiteshvara is portrayed as male on the right side of the body and female on the left.

The second wonder is that from the Bodhisattva's perspective there is no distinction between life and release-from-life, no ascertainable difference between samsara and nirvana, the world of flux and the world of tranquility. Time and eternity are one. This is it. There is no difference between now and life-after-death, no distinction between the longing for God and the experience of living life, no need to long for oneness with God because we are one with God. The point is to live now—like the eunuchs for the kingdom—to choose incarnation, to choose life.

The third wonder is that the first two are the same. Transcending the polarities of male and female is to discover, honor, relish, and enjoy our place, beyond the limits of individuality and the accidents of personality, as embodied in the divine process here and now. Thus the spirituality of the Bodhisattva is called The Way of Joyful Participation in the Sorrows of World.

The Gnostic Jesus of the Gospel of Thomas says the same thing: "When you make the two into one, and when you make the inner like the outer and the outer like the inner, and the upper like the lower, and when you make male and female into a single one, so that the male will not be male nor the female be female, . . . then shall you enter the Kingdom of Heaven." (Logion 22)

Mahayana Buddhists, especially monks, have daily repeated the vows of the Bodhisattva to remain in the cycle of reincarnation and to take upon themselves the suffering of the world out of compassion and generosity. Adopting a literal understanding of reincarnation, shouldn't we expect that many of these generous souls would see fulfillment of their vows in their being reincarnated as homosexuals in the age of AIDS? Shouldn't we expect the present world to be full of bodhisattvas?

Listen close in your meditation. Don't you feel the Christ in you? Haven't you stretched out your arms in willing crucifixion? Haven't you felt the karmic resonances, the ripples in the spirit field? Haven't you heard the faint echoes of the Great Vows reverberating in your soul? Don't you sometimes remember being Avalokiteshvara? I do.[9]

## How Souls Get Reincarnated

There is a notion in Tibetan Buddhism that hints at such a spiritual identity for gay people. After death, souls wait in the bardo for another incarnation. In this disembodied state, they float around, waiting for something to happen, looking for something to interest them. Frequently they become sexually attracted to the sight of human couples in sexual intercourse. (If you could be invisibly present anywhere, wouldn't you go looking for sex?)

If a particular soul happens to be too close, too attentive, and too personally involved when a sperm and ovum unite, that soul will be pulled into incarnation as the offspring of that sexual union. That is how souls get reincarnated.

A homosexual soul, however, floating in the bardo state, can watch lots of acts of homosexual intercourse without ever being drawn into incarnation. In fact, it seems as if it would never get pulled into incarnation at all. Thus homosexual souls must come back only because they choose to. Perhaps they become bored in the bardo and shift their consciousness from lust to compassion for the suffering they observe. We might even say gay people come into the world as bodhisattvas.

## Joy in the Joy of Others

From the story of bodhisattvas, Buddhists derives the four abodes of consciousness, also called the Four Immeasurables. These are the proper attitudes to hold toward life: compassion, loving-kindness, joy in the joy of others, and equanimity.

Joy in the joy of others is the spiritual basis for sexual liberation. Instead of judging other people's sexual pleasures and, wittingly or unwittingly, intending evil on them out of resentment and disapproval, we can be glad for them and wish them well.

As all people begin to wish well instead of ill, the self-fulfilling prophecies of bad things happening will diminish. That is how we save all those sentient beings. If we are compassionate and conscientious about the consequences of our actions, then we do not cause harm to others. If we treat people with loving-kindness, we make the world a kinder place. If we truly experience joy in the joy of others, we release resentment and disapproval and enter into joy ourself. If we experience all things with equanimity, we overcome fear and desire, we let go of judgment and resistance to life, and we create a context for ourselves in which to say yes to experience.

A mantra associated with the bodhisattva goes: "May all beings be happy. May all beings be free." What a good attitude to have all the time!

If you want to find a reason for joy, just be joyful that other people are happy. Be joyful that there are beautiful men in the world. The way to find joy and happiness is to rise above your own situation. You'll never find joy if you have to get everything you can imagine wanting—unless what you want is others' being happy. Then you can get what you want every time.

When you're standing in a gay bar, hoping somebody will talk to you, be happy for all the people who are talking to one another. Wish them well. Wish them love. You might not meet anybody yourself that night, but you won't go home frustrated. You can go home knowing that some of those men did meet one another and experience the joys you wished for them.

## *Follow Your Bliss*

Understanding that afterlife myths are about mystical vision suggests to us that we are seeing the Clear Light all the time—right now. Buddhahood/Christhood is available to us at every moment. The Beatific Vision shines everywhere around us. But we do not see it because it is not what we were expecting. Our beliefs, opinions, likes, and dislikes get in the way. We choose the Beatific Vision by choosing things as they are, being conscious of what is real, not resisting. This is a central teaching of spiritual wisdom.

Joseph Campbell said, "Follow your bliss and don't be afraid, and doors will open where you never knew there were going to be doors."[10]

Bliss is a technical term in Buddhism. It does not mean mere happiness or satisfaction. It means fulfillment of who we really are, realization of buddhahood, accomplishment of the goals that drive us to find meaning in life. To follow our bliss is to disregard the rules that tell us how we are supposed to behave and to seek our own path.

To follow our bliss is to live in such a way that we can always love our experience. It means to make choices and decisions about our life that we will not regret. It means not giving up our dreams and settling for security or acceptability in other people's eyes.

## *Want What You Get*

The adage goes: "Ride the horse in the direction it's going." The way to respond to the problems of gay life—looksism, ageism, shallowness, loneliness, rejection—is to accept that this is the way it is. This is the world we live in. We may not like all the things that are in it. But it does no good to resist things the way they are. We begin by acknowledging the truth of what is so. Once this is accomplished, we can figure out ways to deal with it.

If you are left-handed, what is the point of complaining about handwriting going from left to right? Maybe that is backwards to you, but the only thing you can do is learn how to hold your pen so you do not smear the ink.

After all, looksism, ageism, etc., are projections of your own resistance. They bother you in others because you deny them in yourself. As a community we want to resolve these various problems, but we cannot resolve them by complaining about them or blaming other people. One of the basic rules of life is: "Don't complain about things except to someone who has the power to do something about it." Complaining, kvetching, and making other people wrong just makes you unhappy—and puts out bad vibes.

The wisdom and esoteric traditions tell us that when we choose things the way they are, they will transform. Releasing resistance, replacing it with clear but passive intention and lucid visualization, allows things to change. This is the secret of magic.

Accepting things as they are means accepting our talents, pursuing what we are good at and like doing, instead of what we are supposed to do. This advice also means accepting that there are some things in our life that need changing, some traits that need correcting, some skills that need training.

Working to fix our problems and the problems around us is part of accepting things as they are. The attitude of "no resistance" is not a form of quietism. It is a way of active, serene, disinterested participation.

Most of all, this age-old advice means loving life, loving our life, looking back on all the things that have happened to us and saying: "Yes, wasn't that wonderful—even when it hurt."

There's a quote from Tolstoy that conveys the important wisdom:

The most difficult thing—
but an essential one—
is to love life,
to love it even while one suffers.
Because life is all. Life is God.
And to love life means to love God.

# Conclusion: The Secret

Being gay is a blessing, a higher incarnation, a better way to be. These are notions many of us, especially men involved in the gay spirituality movement, may believe deeply, but seldom say out loud. Perhaps because we are especially sensitive to the problems that follow when one group claims superiority over another, we do not claim superiority over heterosexuals. But at certain moments—perhaps in meditation or prayer, perhaps in sexual arousal, perhaps at a gay bar, a political fund-raiser, or social event—we realize just how blessed we are to be gay.

This discovery is an important part of spiritual maturation. As we understand how blessed we are, we begin to put out good vibes. When we realize that being gay is drawing a long straw in this life, we can forgive the world. We can accept things as they are with all the pain and loss that goes with being human. And when we do that we change the world.

Gay orientation is participation in one of the great thoughts of the planet. We resonate with the lives of all the homosexuals who have lived before us. And we transform their lives by the way we live ours. We affect all the people around us. The world is a different place since gay liberation. No matter how hard anti-gay forces try to prevent it, gay identity has appeared and is changing the world. That is why, as individual gay people, we have a moral responsibility to participate positively in this worldwide change we are creating.

The specifics of our lives may be horrific, like AIDS. But that is the point. To love what is unlovable is to transform it. This is how we participate in the evolution of consciousness.

Being a higher incarnation isn't better. Gay identity implies sensitivity and vulnerability to other people, and even responsibility and expectation of heroic virtue. Being a higher incarnation, in the metaphor of Mahayana Buddhism, may mean being a bodhisattva.

## Transformation of Religion

Religion teaches acceptance and resignation to Divine Will, but all too often it also teaches resistance to the way things are, to the human condition. Roman Catholicism teaches that urges of the flesh and things that give pleasure to the body are sinful and punishable by being burned alive everlastingly. Buddhism teaches that love of life and enjoyment of the senses causes continuing rebirth into life after life of suffering. Protestantism teaches that human beings are miserable sinners only worthy in God's eyes because they are cloaked in the grace of Jesus's sacrificial death. These are not declarations of the wisdom of choosing things the way they are and participating in the beauty and growth of the world. Religion inadvertently ends up being about unhappiness and figuring out who is to blame, not about happiness, understanding, and compassion for other people's struggles.

With the transformation of our understanding of religion we can see that the sex-negative, body-negative, life-denying, punitive notions in religion need to fall into the past—like the persecution of witches and the approval of slavery.

Like the rose that would bend to the pruning knife, mainstream American Christianity should welcome the challenges gay people pose. Here is its chance to transform its attitude and beliefs about the mythologies of the past and to reorient itself back to the teachings of Jesus about love and compassion. It's time to give up Jesus as medieval God and to embrace Jesus—and Avalokiteshvara—as symbols of how humans can relate to one another as loving neighbors, as different manifestations of the same Self of Earth.

The message of the myths is that we can make up our own religion. Indeed, we have to. We may do that by joining a church or by becoming a student of a Master and accepting everything we're told. But we do it, not because it is the One True Church or because the Master is right. We do it because we like how it makes us feel. We may also do it by studying various religions and selecting the metaphors that seem life-affirming and meaningful to us. We can make up our own religion to feel good about our life.

God doesn't care what religion we are. God just keeps shining. We're the ones who have to choose how we think about God—or whether we even do.

## Freedom of Religion

In the modern liberal, democratic world, we have a right to choose our religions and to believe anything about religion we want.

In coming out as gay and being good people who are interested in spirituality, the meaning of life, and the creation of community, we are in fact constructing a religion of gay consciousness, one that has deep roots in the history and evolution of consciousness.

If citizens have a right to choose whatever religion they want, no matter how nutty, and if they can choose religions that object to homosexuality on a moral basis, then homosexual citizens have a right to choose a religion that encourages homosexuality on a spiritual basis. We have a right to make up our religion just as much as Fundamentalist Christians make up theirs.

Since the objection to homosexuality is primarily religious, it has no place outside the churches. Homosexuals have a right to disagree with conservative Christians over the interpretation of the anti-gay texts in the Bible, just as much as Protestants can disagree with Roman Catholics about the authority of the Pope. If they can have splinter sects of Christianity, then we can form a sect of a pro-gay, life-positive religion. This is homosexuality as religion.

## *Time to Wake Up*

It's time to redefine "God." It's time to create a God who lives with us, who struggles with us to love life, even while we suffer, accepting the good and the bad as different faces of reality. It's time for a God who works with us to deal with the problems of life, not one who causes the problems to test us, as he tested Job, or to punish us, as he punished Adam and Eve, for the satisfaction of his immense ego.

The conclusion to reach is not: There is no God. But rather: God is the consciousness that is me. Each of us has to say: "What I am is consciousness experiencing itself and willing its own expansion and evolution." All the stuff that I think of as my ego and my self is just a distraction from the realization that I am God observing my creation from a particular perspective and declaring, unconditionally, "It is good."

We are God acting in the world. How else can God do anything except through human beings? The sun cannot change things on earth except by evolving conscious beings who understand their role as carriers of consciousness and can manipulate matter to serve consciousness. God effects change on earth through our behavior. As we realize we are God creating the universe, we can relax our resistance and create a better world.

To the extent that we can get back to that simple consciousness, we let go of the distractions and allow the will to evolve to operate. The will to evolve is what human beings experience as love. True love is the will to put another's spiritual growth before our own out of appreciation of who the other really is.

The call to remember that you are a momentary manifestation of God is God calling to himself: "Time to wake up."

It is time to change how we think. It is time to love our lives wholeheartedly. We can't waste our lives wishing we were somebody else, somebody we are not. We can't waste our lives feeling guilty or perverted about who we are, regretting that we are not normal, that we don't have children, that we look like we do and not like a dream we have. We can't waste our lives wishing that different people had made us their friends, loved us, and taken us to their beds. It's time to be glad for everything that has happened to us.

During the times of agony and crisis—the times we most need to remind ourselves to love life—we experience pain. We do not say "I like it" when it is awful. But we can say: "This is part of life; this is what I'm getting to experience as my world. It is great even though I'm hurt and crying."

Loving life means looking back on everything that has happened to us and seeing that it was wonderful because it has made us who we are—along with our intentions and motivations to make things different. The point of the whole universal process, from our perspective, is for us to have the experience we are having. This is the "punch line" of life, the "Secret of the Ages."

The act of choosing your life includes choosing to be gay. It does not mean surrender and acquiescence—though that might be called for in the end. It means active participation in the way the universe manifests itself to you and as you. It means recognizing and embracing the karmic patterns that intersect as your life, accepting the possibility of heartbreak and death as part of being human, accepting old age as part of life, accepting that too many of your friends have died. Finally, it means accepting the joy and beauty that are yours because you are alive.

The bodhisattva saves himself and all beings by taking on the suffering of the world. That is to say, in order not to suffer, you must embrace suffering. For when you can say yes to suffering, it isn't suffering. The little summary of hippie countercultural wisdom, *The Lazy Man's Guide to Enlightenment*, says: "When you learn to love Hell, you will be in Heaven."

## Heaven Now

The point is to experience the world as heaven, so that you can say yes to experience. That is the mechanism by which transformation is achieved. This is the secret. See things differently, and they will become different. See the world as great, and it will be great. Do not live for heaven in the future. Get heaven now. Then maybe you will have it after death, too. And if not, then at least, you will have had it.

Heaven, after all, is an attitude: This experience I am having right now—no matter what its contents—is, in fact, God enjoying being alive. Heaven is the sun shining on all that it has given birth to, and—in us—being pleased with what it has become. For us, our homosexuality is our experience of heaven.

## Gay Mystical Consciousness

Gay identity gives witness to mystical ideals. The deliberate choice to live in the present, accepting death with no pretense of immortality through offspring, affirms that we live in the eternal moment. Saying yes to mortality practices detachment from ego. Transcending ego allows us to realize our oneness with greater consciousness, with life.

As we realize this, we see that only our ego will die. Life goes on. And so we overcome death to the extent we overcome attachment to self. To see that you are the universe is to see that you cannot die. To see that the universe mirrors you, and is you, is the essence of homosexual attraction.

In the old days, being gay was something people kept secret. For that reason, homosexuality provided a sense of specialness. It was like membership in a secret club. That has changed. And that's good. Though there is still something special about being gay, and there is still a certain amount of persecution that goes with the specialness.

We do not need any more martyrs, though we shall likely get them. There are people who carry deep scars that cause them to hate us. They project their own self-hate and sexual confusion onto us. They blame us for all the problems in society. They blame the collapse of traditional values on us. They think that by persecuting us they are somehow dealing with child abuse and broken families. And they create a climate in which violence against homosexuals seems almost patriotic.

Crimes committed against homosexuals are crimes against citizens and cannot be tolerated. We legitimately demand that law enforcement protect our rights as citizens. Nonetheless, the persecution is part of what makes us special. Christian churches claim that the persecutions Christianity has faced have proved its legitimacy. So we have to see that the persecution we face is evidence we are a step ahead. Our martyrs confirm our legitimacy and reveal the ugliness and illegitimacy of our opponents.

When people are jealous of you and resent what you've got, you know you've got a treasure. If not, they wouldn't bother with you, would they?

Accepting things as they are necessarily includes accepting the opposition we face. It also includes striving to create a world in which such violence does not happen. Until then, we must not let the opposition stop us. We must not let ourselves be frightened out of the truth of who we are.

We understandably downplay our experience of being gay. We emphasize the suffering and social difficulties we face. We say things like, "This couldn't be chosen; who'd have chosen to be condemned and ostracized?" We say these things to avoid retaliation from the straight people who do not want us proclaiming how lucky we are. We keep a low profile. We poor mouth. But we must tell *ourselves* the truth about our good luck. We must tell our brothers. This is the good news, the boon of our hero journey, that can save us and them.

We have to believe that being in the altered state of sexual consciousness is a good thing. Any other position is self-defeating. We can create our lives so that this is true. We can take care of ourselves. We can maintain our health and vitality, the glow in our complexion and the flexibility in our muscles. We can protect ourselves from disease. We can work on our moral and psychological well-being, letting go of neurotic behaviors and compulsions. We can cultivate good friendships. We can have positive and delightful sexplay with willing, enthusiastic partners. We can have deep, committed, long-term sexual partnerships. In all these we can affirm our essential goodness.

## Gay Community

Central to our awareness of our identity has been the creation of a gay subculture. Many of us have fled our unwelcoming families to move to gay meccas where we can be ourselves and enjoy the support of like-minded people. It is good advice to suggest to young gay men and lesbians that they ought to live in San Francisco or the West Village or West Hollywood at some point in their youth. How liberating it is to find yourself in the majority!

But as we retreat into our ghettos, we may be abdicating one of our most important evolutionary functions.

Homosexuals have always played a role in the extended family as good aunts and uncles. We've been unmarried and unencumbered adults who could act as surrogate parents and available babysitters. By being there to give avuncular, uncomplicated adult affection, homosexuals contributed to the children's mental and emotional maturation. Especially in today's self-enclosed nuclear families, the presence of other adults enhances a child's experience of life. A modern demonstration of the role gay people have had as surrogate parents is the drive for gay adoption and alternative parenting. Gay people make good, kind, and loving parents. Raising a foster child is a way of caring for society's future.

A gay person in the family is someone who understands both men's and women's points of view and consequently can help resolve fights between our siblings and their spouses. We are natural marriage counselors.

We do well to choose safe, welcoming environments, like Greenwich Village or West Hollywood. But we also have a responsibility to the future of the human race. By living exclusively in gay communities, we might lose our influence in the greater world.

The presence of likeable, exemplary, openly gay people in the general population models attractive, virtuous behavior and makes everybody happy. Gay people put out good vibes.

Still there is no right or wrong way to be gay. The assimilationists and the gay separatists all have their points, though some assimilationists might be tempted to silence openly radical queers. The gay movement is about diversity. There is room for everybody. And that is an essential piece of the spiritual message.

Evolution demonstrates that diversity is adaptive. Gaia rejoices in variety. And variety enhances chances for selectability and survival. This is something the Bible's preference for uniformity—no mixing of grains in a field, no blending of fibers in a fabric—is incorrect about. When all the grain in the field is cloned from the same source, the crop is more susceptible to destruction by climatic conditions or parasites.

If this is true biologically, perhaps it is true psychologically as well. Diversity in consciousness enhances the experience and the health of the planetary mind.

## Population Imperatives

The biggest problem the planetary mind faces is that the world is too crowded. The human race has succeeded in filling the earth with its kind. Now there are too many of us for the planet to support. While human agricultural technology can produce enough food for a world even twice as crowded as it is, what are we going to do with all the waste these people produce, the pollution, the garbage, the shit? Where are we going to get all the natural resources they will want? And they all have a right to want the leisure and affluence that we in the First World enjoy.

The human population is going to have to stabilize or decrease. This must happen. The planet's self-regulatory processes are going to bring it about. It will likely happen by war, famine, and plague— the traditional population cutters. Or it could happen consciously and intentionally, as a self-aware planet would choose to do, by limiting growth. In a generation or two, the population could be brought under control by an appropriate embrace of homosexuality as God's natural contraceptive method.

Everybody who has the slightest inclination toward homosexuality, or who doesn't feel the drive to be a parent, or who carries a genetic disorder, or whose parenting skills have been damaged by an abused childhood ought to be encouraged to avail themselves of the pleasures and rewards of being gay. This would reduce the population and take people out of the parental role who shouldn't be in it.

Anti-gay forces fear that allowing homosexuality would mean

everyone would become gay and the race would die out. In fact, even if everyone did become gay, we would still know how to produce a next generation. The evidence of this is the interest among a certain segment of the gay/lesbian population in having children.

Population reduction is going to be disruptive for economies based on ever-expanding customer bases. But it will be far less disruptive if it happens because more and more people are gay than if bombs start falling and vast populations die horribly.

In the Biblical metaphor, the rainbow was given as a sign that God would never again destroy the earth. If the development of gay-consciousness is one possible answer to the threat of devastation from overpopulation and pollution of the earth's environment, then we are a fulfillment of that sign. It is no surprise, then, that the rainbow flag designed as a decoration for the Gay Day Parade in San Francisco in 1978 has become a worldwide symbol of gay liberation.

## Messengers of Gaia

Gay people are and will be models. We are messengers from Gaia. We are part of the call of evolution for the human race to wake up from childhood. It is a mere curiosity that the words "gay" and "Gaia" resemble one another. But the pun is there, nonetheless—a meaningful, synchronistic coincidence. We are people of Gaia. But it is no accident that being "gay" has always meant having a good time and enjoying life.

We experience this by reminding ourselves that everything is alive and we are part of it all. This is what the mystics tell us. This is what our new myth tell us. This is what fills us with wonder.

We have all seen that on a beautiful spring day in the country, the world seems alive and electric. There's an aura around every tree and bush and blade of grass. We experience vitality in the world by consciously conjuring a sense of wonder at the beauty around us. We experience the vitality in our own flesh. We relish the pleasure of being ourselves incarnate. We feel the life in us. We feel the subtle sexual energy that moves up from the base of our trunk—our first and second chakras—and fills our torso, sending thrills through our neck and face, causing us to smile with joy as it reaches our brain—and seventh chakra—and fills our consciousness. This is the pleasure of simply being alive.

The practice of such awareness is a kind of mini-enlightenment, a *satori*, that we can achieve just by intending to. The trick is to remember this vision and to recreate it in our mind when things are not looking pretty and we do not like what is happening.

The world is transforming, attitudes toward lesbian and gay people along with it. Gay rights, even domestic partnership rights, are part of the agenda of liberal democracies around the world. Straight people are letting go of their fears and oppositions. The polarizations are fading into the past. This is making them better people, and the world a better place.

In any specific individual not all the virtues of enlightened consciousness are present. We all know gay people who are not paragons. Even so, the stereotypes of homosexuals are changing. A common joke on TV sitcoms now is that the decent, caring, attractive men are all homosexual.

## The Gay Agenda

Anti-gay forces say there is a "gay agenda" to undermine "normal" society, to overthrow churches and institute devil worship, to break up marriages and sell the children into homosexual prostitution. There is no such agenda.

But, of course, there is a gay agenda if by that weighted term you mean a dream of how the world could and should be. And that agenda is more modern and sensible than the Fundamentalist agenda of reimposing theocracy on modern society.

The gay agenda is a call for human freedom and respect for diversity and otherness, a call for compassion. It is amazingly egalitarian. The movement, often even to its own detriment, embraces the demands of all minorities calling for justice and opportunity. Gay rights includes all rights. Gay people can't be free until all are free. Gay men and lesbians can't be saved until all human beings are saved. (Sounds like the Bodhisattva Vow, doesn't it?)

The gay agenda is the American agenda, the essence of democracy and personal freedom. It is idealism at its best, a demonstration of what a modern enlightened morality and religious attitude ought to be, a remarkable demonstration of what Jesus was actually talking about.

## Why Gay Spirituality

As we heard from E.M. Forster at the outset of our discussion: "There is a secret understanding between them when they meet. They represent the true human tradition, the one queer victory of our race over cruelty and chaos."

Not all of us are called to the roles of kindness and generosity. Not all of us are called to be saints, bodhisattvas, and world-transformers. But we participate in the collective transformation of consciousness whether we mean to or not. It is not so much the behavior of individual gay people as it is the appearance of gay identification itself that conveys the message. Any of us can become aware of what we are doing in planetary evolution. And we can choose to live our lives according to these metaphors. In so doing, we change the world. We ease the suffering in the world by putting out good gay vibes. We ease our own suffering by recognizing eternity in every moment.

This book began with the question "Why *gay* spirituality?"

The answer is that gay people are in the vanguard of a transformation in consciousness. We participate in waking up the planet by calling attention to important spiritual, psychological, and ecological issues. We help reveal the workings of Gaia. We test religion and we help redefine God. We stand on the ledge of the world's weird wall. We are oracles. We are guides. We put out good intentions. We radiate good vibes. We are moved by spirits true. And we are spirits true.

# ABOUT THE AUTHOR

Edwin Clark (Toby) Johnson, Ph.D., is author of several autobiographical accounts of his personal spiritual development, influenced by the thought of comparative religion scholar Joseph Campbell. *The Myth of the Great Secret: A Search for Meaning in the Face of Emptiness* (Morrow, 1982) recounted his leaving Roman Catholic monastic life and discovering a new meaning for religion in the revolutionary days of the late 1960s and early 1970s. *In Search of God in the Sexual Underworld* (Morrow, 1983) described Johnson's experiences—and his interpretation of events as a religion scholar—while working with Harvard-trained gay sociologist (and namesake) Toby Marotta in a federally funded study of teenage prostitution. *The Myth of the Great Secret (second edition): An Appreciation of Joseph Campbell* (Celestial Arts, 1992) combined the most Campbellian parts of the first two books, adding substantial anecdotal material about Johnson's friendship with Campbell.

In the late 1970s, he worked as editor/assistant with Marotta in producing Marotta's two books, *The Politics of Homosexuality* and *Sons of Harvard: Gay Men in the Class of 67.*

Toby Johnson is also author of three gay men's novels: *Plague: A Novel About Healing* (Alyson, 1987), *Secret Matter* (Lavender Press, 1990), and *Getting Life in Perspective: A Spiritual Romance*

# About the Author

(Lavender Press, 1991). *Secret Matter* won a Lambda Literary Award for Gay Men's Science-Fiction the year it was published; in 1999, it was a nominated to the Gay Lesbian Science-Fiction Hall of Fame, the first year of the award.

In 1996, Johnson took over the job of editing and publishing *White Crane: A Quarterly Journal of Gay Men's Spirituality.*

For several summers in the early 1970s, he was on staff at a Jungian-oriented conference center in the coastal mountains north of San Francisco called The Mann Ranch. There he met many of the leaders of new paradigm thinking, including Campbell. To this day, when asked his religion, Johnson—only half tongue-in-cheek—identifies himself as a northern Californian Jungian Buddhist. During the early 1990s, Johnson was on the board of the directors of the Joseph Campbell and Marija Gimbutas Archives and Library at Pacifica Graduate Center near Santa Barbara.

Toby Johnson was trained as a psychotherapist in San Francisco during the time gay-oriented psychotherapy was being developed. As cochair and spokesperson for the Gay Mental Health Task Force of San Francisco's Health Department, he was instrumental in the adoption of a Gay Client's Bill of Rights that guaranteed access to gay or gay-sensitive health care providers—a notion that had major effects in AIDS-related services a few years later.

Johnson practiced psychotherapy in San Francisco and, later, in his hometown, San Antonio. For several years in the early 1980s, Johnson was male co-chair of the San Antonio Gay Alliance. Then, from 1988 to 1994, he and Kip Dollar ran Liberty Books, the gay and lesbian community bookstore in Austin, TX. Partners since 1984, they were "poster boys" for gay marriage in the Texas capital and were the first male couple registered as domestic partners in Travis County. They were also the cover boys on the Spring 1997 issue of *Naked* magazine. They are among the 14 couples featured in Merle Yost's coffee table book from Pilgrim Press, *When Love Lasts Forever: Male Couples Celebrate Commitment.*

In fulfillment of a dream they share with many gay couples, Toby and Kip have been operating a gay bed and breakfast in the Rocky

Mountains outside Denver called The House at Peregrine's Perspective. In 2000, they're moving their dream back to the Texas Hill Country.

Johnson's Web site address is www.whitecranejournal.com.

# NOTES

1 "Everything's Possible" © 1983 Pine Barrens Music (BMI). Words and Music by Fred Small. Reprinted by permission.

2 The nature religions (in Europe, paganism and Wicca; in America, the Native-American Indian traditions) articulate an awareness of the web of life that the modern science of ecology is demonstrating empirically. They play an important role in the development of the new paradigm.

3 Midrash was a Hebrew literary genre of stories with elaborate embellishment using familiar Scriptural symbols. While midrash might sound historical, it was meant to morally instruct and edify, not to recount history. It was often a homiletic device, not unlike "spinning a yarn," to get a point across. The story of the Three Wise Men is an example of midrash. It was a tale about the universality of Jesus's message, not an account of the visitors at Jesus's baby shower.

4 "Paradigm shift" is an expression from Thomas Kuhn's *The Structure of Scientific Revolutions*. It has entered modern parlance as the term for rethinking the world. A paradigm is a model for conceiving how things work: imagining electricity running through a wire as a fluid flowing through a tube gives a pretty good approximation of how electrical force behaves, but electricity is not

a fluid. The great paradigm shift of all time was the Copernican revolution. Understanding religion as metaphor instead of revelation of Absolute Truth is a paradigm shift.

5 Tantra means "warp and woof" or "web," i.e., the interweaving of phenomena.

6 Tibetan Buddhism is called Tantric. But in the orthodox Tibetan religion, headed by the Dalai Lama, that has caught the modern imagination, Tantra does not mean quite the same thing.

7 Jung called this dynamic synchronicity "meaningful coincidence." He suggested that synchronicity is an organizing principle just as real, if not as well-understood or as predictable, as causality.

8 The word "bisexual" has two different uses. To be bisexual means to be sexually attracted to both males and females. It also means to be both male and female, possessing both sets of organs and capable of self-fertilization (as with certain plants). The interplay of these inconsistent meanings is instructive.

9 Toby Johnson's story of meeting a cute fellow at the 21st Street Baths in San Francisco who identified himself as the Bodhisattva Avalokiteshvara appears in *White Crane Journal*, Issue #37.

10 There is a parallel in Campbell's words to the final words of the play *Auntie Mame*. You wonder if he was trying to quote Mame. This archetypally gay character ends the play, luring her grand-nephew to the banquet of life, by saying, "Oh, the doors I will open for you, doors you never even dreamed existed." All gay men need God to be their Auntie Mame.